ON PARADE

The number of Jews to reach the rank of warrant officer class 1 in the long history of the British army can probably be counted on one hand. In this small group were Len Sanitt and Nat Stein. Len became a warrant officer class 2 at the age of 21, and was promoted in the field to warrant officer class 1 when the 53rd Field Regiment RA reached Tobruk after the 8th Army under Montgomery broke through at El Alamein.

ON PARADE

Memoirs of a Jewish Sergeant-Major in World War II

by Leonard Sanitt

SPA
BOOKS

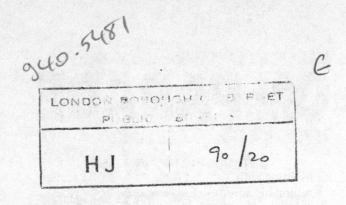
© Leonard Sanitt 1990

ISBN: 0-907590-31-4

Published by:

Spa Books Ltd
PO Box 47
Stevenage
Herts, UK. SG2 8UH

Typesetting by Ronset Typesetters Ltd, Darwen

Printed in Great Britain by Antony Rowe Ltd, Chippenham

To my dear wife Sonia
for listening with love and patience to an old soldier
retelling his adventures over a period of 40 years

Contents

ACKNOWLEDGEMENT

To my charming nieces Carolyn and Karen for all the help and assistance they cheerfully gave to enable me to transfer my story from my head to this book.

Foreword

Our Uncle Len wears many hats and, as you will discover as you read his memoirs, by the age of twenty-five he had already achieved more than most people manage in a life-time. From a loving but humble Jewish East End background he first travelled to Hatton Garden, then to the Leyton Territorial Army and eventually became a remarkable REME soldier during the war. He had many fascinating adventures in the Middle East and Italy and ended his career as a member of that illustrious band of men – The Jewish Brigade.

So, to many, he will be admired as an excellent soldier with a wonderful sense of proportion and the true qualities of leadership.

Nowadays he is renowned for having been one of London's finest manufacturing jewellers but to his family and friends he is undoubtedly one of the kindest and most generous of human beings ever to have been encountered. His patience, good humour and sensible advice have helped so many of us through difficult times and we feel very privileged to have given some small assistance in the production of this book. As will all his readers, we eagerly await its sequel.

Carolyn and Karen.

Preface

Hello Adam, Gideon and Ruth. This is your Grandpa Len's story. I am writing this for you, my grandchildren, to tell you about the many different experiences of life and people that I have encountered.

It has always been a source of sorrow to me that I never knew my grandparents and the type of life that they led. Consequently I will try to tell you a little about your forebears, as well as my early years in London's East End and my adventures during the Second World War.

You don't have to take any notice of anything I say for I've no intention of laying down any rules or regulations for you to live by. The one thing that I think is more important than anything in life is freedom; personal freedom.

*

The majority of this autobiography deals with the years I spent in charge of a REME detachment during World War II, first with 53rd Field Regiment and finally with the remarkable Jewish Brigade. There have been many stories written about the major battles of the war from the commanding officer's point of view but my story concerns the essential but often overlooked technical aspects of war. In particular it explains how massive amounts of vehicles and armaments were actually transported, maintained and repaired.

My success in this field could never have been achieved had it not been for my early experiences. The main influences upon my life were firstly, my Jewish East End family upbringing which gave me a sense of proportion; secondly, my jeweller's apprenticeship which taught me the basics of craftsmanship and, thirdly, the Victoria Boys' Club which provided me with leadership and camping experiences.

L.S.

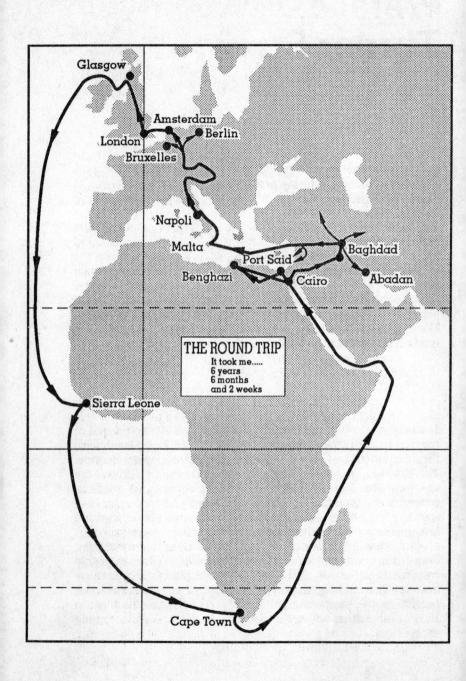

1
Turner Street

My name is now Leonard Sanitt, but when I was born my family name was Sanitsky, which immediately tells you that our family comes from Eastern Europe. My parents, Rachael and Nathan, were known for most of their lives by their Yiddish names of Rochel and Nussen or their Hebrew names of Rachel and Natan. My Yiddish name is Leib ben Nussen. Leib is the Yiddish equivalent to Aryeh in Hebrew and means Lion.

The name Leonard was a most peculiar choice, but by the time I was born my family had become somewhat anglicized. My older brother, five years my senior, was born in May 1915 and was called Mendel, anglicized to Emanuel, though we always called him Manny. Two years later my sister was born. By this time my parents had dropped the type of name used in Poland and named her Dinah. When I came along they considered themselves very modern in their ideas, so I was called Leonard, which soon became Lenny to everybody.

I was brought up in the centre of what was then the Jewish ghetto in East London, commonly known as Whitechapel, where Jewish immigrants lived from about the early 1800s to the end of the Second World War. During my childhood I found the Jewish East End of London to be a most fantastic place in which to grow up. Although we were a relatively small community, it was my whole world and for the first ten years of my life I hardly spoke to more than a handful of non-Jewish people. To outsiders we appeared to be a small group of homogeneous people; all Jews, all foreigners. But within the ghetto there was an enormous variety of people. There were Jews from all the European communities, originating from thousands of miles apart and with completely different backgrounds. There were those from Lithuania, those from the Baltic states, those from all parts of Russia and Poland; country people, city people, ultra-religious groups and those not at all religious but merely nationalistic. Linking us all was a terrific sense of humour and a wonderful sense of being alive amongst the bustle of the East End with its busy street markets.

Our houses were very small, so our streets teemed with life.

13

There certainly wasn't the reticence in talking to neighbours that exists nowadays for these people were used to living in each other's pockets, in and out of each other's houses, knowing everybody else's business. It was a very happy community abounding with remarkable Jewish humour which, to a certain extent, was gallows' humour.

Everybody considered him or herself, however poor, to be expert on military, political and economic matters. Night after night they would discuss amongst themselves how the Chancellor should solve the financial problems that they found so simple, being amazed that he should have such difficulty. If there was a war anywhere in the world or if the discussion wandered to historical events, then these topics were expertly analysed and all concerned would be confident that had their advice been taken, the solution would have been seen as simple. No problem was too complex for our community to tackle and ultimately to solve.

It was this sense of equality that kept everybody alive and from realizing the terrible truth that we lived in appalling economic and social conditions. But, like so many things in life, if you don't want to know your problems, it's much easier to live and be happy.

We certainly were a very happy family. My father, who named me after his father, David Leib, was a really wonderful man. He was quiet, respected by everybody and I can never remember him raising his voice to us nor to anybody else. Although he could hardly speak English he seemed to understand anything anybody ever said.

I remember that my father used to take me to lantern slide lectures on the most peculiar subjects. He could have understood very little about these talks since they were given in English but he must have appreciated them enough to take me along. The subjects included 'Trekking in Middle Africa', 'Expedition to the Andes' and discussions on the political events and happenings that were beginning to shape the future of the post-First World War times.

A few years earlier the Soviet Union had become a Communist State. My father was brought up during the time that most intellectuals considered that the answer to anti-Semitism was a form of 'socialism that would not allow the aristocracy to use the Jews as a scapegoat for the harsh, slave-like conditions the peasants had to endure.

I can remember my father taking me to the Yiddish Theatre – a wonderful part of East End life – when I could have been no more than three or four years of age. The main Yiddish theatre was at the Old Pavilion in the Whitechapel Road and the other was at the Grand Palais in Commercial Road. If ever there was a misnomer it was the title Grand Palais, but I suppose when you go to the theatre it is not what you see but what you want to see that is the important thing.

14

My father had worked as a young man in Poland in the small town of Gombin near to the Prussian border. It was a very remote part of the world, deliberately kept that way by the Russian Empire to attempt to cut off and prevent armies marching across into Russia from the West. My father was a leather worker and his family had apple orchards. Most of the land in that area belonged to the Germans and I remember my father and mother always said that they had been treated better by the Germans than by the Polish authorities. When eventually roads began to be built in the villages, the need for the Wellington-type boot, worn by everyone because of the mud, disappeared and with it that type of work that my father used to do.

My mother's family were the bakers of Gombin and she had been brought up in the bakery. She used to tell me stories of how, during the very cold Polish winters, the whole family slept in the bakehouse keeping warm from the heat of the oven. Naturally she knew all about baking bread and cakes as did her brother, Isaac Gilbert, who had come to London a few years before my parents and had opened a bakery in Philpot Street. (The name Gilbert, my mother's maiden name of course, was a derivation of Gail-bert meaning yellow beard. Running through my maternal family, every two generations, one of the children turns out to be ginger-haired.

The name of Gombin played a very important part in our childhood. There were many legends about the Gombiners because, like most rural communities, they were very practical people. Although they observed the usual religious practices they were nt the Talmudic student type of people; they were earthly folk.

As an illustration of the insularity of Gombiners there is a story about a man who was travelling on a horse through Gombin. As he reached the small town he wasn't sure where he was so he called to a bystander in Yiddish, 'Chava! Can you tell me where I am?' The bystander, being a true Gombiner, looked at him, realized that here was an outsider, a stranger and replied, 'What's in it for me?' The traveller immediately retorted, 'Ah, this must be Gombin!'

I remember that when I was about six years old there was great excitement in Turner Street because a public lavatory had been built at the corner of Philpot Street and Commercial Road. The whole community discussed it for weeks on end and my mother, who was very proud of her Gombin ancestry, said to her neighbour Mrs Isenberg, 'I don't know what all the fuss is about because we had a public lavatory in every street in Gombin. Here there is only one in the whole district!'

This to my mother illustrated what a modern up-to-date place Gombin was in her eyes and I was very impressed. It was one of these odd items that stick in a child's memory and many years later I reminded my mother of how progressive Gombin must have been to have a toilet in every street.

'Oh yes,' said my mother, 'but I forgot to mention that we never had a toilet in each house!'

At the outbreak of war there were 2,312 Jews living in Gombin. When the Germans entered the town the Jews were immediately subjected to compulsory hard labour. At the end of September 1939 German soldiers set fire to the synagogue and to nearby Jewish houses. The Germans imposed a fine on the Jewish community, placing the blame for the blaze on the Jews themselves. In October 1939 a *Judenrat* was formed consisting of six members presided over by Moishe Want. Early in 1940 a ghetto was created for 2,100 Jews, 250 of whom were deportees from surrounding localities. Most of these ghetto inhabitants continued to perform hard physical labour for the Germans and were compelled to pay some contributions. When the collection took too long, hostages were seized and the Jewish houses were plundered.

In the first half of 1941, the Germans began sending transports of Jews to labour camps; the majority of these were sent to Conin. In the beginning the *Judenrat* called up young men by lists for the transports and they appeared, but when the tragic conditions of the camps became known, the men began to hide. German police with the help of Jewish policemen raided the streets and houses. In 1942, 2,150 Jews lived in Gombin and, despite transports to labour camps, the Jewish population grew because of an influx of Jews from other parts of the region.

On 12th May 1942, all Jews in Gombin were despatched to the death camp at Chelmno. Only 212 survived, 32 on the Aryan side and in concentration camps, about 180 from the USSR; nearly all of them subsequently left Poland. At the end of the war I discovered that there was not one single Jew living in the town of Gombin.

My uncle Isaac married my Aunt Yetta and they had three sons: Percy, (who died just after the war, as a result of an infection he caught as a soldier in Sierra Leone): Monty, who was my age and a great friend; and the youngest, Philip, who was the one who inherited the greatest sense of humour. They also had a daughter named Stella.

My mother's sister, Ruda, lived just round the corner to us in Varden Street and she was married to my uncle Hyman. Their name was Helman, and they had three daughters, Lily, Minnie and Sadie, and three sons, Alf, Benny and Johnny. Johnny was also my age so consequently Monty, Johnny and myself lived in each other's houses and shared all our adventures together as youngsters.

My uncle Hyman was a tailor with a workshop which had been built in his back-garden. There was nothing unusual about this because the whole of the Jewish East End was a hive of industry with small workshops everywhere. These workshops ranged from a single sewing machine in the corner of the bedroom to other quite large establishments capable of housing two or three hundred workers. Everything revolved around the workshops and the season. If trade was good, everybody was happy, everybody was eating, the men were working and things were prosperous. Should it be slack the opposite was the case, but somehow or other everybody managed.

During my childhood our lives seemed to revolve around trade, the synagogues and the *Yomtovim* – the days of the festivals. From a child's point of view, the greatest festival was the Passover (Pesach) and the most awesome was Yom Kippur, the Day of Atonement.

To a child Pesach was an enormously thrilling and exciting period and the *seder* (festival meal) nights were wonderful. As the youngest. I would rehearse for weeks beforehand the four questions I would have to recite during the service. The atmosphere of the *seder* itself in our kitchen was incredible with everything so brightly polished and cheerful. Every child in the neighbourhood wore new clothes somehow bought by their parents and, from top to toe, we were scrubbed, polished and washed. The amount of scrubbing and cleaning that went on in preparation for the festival was unbelievable. All the best crockery and cutlery which were only used for the Pesach period were brought out of storage, cleaned and scrubbed and all the *chometz* (leavened food) was put away, since no leavened foods were eaten during the eight days of Passover.

In my parents' shop, every trace of sweets and chocolates was completely removed, the counter was bare and everything was 'sealed. There was no such thing as special 'Kosher for the Passover' sweets or chocolates at the time, so we children had to forgo these types of goodies, but we more than made up for it with a variety of nuts. Nuts played a terrific part with the children. There were all sorts of games that one could play with them. The shoeboxes from our new shoes were pierced with small holes which we would number 3,5,2,7 etc. One child would be the banker while the others would use it as a sort of coconut-shy, trying to throw the nut from a distance into one of these holes in order to win the number of nuts marked on a particular hole.

Another entrepreneur would put a farthing on the pavement with a small piece of nutshell on it while the others would stand a few feet away and try to knock off the piece of shell by aiming nuts at it. If the aim was successful the farthing would be won; if unsuccessful the entrepreneur would keep the nuts that had missed. Some boys were obviously more successful than others and, by the time Pesach was over, had collected an enormous number of nuts. I never knew what they did with them because somehow or other I wasn't very good at this and always seemed to lose what nuts I started with!

'The other notable thing, as far as I was concerned, was that we used to deliver orders of fruit to our various customers just before Pesach began. The shop was very busy so my brother and I used to hire a barrow from a stable just round the corner in Varden Street. When we delivered the orders, as likely as not, the housewife would give us a halfpenny or a penny as a tip for our services.

On the eve of Pesach a friend and I used to go around swinging a bucket on a rope. Inside the bucket would be a fire and as we toured the streets we would shout, *'Chometz, chometz!'* At each door the housewife would bring a cloth wrapped around a wooden spoon, a feather and some pieces of leavened food that she had carefully collected from the various parts of her home. We would put this cloth into the bucket to burn; for this we would also get a tip. It was all very exciting indeed although, no doubt, our area must have been very similar to other Jewish areas all over the world and at all periods in history.

I went to *Cheder*, or Chyder as we cockneys pronounced it. *Cheder* simply means room. Ours was a small school run by a *Melamed*, the teacher who taught us our Hebrew lessons. We used to go each day of the week after we had come home from school and had our tea. From five to six p.m. I would go to the dilapidated, small, disused synagogue where there were about twenty students – a very grand term for an assortment of scruffy boys between the ages of five and thirteen. Nevertheless we had a bond in common and many of my *Cheder* pals still remain lifelong friends of mine. We never learned very much as far as Hebrew or Jewish affairs were concerned but we had a great time playing all sorts of games with the likes of cigarette cards that were the vogue of the time.

I started to go to school when I was two and a half years old. Since my mother and father had the small shop to run, they were busily occupied trying to earn a living and bringing us up adequately, so the earlier that I could go to school the better it would be for my mother. Miss Harris, the schoolteacher who lived at the top of Turner Street, used to pass by the shop every morning and she would collect me and take me to the Baker Street Infants School. Consequently, instead of starting school at the normal time, I had an early start because Miss Harris could escort me there and home again. One of my earliest memories was when, one winter, Miss Harris slipped on the ice and fell over in the street.

Perhaps going to school so young helped me with my reading because I honestly do not remember any time in my life that I could not read. Undoubtedly reading and books have been the greatest hobby of my life. I always say it doesn't matter what books young children read, because if they start with comics they will gradually move on once the reading bug has bitten them. Books are the gateway to all knowledge, especially for people like myself who have had a very short and limited formal education.

18

When I was five I left Baker Street and went to Myrdle Street School. I was ten when there was one of these periodic changes of educational systems and I was transferred to Rutland Street School until I was eleven. At this age it was probable that only one child out of about thirty in the class would get a scholarship to one of the foundation or grammar schools – the only route to higher education at that time. A preliminary scholarship examination was taken at about ten years three months of age and those children that passed were then allowed to go on to take the finals of the Junior County Scholarship. I passed the preliminary and was eventually offered a half-paid scholarship to the Raines Foundation school under a special in-between system for bright children. However, by this time my father, who had been suffering from bronchitis for many years, unfortunately became worse and it was not possible for my family to pay the fees.

In actual fact I did not want to go because I had decided by this time that I was going to be a jeweller. This was a most peculiar ambition for a boy in my position because the vast majority of my contemporaries were either destined to go into the tailoring trades or to the Houndsditch which was the beginning of a career in retailing. The Houndsditch was a district where a large number of wholesale drapers were concentrated.

Next door to us, however, lived the Isenbergs. The father, whom I never knew, had come from Vienna and was a goldsmith. His son, Willy Isenberg, was also trained as a goldsmith and worked in one of the local shops in Commercial Road opposite the Kutchinsky jewellery shop. (Many years later the Kutchinsky family were to become one of my largest customers.)

Willy had fixed up a small work bench in the kitchen of his house. When I was about six or seven years old I used to stand and chat to him while he was working, my nose barely being high enough to touch the bench. It was then that I decided that I too was going to be a jeweller and I can never remember having any other ideas about a career.

When I was eleven, I went to Mile End Central School which was really a very good school. We were expected to remain there until we were sixteen but most of the boys left at fourteen, for there was a deep, implicit understanding in boys that it was their duty to go to work to help the family finances as early as possible.

Our headmaster was a very enlightened educationalist, years ahead of his time. As an example, it was a very rare thing for the cane to be used and only the headmaster could administer it. I think that in the three years I spent there, the cane was used only upon two occasions which was in complete contrast to the other schools I attended where each teacher seemed to use the cane completely indiscriminately. The standard of discipline was very high in my youth and part of the reason, I believe, is that the whole moral attitude of youngsters in the East End was amazingly high. I do not ever remember hearing my father or my uncles use a swearword; the love, affection, harmony and respect that the youngsters had for even their elder brothers and sisters was quite remarkable. My brother, Manny, five years older than I, was looked upon by me as a junior parent and it was unthinkable for younger children to disobey any instructions issued by any elders in their family. A large part of the upbringing of the younger children fell upon their siblings with the father being very busy working and the mother cooking and cleaning.

Morality among the girls in our community was virtually one hundred percent. Obviously there must have been the occasional lapses but such incidents were kept very quiet. Before the war I never heard of any couple being divorced for these people simply did not exist. Should a husband or wife be unhappy with each other or be unfaithful, it was certainly kept a secret.

My great aversion to gambling stems from what I saw as a youngster where betting amongst certain people in our district had terrible effects. Opposite our shop was a factory called Goldblatt's, and each day I would see the workshop's representative go out into the street to talk to the bookmaker who hung around waiting for custom. Betting was highly illegal and I certainly could never have dreamt then of a situation like to today where it is a business like any other.

At the time gambling had to be hidden from the eye of the law, so it was the custom for one man from each workshop to take all the bets and place them with the street bookie. After the race – most of the gambling was on horses – and once the evening paper had come out with the results, the bookmaker would return to pay out to whoever was fortunate enough to win. Many men backed horses every day of the week, doing it 'on tick' so that they did not have to settle up until pay-day. At the end of the week there were always one or two wives to be seen standing alongside the bookmaker outside the factory. These women knew that unless they reached their husbands to take part of their wages from them immediately they left work, the bookmaker would collect most of it, and there would be nothing left for the gambler's family to live on for the next week.

Sometimes I saw some terrible sights with some awful scenes of crying, shouting and arguing between husbands and wives. The main culprit was usually the workshop runner but, invariably, even the small commission that he received for this service would be lost in one of the bets that he himself placed. Alcoholic drink was never a problem amongst the Jewish community but gambling certainly was. It caused more unhappiness and more trouble than any other one particular factor.

Stealing was also unheard-of, and it was perfectly safe to leave our shop with nobody in it. Should my mother or brother have to leave it unattended for five minutes or so, the door would remain unlocked. If a customer walked in, he would either wait for them to return or he would take what he wanted and pop in later to pay. There were no regulations about children serving in shops and so I helped out from about the age of three. In fact any member of the family who happened to be about would automatically serve a customer. Our shop at number 41 Turner Street sold more things than Woolworths do today in an area which was probably no more than twelve foot square!

In the back parlour, which was even tinier, I slept on a put-you-up for part of my life, but then few people slept in real beds for there simply wasn't enough room. At night a whole variety of incredible beds appeared. Sofas turned into beds, chairs turned into beds, probably pianos turned into beds – it was the only way it was possible to find enough room for everybody to sleep.

When I was six my parents, who had previously only sold fruit and vegetables, split the shop in half – tiny as it was. They introduced confectionery, tobacco and cigarettes. In the summer they would make ice-cream and soda water drinks with various coloured syrups. At a very early period we had a Lyon's refrigerator installed which came in handy because my mother was able to use this to store various groceries that would otherwise deteriorate. In the summer a horse and cart would deliver a large block of ice which went into our ice-box also to keep things cold.

My father was able to do most things. He rigged a water tank in the cellar and attached a gas cylinder. This gas and water would then be mixed going through a weird arrangement of lead piping which, by what appeared to me to be a miracle, meant that when a tap was turned on in the shop above ice cold soda water would appear. The cellar was also where we made our homemade ice-cream. Laboriously, we would all take our turn at the churn, rotating the handle until the ingredients gradually turned into delicious ice-cream.

My mother made toffee apples. My father would cut the sticks, we placed the apples on the stick whilst my mother made the pot of toffee into which we children would dip one in at a time. My mother also pickled her own cucumbers buying them in the market and storing them in barrels in the cellar. She made wine as well so in our cellar there were always wine jars, pickling jars, the ice-cream churn, toffee-apple manufacturing and the soda water being produced; it really was a hive of industry with the whole family taking part in everything that happened.

My first lessons in economics were learned in our shop. I certainly learnt that the money that came over the counter was not destined for spending but first had to be used for stock replacement. I also learnt that whilst a card containing five safety pins sold for a penny, it was perfectly legitimate to sell single safety pins at a halfpenny each to the customer who only required one. Therein lies the root of all economics.

Mile End Central School had one of the scout troops of the district which was named Harland's Own Troop, or the 33rd Stepney. (Mr Harland was a master at the school who had been killed in the First World War and the troop was named after him.) I joined the scouts when I started at the school but my parents were not very happy about it because they had the old idea that was prevalent in Poland; the less the authorities knew about you the better and that the wearing of a scout uniform would lead to military service of some kind. However, I was a very determined youngster and I talked them into allowing me to join. It was a wonderful experience and taught me so many things.

The scoutmaster and the assistant scoutmaster of the troop were brothers from a local family that I got to know very well. In typical scout fashion one we called Cougar and the other Thundermoose. The latter, whose name was Simon Domb, I knew extremely well after the war because he became a welfare worker at the Jewish Board of Guardians and via him I was able to arrange for many boys to obtain jewellery apprenticeships.

Travel being financially limited meant that there were very few green areas we could see or could play in. Most of the small, cottage-type houses (two up and two down) had small back yards containing a tiny earth patch where grass grew and, occasionally amongst the weeds, there would be other plants. In the tenements and schools the play areas were completely cemented over.

We had a tiny grass patch in our yard, where my parents used to attempt to cultivate various flowers but with very little success. However, the one flower that grew without any encouragement whatsoever was the sunflower. I was quite grown up before I realised that other flowers existed to any extent. Everywhere we went the sunflowers flourished and the larger the blooms, the happier we were to see them.

There was one small green square in our area, Ford Square, in a section of which we were allowed to play. The other part of it was cultivated with various flowers by a keeper whose main job appeared to be to keep the children off the grass.

There were two parks that were used by the entire East End, of which the nearest was Victoria Park. As soon as I became old enough to go there without grown-up supervision, my friends and I would go at every opportunity to play football, cricket and other sports. As we got older and were allowed to travel further, we would visit Springfield Park, which was a beautiful place, much more cultivated and landscaped. It used to cost twopence on the bus for an adult so family visits were confined to a whole day, usually a

Sunday, when the weather was fine. We used to take some food with us but when my father accompanied us I was allowed a large round biscuit and a glass of milk from the cafeteria. It was unthinkable to buy any other food whatsoever in a non-kosher restaurant so it showed how progressive my father was in that he allowed me to have biscuit and milk because he thought it would be good for me.

When I was twelve my father died. His illness had begun just after his arrival in England, when to earn a living he sold fruit and vegetables. He hired a barrow, bought his produce at Spitalfields Market and pulled the barrow round the streets to sell his wares. This was very common at the time, but it meant being out in all weathers. The first few months after they had taken the shop in Turner Street, my mother had sold indoors whilst my father continued with the street-barrow until they reached a point where the shop alone could support us. However, by this time my father had contracted pneumonia; he was very fortunate in surviving it, but was told by the doctors that he had to give up the barrow.

To supplement the income from the shop, my father then took in work from the local tailors. He set up a pressing establishment, using a gas method of heating the irons, working for a period of time as an outdoor presser. The pneumonia had left him with bronchitis, which the steam aggravated, and he developed an abscess on the lung as a result of the coughing. After a few months in hospital he died in February 1933.

I have vivid memories of his final illness and his death. He suddenly announced that he wanted to come home from the hospital and my mother agreed. It is funny how small things stick in the mind. Since his bedroom was on the upstairs landing it was felt that it would be a good idea to have an electric bell fitted by his bed so that my mother, who was serving in the shop, would know when he required assistance. I remember that a young electrician from Philpot Street came round to fix this bell. I was very excited about it because, to my simple mind, I thought that as my father was coming home, he was recovering.

He arrived home about 11 a.m., was put to bed and about 2 p.m. that same day, the bell rang just as it had done a few times previously. On this occasion my mother went up and then shouted down to me to run round to New Road to fetch the doctor immediately. I rushed round for the doctor and waited downstairs with my sister and brother. A few minutes later the doctor came down the stairs and told my brother that he was very sorry but our father had died.

We sat *shiva** for the week and for a further eleven months we were in strict mourning. This meant that my brother and I had to

*Very strict regulated mourning

go to the synagogue each morning and evening to say prayers for my father. We did not go to the cinema or to football matches, we did not listen to any music and life was very difficult. My father had lived in England for something like eighteen years before he died at the very early age of forty-one. I was twelve, my sister was fifteen and my brother, now the man of the family was seventeen.

During our year of mourning my barmitzvah came round but we had no festivities at all. When my cousins were barmitzvah'd round about the same period there had been big parties, lots of activities and presents with everybody being very happy. When I got barmitzvah'd nothing happened at all.

I remember sitting in Philpot Street Synagogue next to an old man who was one of the daily worshippers, always present each morning and evening when I went to say *Kaddish* – communal prayers – for my father. Whenever there was a barmitzvah in the synagogue a different coloured, embroidered tablecloth would be placed on the prayer table that held the Sefer Torahs or Holy Scrolls. There was no religious significance to this; it was simply that the table height had to be raised for the small boys to be able to read. An additional box was thus put on to the table and then it was covered with the cloth.

This old man next to me said, 'Ah, we are going to have a barmitzvah this morning!'

I turned to him and said, 'Yes, it's my barmitzvah.'

My name was called, I went up and was given an Aliyah, which means I could now partake in the service by reading a portion of the Law. I said my portion of the Torah and went home, exactly the same as every other Saturday of that year.

At the end of the year's mourning I remember going to the Foresters Cinema in Cambridge Heath Road. It seemed a thrilling experience after a whole year of being denied any festive activities.

There were other incidents that come to mind about my very early youth. I remember when electricity was installed, replacing the gas lighting. We were one of the first houses to have electricity, because we ran a shop and my mother and father thought it would bring more business. I was about six and from that very early age was impressed that every time I went out of a room, I had to switch of the light; it would be a terrible waste of electricity to leave the lights burning when nobody was in the room. Consequently, I got into the habit of thinking that it was economically necessary to switch off lights. This has stayed with me all my life and even to this day, even if I know I'm going back in a few minutes, even when I'm in other establishments or houses, I have a compulsion to turn off the light in an empty room.

Another very important part in my young life was kosher food. This is really a whole way of life, because it limits one's activities. It certainly stopped me going into any restaurant until I was an adult.

Before I went into the army I had never eaten anything that was prohibited. On the one or two occasions that I went into a place like Lyon's Corner House in Coventry Street when I was about seventeen, all I had was a cup of tea and a pastry. The thought of eating any food that had been prepared in a non-kosher manner never occurred to me.

The only exceptions to home-cooking were the Jewish restaurants or, as we called them, 'salt beef shops'. Blooms was the most well-known, but, in our family, we could not afford to go into somewhere like that to have a sit-down meal. Our treat was to be sent, perhaps at a Sunday lunchtime, to buy a quarter or half pound of salt beef and my mother would make sandwiches which we would all eagerly devour with pickled cucumbers.

However, we did regularly use the chip-shops of which there were several in the East End. For one penny one could buy a portion of chips, for another halfpenny we bought a bagel and a pickled cucumber also cost a halfpenny. Therefore twopence bought us a really enjoyable meal. The chips were held in newspaper and one helped oneself to salt and vinegar from the receptacles that were attached by a chain to the bar. Every now and again some comedian would unscrew the top of the salt-cellar so that some unfortunate person would receive a deluge of salt which ruined their chips. The same was done with the vinegar bottle by loosening the cork, but this was all part of life and, as regular visitors, we knew all these tricks and made sure they never happened to us.

Our shop opened at 7 a.m. to catch the early morning trade and did not close until midnight. It was open seven days a week and fifty-two weeks a year. The only three days in the year that we actually closed were the day of Yom Kippur and the two days of Rosh Hashanah, the Jewish New Year. After my father died my brother looked after the shop with my mother.

When I was eleven I had my first holiday at scout camp at Goring-on-Sea. I had also been to Southend-on-Sea on two separate day trips that summer and found it very exciting. We went by coach and it was a new world to my eyes. I thoroughly enjoyed looking at the sea, paddling, going to the Kursaal fun fair and buying a stick of rock. There was a scheme whereby children could go to the country through the Country Holiday Fund but my mother and father were not keen on the idea. Thus the scout camp was the first time I had been away from home on any sort of holiday.

It rained for the first couple of days so we were not at all happy, but then the sun came out and I took to the camping life like a duck takes to water. This was probably a good thing, because I was to spend a great deal of my army life under canvas.

I remember one incident at this scout camp when my cousin

Monty and myself were told to take two dixies and to fill them with water from a trough in the next field. To our horror we saw a bull drinking from the trough and, having no previous experience whatsoever of the countryside plus having heard about the ferocity of bulls, we decided to stand by the gate and wait until the animal went away. After about an hour we were still too scared to venture into the field and the scoutmaster came dashing over wondering what on earth had happened to us. We showed him the bull and explained that we were being very prudent in not going into the field.

He looked at us, 'That's not a bull, it's a cow!' He promptly went over to the animal, gave it a friendly smack on its behind and off it went happily.

I must also mention another memory I have as a child, that of the first book that ever belonged to me. I don't recall how old I was, but the book was about eight inches square with a brown leather covering. It was about a family where a young child used to go to bed at the top of a house, in the attic. As it was my first book, it made such an impression on me that I remember carrying it around very proudly. I am sure that this book opened up for me what was to be the most wonderful thing of my life: the reading of books, as I mentioned earlier. Certainly, reading has often saved my sanity. Throughout my life, in times of stress and distress, I was always able to pick up a book, immerse myself for a few minutes, come out of the present and enter into a world of limitless time and space.

At this juncture I must write a little more about my mother. Rachael Gilbert was one of several children in a large family. As a young woman she married my father, travelled to a strange country and left behind everything she knew. London was a teeming metropolis, the largest city in the world at the time, and here she made a home and reared three children in the finest way any mother could. She was a most fantastic person who coped admirably with various economic difficulties and the misfortune that her husband, whom she loved very dearly, left her a widow at the age of forty. She then had to earn a living, see that her young children were looked after, educated and made fit in all ways to become adult members of society. All this she achieved in a most remarkable manner, always cheerful and never complaining to anybody about her difficulties.

She taught us all in a manner, in which I can only hope I have taught my son and that he will teach his children. She had a wonderful philosophy of life and, after any particular difficulty, she would turn and say, '*Ich hob zei alle in Varshe.*' (I've got them all in Warsaw.) Thus, with that one sentence, she was able to clear from her mind all of life's problems. I, too, have found it very useful in my life. Often, during a particularly difficult period when very concerned or worried, I would remember my mother's words and I too would stand, shouting in Yiddish, 'I've got them all in Warsaw!' In other words, 'To hell with everybody, they can do as they please, say as they please, I will still carry on in my own way – undeterred!'

The other thing my mother taught me was the Sanitsky family motto which is, '*Gesogt is getun*' – 'No sooner said than done'. Once she had made up her mind that something had to be done, irrespective of all the problems and excuses that could be made, she immediately got on with it. Her attitude was that if a thing needed doing, get it done with; good, bad or indifferent. That is again a philosophy I have followed all my life.

My mother enabled me to become an apprentice when I left school, after I had had a long discussion with her about it. It meant that my contribution to the family funds for five years would be virtually nil and on my occasions it would mean that I would have to call upon her help for both the initial apprenticeship course costs and for some financial support during this time. She was totally in favour of my plan and did everything possible to help me, firmly believing the old Yiddish philosophy: that a boy or a man without a trade is a thief.

When I went into the army, I automatically made a weekly allowance of part of my earnings to my mother. Unknown to me, for the six and a half years I was away, she put this money aside and when I returned home she gave me a Post Office Savings book with over £600 in it. I had sent this money to help her during the war but, however desperate things may have been, she had not used a penny of it. It had all been saved for me to help towards starting my own career and achieving what success I could.

I remember that when I was quite small the Gilberts, my uncle and aunt, had a girl as a living-in home help. She came from Wales and taught us children the Yaga language which is formed by separating the consonant and vowel sounds and adding 'ag' before each vowel sound. It sounds simple but, after a lot of practice, when it is spoken very fast it is not easily understood by the uninitiated. All the members of the Sanitsky, Gilbert and Helman families became very proficient at this and so I taught it to my son and am trying to teach it to my grandchildren. It is very useful if one wants to say something to a member of one's family without anybody knowing what one is saying. Of course one mustn't be rude about it; it must be used very discreetly.

The Yiddish language played a very important part both in my whole upbringing and in the tone and character of the Jewish East End. Yiddish is a relatively new language, which presumably originated from German having a similarity with German, just as medieval English has with modern English. Yiddish also contains Hebrew and Polish words since it evolved during the 300 years that the bulk of the Jews lived in Poland where they all spoke the language. Yiddish finally became established when it began to be written with three or four famous authors, such as Sholem Aleichem, becoming well known.

My parents always spoke Yiddish to each other, but as the children grew up a gradual change came about as more English words were introduced into their vocabulary. As children, we always spoke English to each other and would reply in English to adults addressing us in Yiddish.

The English that we spoke was very liberally sprinkled with Yiddish words and expressions like: *meshugge, lobus, yom tov,* good *shabbes, haimisher* cucumbers. Phrases containing one English and one Yiddish word were frequently used, mostly because there were several words in Yiddish that never quite meant the same thing in translation. *Meshugge*, for instance, literally means 'mad but it doesn't quite mean insane, more like 'silly' as in, 'Don't be *meshugge!' Lobus* means 'bad boy' but bad in a nice way; naughty but nice!

Expressions such as 'Good *yom tov*' or 'Good *shabbes*' came naturally to us and we presumed we were talking English because it would never occur to us to say 'Good Sabbath' or Good Holy Day' and thus certain Yiddish words became part of our English language. One example is the way the whole world refers to the 'Yom Kippur War' – it is never the 'Day of Atonement War' – so Yom Kippur is now part of the English language. *Beigel* (or bagel as the world pronounces it) is now part of English and in America other words such as '*chutzpah*' (meaning cheek or liberty) are commonly understood.

Some of the Yiddish in the East End was different to that used in other parts of the country, presumably because people originating from different European communities introduced their own local words into the area that they had emigrated to. For example, we never used the word '*yarmulkah*' to denote the headcovering that men wore. We always called it a '*cupple*'. However, I have discovered that anywhere out of London most Jews do not know to what I am referring.

Most long-standing immigrants spoke accented English with a few Yiddish and Hebrew words and we had a lot of characters around whom we used to imitate. If you asked somebody in the tailoring trade what business was like, you would probably get an answer like,'Hop to nar it's been busy, but nar it's gitting slack!'

There were two locally printed newspapers, *the Times* and the *Evening News*, edited by a very famous character, a real, old-fashioned journalist called Moishe Myer. It was very common when his editorials or articles were being discussed, for my father and others to say, 'Moishe Myer says this or Moishe Myer said that!' It was as though people thought that everything printed in the newspaper was the opinion of the owner.

As a child, I used to read the *Evening News* very slowly and laboriously, but I could understand it. The script was in Hebrew, the same I was learning at *cheder*, but the language was Yiddish and, although I could not translate Hebrew, I could pronounce it and comprehend the Yiddish. I thus learned to write Yiddish using the Hebrew written characters.

I remember telling my son Nigel, when he was about ten, that when we translated parts of the Bible from the Hebrew, we translated them into Yiddish because our *cheder* teacher could only understand a few English words. Nigel asked me what happened to the boys who couldn't understand Yiddish. I told him there were no such boys for, before the war, every young Jew living in a Jewish area understood spoken Yiddish. Very few of us could speak Yiddish to any extent because we simply didn't practise it. As I always say, '*Ich kon raden mit a tzybrochener tzyng!*' in other words, 'I can speak but with a broken tongue.'

The sad but inevitable thing is that the use of Yiddish and the Yiddish language itself is almost certainly not going to exist in a hundred years' time. Inevitably, Hebrew has to take its place. Yiddish probably never really had a chance of surviving once the early pioneers, the first modern Zionists, decided that Hebrew (*Ivrit*) was to be the language of Israel. It was then that the language of Yiddish was doomed. It is probably not all that important and it is really just from a sentimental point of view that it is to be regretted.

When I was young I always thought that sugar was obtained either as small cubes or in a fine grain form known as 'lumdust' – I only realised later that the real name was 'granulated sugar'. Most East Enders called the dust that the sugar left at the bottom of the bag 'lumdust' because it was sold cheaper than cube sugar and was thus the type that they bought. Instead of being referred to as 'lump dust', it gradually became 'lumdust', the 'p' being dropped, so that most people thought that this was the English name for the product.

In the same way, broken biscuits were cheaper than whole ones and everyone I knew only bought this kind of biscuit. I remember that Peek Freans used to make shortcake biscuits in the shape of Punch and Judy and the various animals. Not until I was almost an adult, did I realise that you could actually buy the characters as whole biscuits.

As a Jewish community in a non-Jewish country, some odd things happened with regard to certain names – for example, St John's Wood Synagogue – an unusual name for a synagogue, which happens to be in the St John's Wood district of London. In addition there are 'Vicarage Lane' and 'Whitechapel' Synagogues – the latter we used to say very quickly so as not to think of it as a white chapel!

There is also the Waltham Abbey Jewish Cemetery which really is mind-boggling as one wonders what on earth a Jewish Cemetery is doing in an abbey.

A few months before leaving school, a major event that shaped my life occurred: I became a member of the Victoria Working Boys Club. Then came another milestone: I became an indentured apprentice to become a jeweller; a diamond-mounter as the indenture said. These two events, my life at the club and my life as an apprentice in Hatton Garden, ran side by side during the five years from the age of fourteen until I went into the army when I was nineteen.

2
Apprenticeship

In order to become a jewellery apprentice I went along to the Jewish Board of Guardians, which had a local Boys Industrial Department run by a gentleman called Mr Gee. I told him that I wanted to be a jeweller and, after a long examination of the reasons and my background, he said that as soon as I left school, I should visit him again and he would see what he could do.

It was very difficult to get an apprenticeship in one of the large, important jewellery firms like Cartier, Boucheron or Garrards, not because they would not take on Jewish boys – although it certainly played a part in limiting the number of jobs that we could expect – but because there were only a limited number of apprentices required. It was the nature of the trade that there were always relatives or friends of the people already working in these firms who were on the waiting list for the few vacancies that became available. Despite all the efforts of the Board, Jewish boys mostly went to jobs in very small firms where the quality of work was usually of a lower order than the large West End firms.

Thus, when I left school, I saw Mr Gee as promised and he sent me to a small firm in Hatton Garden. I went along merrily for a month's trial to a tiny room, in a back street off the Garden, which contained only a single work-bench since it was a one-man business. The owner was the only craftsman although there was another apprentice who had already been there for two years.

I started work immediately and at lunch-time, just before one o'clock, the governor told me to go out and buy him a sandwich for his lunch. I was perfectly happy to do so as cleaning and errands were part of my duties. He told me to fetch a ham sandwich from one of the local cafes in Hatton Garden. I got him his sandwich and in the afternoon I told him that I was very sorry but I was not going to be able to return the following day.

The next day I returned to Mr Gee, who was somewhat surprised to see me; I told him that I couldn't stay at that firm and requested that he should please send me to another. Naturally he asked me for an explanation. I told him that the firm was okay, but as they had sent me out to buy a ham sandwich, I didn't feel as though I

This Indenture

made the **FIFTH** day of **NOVEMBER** One thousand nine hundred and **THIRTYFOUR** BETWEEN **RALPH GLICK,** 40, Hatton Garden, Holborn, E.C.1.

(hereinafter called "the Master") of the first part **RECHEL SANITSKY** 41, Turner Street, Commercial Road, London, E.1. of the second part

LEONARD SANITSKY son of the said **RECHEL SANITSKY** (hereinafter called "the Apprentice") of the third part and THE BOARD OF GUARDIANS AND TRUSTEES FOR THE RELIEF OF THE JEWISH POOR Registered of Middlesex Street in the City of London (hereinafter referred to as "the Board") of the fourth part WHEREAS the Apprentice has agreed to bind himself and the Master has agreed to accept him as an apprentice upon the conditions hereinafter mentioned AND WHEREAS the Board has at the request of the said **RECHEL SANITSKY** (hereinafter called "the Parent") agreed to advance out of funds belonging to the said Board the premium required for such apprenticeship the same being charity moneys AND WHEREAS by an Agreement of even date herewith and made between the Parent of the one part and the Board of the other part the Parent has agreed to repay to the Board the moneys so advanced by weekly instalments as therein mentioned NOW THIS INDENTURE WITNESSETH that in consideration of the sum of _____ **SEVEN POUNDS TENSHILLINGS** by the Board to the Master paid on the execution of these presents and of the agreement to pay the further sum of **SEVEN POUNDS TENSHILLINGS** hereinafter contained and of the covenants and agreements entered into by the Parent and Apprentice he the Master hereby covenants with the Parent and Apprentice and also as a separate covenant with the Board in manner following that is to say: THAT he the Master will take and receive the Apprentice as his apprentice from the day of the date of these presents for the term of **five** years and also will during the said term to the best of his knowledge power and ability teach and instruct or cause to be taught and instructed the Apprentice in the trade or business of **a DIAMOND MOUNTER** and in all things incident or relating thereto AND will pay to the said Apprentice wages at the rates and in manner following that is to say during the first year

first six months **SEVENSHILLINGS** and **SIXPENCE** per week during the second second six months **TENSHILLINGS**

first six months **TWELVESHILLINGS** and **SIXPENCE** per week during the third year second six months **FIFTEENSHILLINGS**

first six months **SEVENTEENSHILLINGS** and **SIXPENCE** per week during the second six months **TWENTYSHILLINGS**

fourth year first six months **TWENTYTWOSHILLINGS** and **SIXPENCE** per week during second six months **TWENTYFIVESHILLINGS**

the fifth year first six months **TWENTYSEVENSHILLINGS** and **SIXPENCE** per week last six months **THIRTYSHILLINGS** per week

Provided that if the apprentice shall absent himself from work owing to illness or incapacity contracted or arising otherwise than out of and in the course of his employment hereunder for a period exceeding two weeks the wages hereinbefore specified or such part thereof as with the value of any benefits receivable by the Apprentice under or by virtue of the National Insurance Acts will make up the full amount of such wages shall on the expiration of the said period of two weeks cease to be payable until the Apprentice shall present himself for work. AND that he the Master will not assign the Apprentice to another master without the

Part of my Indenture Agreement.

Consideration of the BOARD OF GUARDIANS AND TRUSTEES FOR THE RELIEF OF THE JEWISH POOR (Registered) having paid or agreed to pay **FIFTEEN** Pounds as a premium for the Apprenticeship of my son I hereby undertake to repay to the said Board the said sum of **FIFTEEN POUNDS** or so much thereof as the Board shall have paid by the instalments following that is to say: during the first year after the commencement of the said Apprenticeship the sum of

ONESHILLING	per week, during the second year
TWOSHILLINGS	per week, during the third year
THREESHILLINGS	per week, during the fourth year
FOURSHILLINGS	per week, during the fifth year

per week until the entire sum paid as a premium as aforesaid shall have been repaid, such instalments to be paid between the hours of 9.30 a.m. and 1 p.m. on each successive Sunday at the Offices of the Board or at such other time and place as may be appointed therefore AND I FURTHER AGREE that if default shall be made in payment of any one or more of such instalments I will, if required by the said Board, forthwith, pay the whole of the unpaid balance of the said sum paid as a premium as aforesaid AND it shall also be lawful for the Master of my said son upon notice in writing from the said Board to deduct from the wages payable to my said son the instalments for the time being owing and pay the same to the said Board.

Dated this **Fifth** day of **November** One thousand nine hundred and **Thirtyfour**

WITNESS

[signature]

Rechel Sanitsky

33

could remain there. Mr Gee looked at me and explained that the purchase of a ham sandwich did not mean that I, myself, had to eat non-kosher food; life was not as simple as that. I must expect, in the new world into which I was going, to adjust and adapt the ideas that I had been taught as a child. While he was lecturing me, a telephone call came through from another Hatton Garden firm with a vacancy for an apprentice and the next day I returned to the Garden to a firm called 'Ralph Glick'.

Ralph Glick was a larger organisation consisting of about eighteen men and boys of various ages – I was the only Jewish person among them. I started to work, cleaning and so on and, at twelve o'clock I was instructed to go round with a list for the lunch-time orders. By the time I had completed the list, instead of one ham sandwich from one café, I had a variety of ham sandwiches plus other non-kosher foods to obtain from a variety of cafés in the area. However, by this time I had learnt one of the first lessons of life and cheerfully accepted it, fetching everybody's orders.

I settled at Glick's very quickly, making many friends some of whom became lifelong friends of mine. It was a completely new world to me because this was the first time I had lived as a Jew in a non-Jewish environment.

The system in this company was that each year (an apprenticeship lasted five years from the age of fourteen to nineteen) a new apprentice would be employed as the senior one finished his time and became an improver. It took five years to become a mounter, then one was an improver until the age of twenty-one. I took to the work immediately, having no difficulty whatsoever and I thoroughly enjoyed my five years there.

The senior apprentice, an eighteen-year-old named Horace Craddock, sat next to me and was responsible for teaching me in my early years. The mounters were on two benches not more than five yards from each other and each bench had seven places. Most of the time everybody was talking to everybody else and we could all hear each other's conversations whilst we were working, since the nature of the work was that it was fairly quiet. It was very cosy and under these circumstances we got to know everything about each other.

Bill MacDougall came from West Ham, Eddie Sayer from Plaistow and Sid Harvey came from the Alexandra Palace area. Sid left before his apprenticeship finished to join the Merchant Navy. During the early part of the war he achieved some fame because he was on an armed merchantman that engaged a pocket battleship, and I was very pleased when I read about him in the newspapers.

Other apprentices at Glick's included Mick Schlain (who afterwards became Mick Slade of Slade & Woolf, one of the leading manufacturing companies) and Archie Cooper who had two older brothers, Alf and Frank. I was very close to Alf because we had the hobby of weightlifting in common. Frank Cooper was a composer in his spare time and was one of the first men in the jewellery trade to recognise the importance of the 'lost wax casting system'. This was a modernised system for economic jewellery production, which I was able to develop many years later for producing very complicated jewellery of international quality. Just before the war, Frank left Glick's and went to one of the large firms in the Garden to set up a casting workshop for them.

The foreman was Bill Whittlesey who, a few months before the war broke out, got some form of food poisoning and, to our great astonishment, died. His funeral was the first non-Jewish religious ceremony that I had attended and it impressed me greatly. It was so simple for he belonged to a Protestant sect that did not believe in anything ornate, using a very sparse bare church.

I often went to the houses of my co-workers, joined them socially and never found any difficulty because of the fact that I was brought up in a completely Jewish environment. During my apprenticeship I led two separate lives: one revolving around the Jewish family and Jewish boys' club life and the other a normal English working life.

At first I was paid 5s 0d (25p) a week which increased by 2s 6d, then by 5s 0d each six-month period until during the final six month period of my apprenticeship, at the age of 18^1/2 and a half I was paid £1 10s 0d (£1.50) a week. The cost of being apprenticed was £15, which my mother had to pay half on the day that I signed the documents; 5th November 1934. The Board of Guardians loaned my mother £7 10s 0d at the start of my apprenticeship and, two and a half years later, the second instalment of £7 10s 0d.

I had to buy a kit of tools, costing £2 5s 0d and both the money for the apprenticeship and the money for the tools were loaned to my mother by the Board of Guardians. I remember the ritual of going along to the Board of Guardians' offices in Middlesex Street each Sunday morning where I would repay them 6d. (2½p) for the premium and 3d for the kit of tools.

My 5s a week was used as follows; the fare money from St Mary's Station to Farringdon Street was 10d (5p) for a weekly season ticket, the national insurance stamp was 2d and then there was the 9d repayment money. I was left with the princely sum of 3s 3d. My mother allowed me to keep 6d for myself and the rest I duly gave across to her each week to contribute to my support and clothing.

My working day started at 8.30 a.m. and finished at 6 p.m. including a one hour lunch-break and a short tea-break. On Saturdays we worked from 8.30 a.m. to 1 p.m. but most of the time I tried to work overtime. Overtime was optional for most of the year and, after a few months in the firm, I had made myself useful enough to be included in the overtime rota. At first I was paid one penny an hour but, towards the end of my apprenticeship, this had risen to 6d an hour. Two or three hours' overtime a week supplemented my personal income, for my mother would not take any of this extra money from me. Thus, with my 6d allowance plus 3d for three hours' overtime, I had increased my spending money by fifty per cent.

Most of my leisure time was spent at the boys' club but, often on a Saturday night, I would go to the Paragon Cinema at Mile End. Here, in a former music hall, there were stalls, a dress circle, an upper circle and a gallery. The gallery was not considered very suitable for watching films so a ticket here only cost 4d for which one could see a programme consisting of two major films and a stage show. After the cinema my friends and I would go over to Johnny Isaacs to buy a penny portion of chips, a halfpenny bagel and a halfpenny pickled cucumber. This sixpenny night out was thoroughly enjoyable yet still left me with a further 3d for the rest of the week.

Most of the work that I was being trained to do was with platinum since very little gold was used for jewellery at that time; platinum was the modern metal. As a junior my chief tasks were to keep the workshop clean, to make the tea at lunch-time and tea-break and to wax and clean the benches each morning before the senior men started work at 9 a.m. During the day I would be given some simpler tasks to do with jewellery-making such as milling out metal or drawing out wire, doing the pickling and bending round circles of metal wire for collets. Gradually, as I became more experienced, so I would be given more complicated work.

I also had to do all the necessary errands such as going to the Bullion Merchants Johnson Matthey or Baker Platinum and ferrying work to the outdoor workers such as polishers, setters, engravers and any of the other splinter trades that were part and parcel of the industry in the days before such craftsmen would be incorporated into the main firm.

Occasionally I would deliver to customers in Bond Street or other parts of the West End, thoroughly enjoying these expeditions and feeling very proud when I recognised articles in their windows which had been made in our workshop. Later on, as I was more senior, I would be thrilled to note items in shop windows which I had made myself.

Twice a week I attended evening classes at the Central School of Arts and Crafts. In the mounters' class some of the people were not jewellery apprentices, but were people like school-teachers who wanted to make jewellery as a hobby and many of them were very amateurish. I stopped going after about six months simply because I was far ahead in my knowledge gleaned from my daily work. The first few months did help however.

After a while I became very familiar with the whole of Hatton Garden and the area around it, getting to know the character of areas such as Leather Lane, Cross Street and Clerkenwell. I became acquainted with other apprentices from firms in the Garden that were similar to ours, the suppliers of gemstones or lapidaries or the host of small firms that went at that time to make up the jewellery industry. Most of them have disappeared now.

At Christmas we were able to supplement our income with Christmas boxes from the polishers, setters and customers with whom we dealt. The custom was that the two junior apprentices who had shared the work during the year, shared the bonuses. We used to get a small notebook, take it round to the various firms, hand it in and say, 'Happy Christmas'. The polisher or setter would look at the previous names in the book to see how much had been given, write in their own names and put down the amount that they were going to donate; 6d or 1s 0d. Every apprentice in the Garden discussed this book, trying to estimate what the take was going to be. There were many systems to try to increase the amount of money that would be given, the most common being to write a number of names of different firms and put by the side a larger sum of money than was reasonably expected. It may have appeared to us that we were fooling the people we went to but, as the custom had probably gone on for the last hundred years, they were all well aware that the books were being padded out to try to entice them to give a higher Christmas box. This was all taken in good clean fun as were the various other things to do with apprentices.

Every apprentice, at some time or another, would be sent to a local firm that sold tools to buy a diamond magnet. A diamond magnet in the jewellery trade is the equivalent to the left-handed hammer in engineering. A diamond is a mineral that has no magnetic properties. Apprentices would often have to spend hours every time a diamond dropped to the floor searching for the valuable missing stone. It was not unusual to spend two or three hours hunting since ultimately the gem had to be found. Therefore the diamond magnet would have been a wonderful tool. All the shops in the area knew of the diamond magnet ruse so it was common practice when a green apprentice went in to buy one that Coopers, for instance, would say that they were sorry but they were out of stock but they would suggest going to Salvo's. Salvo's would send the boy to Pike's and so on until finally the boy would make the rounds of all the tool shops in the area before returning to the workshop and discovering that no such thing existed.

Underlying this fun was a determination to spend as much time as possible at the bench for all apprentices realised that it was only by sitting at the bench that the trade could be learnt. All the errands had to be done but the sooner one got these out of the way the more time one could spend learning one's craft so that when the five years were finished one could be a good enough craftsman to obtain a job.

Our workshop, like all the others, was tiny relative to the number of men in them but was kept scrupulously clean and tidy. Every tool that was for general use had a place of its own and woe betide any apprentice if any of these tools were either missing or absent from their proper places, hanging upon their correct nail. We all wore leather skins, tied with strings round our necks, to catch and conserve scraps of metal that might fall as we worked. The rules of conserving losses of metal were so strict that nobody, not even the foreman would dream of ignoring them for fear of being dismissed. Metal conservation was of paramount importance. Nobody left their seat until they had vigorously brushed their hands and the front of their working coats to ensure that any metal was captured in the skin.

We had to wear these brown working coats, which we had to supply ourselves at the cost of about two weeks of a new apprentice's salary. Most junior apprentices made do with any that were no longer considered as suitable by previous owners who may have discarded coats because they were too tattered, or left them behind as they were not worth taking. Such coats were usually far too large and invariably patched, so boy apprentices were easy to recognise as they walked around in what looked like tattered brown rags which went right down to the ankles.

When Baker Platinum opened in a smart new building in High Holborn, the word soon went round that it was possible to go to their cloakroom where, apart from hot water and washing facilities, there was a boot polishing machine and a free dispenser of Brylcream hair cream or something similar. All these were available to anybody who had a reason to go to the building. This was a sensation among the apprentices and, for a few short weeks, all the boys could be seen still in their ankle-length raggedy coats but with highly polished boots and hair liberally plastered down! Needless to say, the powers that be soon put a stop to that nonsense.

There was also a continual battle of wits between apprentices and some of the caretakers of the various buildings. Most of the caretakers also acted as lift operators and considered that they had so much work to do that unimportant people, like apprentices, could jolly well walk up and down the stairs. The apprentices tried to outwit them in every way they could usually by trying such subterfuges as having a large parcel in one's hands which then required the use of the lift. We used to collect together empty boxes so as to pretend that a heavy parcel had to be taken up to various offices.

I remember on one occasion someone dared me to use the lift at No 1 Hatton Garden, right on the corner. Here we used to visit an office on the sixth floor and I took a very dim view of walking up and down six floors when there was a lift on the premises. I pretended to have a limp and told the carefully questioning caretaker that I had hurt my foot playing football. I informed him that the doctor had told me to take it easy so I really needed to use the lift. He only half believed me, grudgingly took me up to the sixth floor, watched me hobble along the corridor, took me back down to the ground floor, continued to watch me as I limped to the front door and then, like a shot, saw me run down the road laughing my head off.

There was a disadvantage to this because for a period of time, on the occasions I was sent to this particular office, I had to reconnoitre the ground, go to the front of the building, wait until the caretaker was busily occupied in the lift, so that I could nip in and run up the stairs making sure he couldn't spot me.

Leather Lane was a fascinating place containing a market. My early apprenticeship ran concurrently with the gold break-up, coming off the gold standard. Enormous amounts of gold articles were sold and broken up and a lot of them found their way to one or two stalls in Leather Lane. I became friendly with one of these stall-holders and was able to oblige him by doing small jobs for him. As a result, whenever he got a pocket-watch to break up for the gold content, he would allow me to strip the watch and keep the parts.

These movements were pretty useless because there were thousands and thousands of broken movements around, but I got very interested in the dials of some of these watches. Some were Victorian or Edwardian, some perhaps were even Georgian and the dials were absolute works of art. They were mostly enamel with flowers, motifs, decorations of all kinds and usually they were in perfect condition so I used to collect them as a hobby. By the time war broke out I had about 200 of these beautiful dials which could never be obtained again because the watches had been destroyed and it was the end of an era. Nobody thought they would have any value but I simply kept them because I enjoyed the look of them. When I went into the army I left the box of dials in the cellar which was later converted into an air-raid shelter.

Some months after I was demobbed I remembered the dials, searched for them but never found them. Nobody at home knew what had happened to them although my mother remembered my collection. That should have been the end of that story but, oddly enough, about ten years later during the mid-fifties, I read that there was going to be an auction of a collection of dials at Sotheby's. I went along, looked at the dials and, although it was many years since I had seen them, I was pretty sure that they were my property but could do nothing about it. They fetched £1,500 – at the time an enormous sum of money.

In the workshop, as I have explained we were always having problems with dropping stones. When one is handling tiny objects, it is obvious that at times a stone will flick out from the tongs and land either in the leather skin in which filings etc were collected or on the floor. The apprentice would have to get on his hands and knees to look for it every time a man dropped a stone. This was disruptive to us all.

On one occasion I remember I was sizing a single stone ring. I had cut out a piece at the back of the shank, had the ring in a pair of pliers in my left hand and another pair of pliers in my right hand. As I was closing the two ends of the shank together ready to solder it, the governor came by, saw me doing this and said, 'Give it to me and I'll show you how to do it.'

I handed him the pliers and the single stone ring. After I had passed it to him he looked and said, 'Where's the ring?'

I stood up thinking that the ring would have gone into the skin but it wasn't there and he said that it must have fallen on the floor. We searched and searched but the ring had disappeared. The governor had put the pliers back in place where they sat with the rest of my pliers, about ten of them in row by my skin, all hanging on a piece of wire.

Everybody began anxiously to search for the single stone ring which, containing a one carat diamond, was nowhere to be seen. Suddenly someone noticed that the window near to us had been opened about three inches at the bottom as it was a hot summer's day. This was not supposed to happen for fear of things jumping out of the window and normally only the top of the window should be opened, but it had been very warm indeed. Every individual in the workshop got up and went down the street to search the pavement. After two or three minutes – in Hatton Garden everyone was interested in everybody else's business – there were people from all over the Garden. Once we said we were looking for a single stone ring, the crowd grew larger as everybody joined in the search. The governor started to become anxious in case somebody was to find the valuable ring and keep it. He kept saying, 'Thank you very much, we don't need your help!' but nobody took any notice of him and there must have been a crowd of about a hundred by the time we abandoned the quest.

Finally we returned to the workshop, desperately looking there again. I sat at my place and, hanging on the pair of pliers that the governor had put down, was the ring. A sigh of relief all around – he just hadn't noticed the shank on the pliers as he had replaced them on the wire.

There are many incidents I could recall about the years of learning the trade. Any individual who takes a piece of raw material, turns it into an article, especially one that is admired and treasured, changes his character once he becomes a craftsman. I personally believe that every person should produce something, even if it is simply putting seeds into a garden and growing flowers. There is in each human being a need to make something out of nothing. It is my experience that craftsmen, whether they are carpenters, fitters, welders, polishers, mounters, setters etc are a different breed to people who simply work in offices and don't produce anything. Non-producers are necessary but are a different breed.

There were so many characters in Hatton Garden that are remembered to this day. I recall one engraver that I used to visit: the first time I went into his workshop, he sat down at a similar bench to ours and merrily continued engraving a silver plate. In his hand he held a sharp-pointed instrument (a scorper or graver) and began to talk to me as I stood by him. Suddenly the instrument slipped, he said, 'Blast!' and, with one thrust of this sharp scorper, he went smack and dug it into his leg. I nearly jumped out of my skin but he laughed his head off and I discovered that the leg was wooden! He had lost the limb during the war. He was known throughout the Garden and it was the usual thing for every new apprentice to experience this act of his.

There were various characters who paraded the streets as one man bands, or groups of people playing banjos and other instruments. Everyone in Hatton Garden would throw money to them out of the windows. We would often heat the halfpenny with a blowpipe, watch the man from the street pick up the coin and promptly shout out curses to whoever had sent the coin down. Any busker in our area knew full well that the coin would be hot, so the cursing was only an act, for the buskers either wore gloves or would hold something in their hands into which they could scoop up the coin.

In 1936 Dinah, who had been a wonderful loving sister to me, got married to Mick Pittenberg. Being three years my senior she had taken care of me from babyhood and was everything a brother could wish for in a sister. I was now sixteen and, together with my mother and my brother Manny, felt responsible for looking after my sister and ensuring that she was properly married. The fact that our mother was a widow was not to harm her chances of having a proper marriage.

You cannot imagine what a big event that marriage was in our life. Probably marriage was the largest event in any Jewish family; certainly it was in our circle. For many months before the wedding all sorts of arrangements were discussed, revised, revised again, finalised, finalised again – especially the number of people who would be at the synagogue. This was the large synagogue in Philpot Street where we had been members all our lives. The reception took place at the Shoreditch Town Hall, and we hired an outside caterer. Over and over again, we discussed the number of people who would be coming to the dinner, the clothes we were to wear, where the various members of our very large family were going to sit, the order of importance of their position from the top table downwards and so on and so on. It was a wonderful year.

Some months before the wedding itself, as we discussed the small gifts to be given to the six or seven bridesmaids I, in my new-found enthusiasm as a halfway apprentice, said that I would make silver name brooches for them. This took me weeks and weeks in my spare time as the governor allowed me to stay late and make them in the workshop when I explained to him that it was for my sister's bridesmaids.

Finally, the great day came, the weather was lovely and we looked splendid all dressed up in our hired suits. We didn't wear mere dinner suits but top hats, white ties and tails, as we very proudly escorted my sister to the ceremony. The festivities continued until 2 a.m. the next morning and we returned home tired, happy and with a sense of a good job well done.

By and large, life was very exciting, time went by quickly for we all had a terrific sense of humour considering the conditions – but then, this was the only life we knew; we were happy to be alive.

I was happy to be rapidly learning a very complicated craft which has stood me in good stead for all of my life. I found that I had a natural instinct to working with metal, having always been completely at home with any metal object whether it required repairing or manufacturing. To this day, if I see anything made of metal, I understand immediately its advantages, its disadvantages and all its problems. Over the years I have worked on things as tiny as a one-pointer diamond (a stone not metal) and as huge as ten-ton lorries or six-inch guns or military tanks. Thus whether it was tiny or enormous, a hand object or a lathe, a milling machine, soldering with a small blowpipe on precious metals or welding with an oxyacetylene pipe on sheet metal, cast bronze casting or cast iron casting, it was all the same to me: all metal.

I have always looked back with joy on the years that I spent as an apprentice before the war. I think it was the finest decision I ever made in my life to become a jeweller and have never ever regretted it. Nor did I consider doing anything else in my early years.

3
The Victoria Boys' Club

In my early years Britain was faced with the new international political elements of Hitler, Mussolini and Franco, whilst at home there was the Fascist, anti-semitic Mosley and the Blackshirts. This, against the backcloth of the terrible economic depression of the thirties, and such events as the Japanese invading China, Mussolini invading Abyssinia, the Spanish Civil War, Hitler, the Anschluss with Austria, the takeover of Czechoslovakia, the Munich crisis and finally Hitler's German invasion of Poland and the outbreak of the Second World War.

All of these activities and events were interwoven and intermingled in the whole fabric of my life. The key to it was the Victoria Boys' Club, or simply 'The Club' or 'The Vic' as we called it. Nobody could possibly realise the lifelong effects that these East End Jewish clubs had upon their young members.

Our club was founded when the Bishop of Stepney contacted Herman Adler, the Chief Rabbi, to ask that something be done by the Jewish community leaders about the gangs of young Jewish boys who had been creating problems whilst roaming the streets in the Commercial Road area. Consequently, Dr Adler, in conjunction with Charles Montefiore, a member of one of the most renowned Jewish families in the country, opened premises in March 1901; the club being named in the memory of Queen Victoria, who had just died. Within a year it had moved to new premises in Fordham Street and this was the building that I first entered when I was about thirteen and a half, a few months before I left school.

The spirit of the club combined with the respect and affection connected with it was so great that no old Etonian nor any old Harrovian could possibly have been more proud of their illustrious schools than the boys of our club were of the 'Vic'. During all the years that I remained a member, whenever any of the boys were skylarking about, it was only necessary to say, 'Remember the Club's good name. You are representatives of the Club!' and immediately the boys would behave themselves.

44

Its influence on me was enormous for, like most young boys, I had often read publications like *The Magnet* and *The Gem* which depicted the way of life in public schools, propagating such ideas as fair play, sportsmanship, manliness etc. Our clubs, in many ways, replicated the ideals of these large public schools. Many of the managers, as the people who ran the club were termed, were themselves public schoolboys. Charles Montefiore himself had originally attended Clifton College, which was the only public school to have a Jewish House – Polack's House – and he was responsible for getting some Clifton old boys interested to come to the East End.

This association of Polack's House and the Victoria Club lasted right through to the end of the war and beyond manifesting itself in a number of ways. Our club colours, chocolate and white, were the same as Polack's House and each year a large hamper used to arrive full of partly worn football jerseys and other sporting kit which we proudly wore as we carried out the club activities.

The activities at the club were divided into two basic parts; physical and cultural. The former included athletics, gym, boxing, football, cricket, badminton and table-tennis whilst the latter consisted of reading circles, debating groups, amateur theatricals, concert parties, a library and various other social gatherings.

By far the largest, happiest and most eagerly anticipated event of the year was the summer camp on the Isle of Wight. Here we stayed at Nettlestone Farm near Seaview, where we experienced a completely different world from the one we lived in for the rest of the year. We saved our money as best as we could throughout the year to collect the very small cost of the camp. Some weeks beforehand a committee of managers would meet to assess each boy and decide how much each should be asked to contribute. Those who were studying, apprentices or unemployed, were only charged a token sum whilst others might have to pay up to the full figure of perhaps £1 for the holiday.

Our tents were old army bell tents from the First World War and accommodated either seven or eight boys. We also had a big dining marquee where one table for each bell tent was laid out. There would be one young manager – generally boys only aged about nineteen themselves, just down from Clifton College – in charge of each tent and we considered it our duty to find as many ways as possible to pull their legs and rag them as best as we could.

On one occasion as we sat down for the first meal of the camp, one of these managers introduced himself to us as being in charge of our group. He announced that he was going to collect our food from the cookhouse and wanted to know how many boys there were in our tent. One of the brighter boys at our table said that there were eight of us so the manager promptly went away and brought back food for eight. However, our group this year only actually consisted of seven boys but we very quickly made short work of the extra portion.

When this young chap (who shall remain nameless as he later became one of the most popular managers at our club) had not seen the eighth member of our tent after a couple of days, he began to get quite worried and asked the name of this eighth boy. One of the boys piped up and said, 'Fineberg,' to which somebody else added, 'Chunky Fineberg!' Thus Chunky Fineberg was born. After two or three days the whole camp was in on the joke and we continued to happily share Chunky Fineberg's extra portion of food amongst the seven of us.

All the other managers and boys joined in the fun with all sorts of ingenious excuses being made to our manager as to where this boy was at any particular moment and why he was never seen. We managed to drag this out until the end of the week when the truth finally dawned on our victim. But Chunky Fineberg didn't die. He was enrolled as an official club member and from that day to this, whenever any unpopular chore is required to be done, it is still the custom in the club to say, 'Give it to Chunky Fineberg. He'll be delighted to do it!'

The club also held a weekend camp at Broxbourne in Hertfordshire to which I used to go regularly with my friends during the summer. We had a fantastic time and it gave us a lot of healthy outdoor activities as well as being very inexpensive – obviously quite important. For the months before I left school in 1934, most Friday evenings would see me catching the 6.30 train from Liverpool Street which took half an hour to travel to Broxbourne. Then there was another half hour walk along the towpath to get to the camp. This was a permanent site that the club had been given by one of its managers. There was a small hut which we had built to store the blankets and cooking utensils etc and again we slept in old army bell tents. We would return home on Sunday at about 7 p.m. and the cost of this was 1s 3d (6^{1}/2p). I would do any sort of extra activity to raise the amount necessary to be able to go down to week-end camp.

As I have mentioned before, we had several managers and amongst them was Denzil Sebag Montefiore, another member of the famous family. He was very generous whenever he took his turn to take charge of our week-end camps. Denzil, like some of the other managers, brought with him what we considered to be delicacies to supplement the food provided – all of which was cooked over an open fire. His particular contribution was something that was always very popular: roly poly pudding liberally filled with currants and fruit. All we had to do was to boil a dixie of water, put the canvas-wrapped pudding in to heat and, after ten minutes, we would have a delicious sweet served with tinned custard.

On one occasion there were only about ten of us at a particular week-end camp since the weather was poor – not that that made our trip any less exciting. Denzil, however, had brought far too many of his puddings, one being sufficient to share between four boys. He had about two dozen of these which was ridiculous. I said to him that it was very kind of him to bring these along but it was a waste of food. He told me that it was his mother who made them for us all to eat. I said that it was not fair for her to be so busy, making far more puddings than we could possibly eat but, to my amazement, he said that I needn't worry because she was helped by the cook.

I said, 'Oh!' in a surprised tone and added, 'But surely the cook has other things to do?'

He replied, 'To be truthful, Len, in my home we employ thirty-six staff.'

As far as I was concerned that was the end of the subject. It had not occurred to me that any private home could possibly employ so many chauffeurs, gardeners, maids and under-maids so it was an insight as to the different types of lives led by the very wealthy families compared to the members of the club from Stepney.

I admired people like Denzil and his brother for having the guts to give up their time and to mix with youngsters to try to pass on some of the better ideas that they had been brought up with. Not all these ideas were good and not every one was successful but, by and large, most of these fellows – despite their wealth, I am tempted to say – were extremely popular and did an immense amount of good.

These camps were a fantastic way of learning how to live under canvas. This was one of the reasons that I and many of the rest of the boys took to army life without the slightest problem. We were used to the types of activities involved in camping and to the idea of living and working with a group of young men of similar ages but different characters.

Throughout the winter we regularly played football in various leagues against the other clubs on Sundays, usually at Eltham. Occasionally we would be top of the Association of Jewish Youth league for our age-group and should we reach the cup final, there was more excitement amongst us than with the Football Association cup final.

Cricket was also played enthusiastically, although those of us who went to camp had little opportunity to compete for the club but would play amongst ourselves whilst away. On Saturday nights we often played badminton and during the week there was boxing, PT, table tennis and road running.

Oddly enough road running was my favourite as I much preferred it to more formal sports. We used to run from the club down the side turnings of Commercial Road and Whitechapel Road up through Leadenhall Street, past the Bank of England and into the city which was deserted in the evenings. Then we would probably run to Ludgate Circus and back again to the club where we would have a shower.

Alf Cooper, a friend of mine at the workshop in Hatton Garden, was an asthmatic who had been told by his doctor to take up weight-lifting as a means of counteracting the effects of the asthma. As we were great friends, I began to take an interest in weight-lifting when I was about seventeen. Together with a few other boys in the club, including Billy Raven and Sonny Warrenberg, we joined the Bethnal Green Men's Institute where they had a weight-lifting class of a very high standard. On one occasion I acted as a catcher in a competition against another club. There were two catchers who used to stand one on each side of the competitor. Once the weight-lifter had achieved the two-second hold in the air, he simply dropped the weight as if it was nothing to do with him any more, so then we had to catch the weight to stop it falling on to the floor. I didn't like this very much since it was a bit too dangerous!

I got so interested in this hobby that I decided to buy a barbell of my own. There was a firm in Holborn called Gross and Co. and during their sale I bought a set of barbells for fifteen shillings including delivery. I had saved the money myself but I knew that my mother would not be very happy to see a set of weights arriving since it was a frightening looking thing weighing 140 lb. I had to rely on a *fait accompli* that when the weights had been delivered my mother would not object too much to having them in the house.

The weights were delivered one day by horse and cart and my mother looked in astonishment when the delivery man told her that they had been paid for by a Len Sanitsky. My mother then said, 'Fine!' and allowed them to be taken into the house. When I returned home I explained to my mother that the exercise was very good for me, that I would be able to practise my weightlifting in our back garden instead of having to go to Bethnal Green Club and she was quite happy with it after a while, often watching me as I practised. Eventually, so many of the other boys became interested in my new hobby that I transferred the barbells to the club and we had our own very small weightlifting circle which happily continued until the outbreak of the war.

Every now and again the club invited the local people to come to watch our activities such as prize giving, concert parties and drama which we held in the gym. Spectators were also welcome when we had table tennis tournaments as our standard at this was very high; we had one boy, named Schlauss, who played for England. The locals were particularly keen on watching our boxing tournaments, one of which I had to organise. Unfortunately we were a couple of bouts short on the programme so I went around the club asking various people if they would care to participate but generally received quite frosty answers. Eventually I approached a friend of mine called Henry Vagoda saying 'Come on, Henry, you're a tough guy, what about taking part in our boxing tournament?'

Henry, who was much bigger than I, said, 'No, it's for mugs only!' As I tried to persuade him a gleam came into his eye and he asked me if I was going to box. I told him that I wasn't because I was not very good at it. He said that if I boxed, he would box me. The die was then cast for I couldn't back down after that.

I put on as good a face as possible and said, 'Certainly, Henry, I'll box you.'

The great night came along, I had my old friend Ginger in the corner with me and it was finally my turn. The place was mobbed and some of the bouts had been very good indeed. Well, although I had taken part in club boxing, I had never boxed in a ring in front of an audience before and this was an entirely new experience. I never realised how good Henry Vagoda was.

After about fifteen seconds of dancing round him, from some unexplained area a boxing glove hit me on my chin, another hit me on my nose followed by a succession of what appeared to me to be sledgehammer blows. For two more minutes whatever I did was to no avail. Not to put too fine a description on it, Henry half killed me! I came round, sitting on my stool in the corner of the ring with a peculiar feeling in my head. Water was thrown over me for I had actually been knocked out! I must add that before I had blacked out, I had frantically made signs to my pal Ginger to throw the towel in for me but all he did was to give me an encouraging shout saying, 'You're doing fine!'

It was a terrible experience but it taught me a lesson; to be very, very careful before asking anybody else to take part in our boxing tournaments.

Our social life revolved around the various girls' clubs in the district and our own Sunday evening dances which we held monthly in the gym. We used to spend a great deal of time decorating the gym hall with streamers to make it look attractive but it was always a problem to know what was the most effective method of advertising these dances. By trial and error we discovered that the best way to get a crowd was to admit girls by invitation only. We used to send a number of smartly printed cards to each of the girls' clubs and, because they were couched in the form of an invitation, the girls that were selected by their own manageresses to be given these cards, thought they were getting something which was valued. We also gave a number to several of our own boys who would give these cards to girls with whom they were friendly. By persuading a good crowd of girls to attend, the boys then followed automatically.

At one period we had short entertainment during the evening. Some of our boys were extremely talented, producing, writing and directing their own comic shorts. Jackie Goodman, known lovingly as 'Flappers' due to the size of his ears, was the leading light behind this together with his friend, Abie Tilovitch, (who afterwards became Alan Tilvern, went on to the professional stage and is still quite well known).

These activities, plus the fact that our boys were friendly and well-liked, meant that our club became very popular with the girls and, at one period, we actually had to turn girls away simply because we didn't have sufficient room in the gym.

To cover the cost of the three-piece band, 30s (£1.50), and the invitations, we decided to charge sufficient to break even. We made tea and cakes in the interval but we never managed to find a way of making it pay since the boys in charge of the catering were either running it as a private business or were more fond of eating the cakes than selling them!

The girls' clubs – Brady, Stepney, Butler Street, Oxford & St George's, Cambridge & Bethnal Green – all regularly ran their own socials. As we got older and travelled further there was also West Central Club and Stamford Hill Club, who would invite us to their dances so there was no shortage of places to go. We therefore got to know many of the local girls at the various clubs without the expense of dating which would have been very difficult for those of us on a low income or still studying.

In 1935, to my complete astonishment, I was made club captain. I had been for some time promoted to monitor position which meant that I assisted in the general running of the club for the whole idea behind the club system was that as much responsibility as possible should be given to us to manage our own affairs. We had a very elaborate committee system, where we learned all the democratic forms of how to act in committee and how to divide responsibilities into sub-committees. We elected our chairman, our monitors and finally our club captain. I was very proud to be thus honoured and, looking back on my life, of all the various achievements I have had I think being made the club captain of Victoria is at the top of the list.

In 1937 I left the boys' club and went into the senior part of the club, which was still in the same building but called the Victoria Intermediate Club and was for boys aged from seventeen to twenty-two. After some months I was elected as one of the two co-secretaries so during my club life I learned a great deal about the running of organisations, how to get on with people and to get the best out of them. All these experiences were to help me greatly in my adult life.

When I was about sixteen, as is usual with young men, we became interested in social activities and became good friends with many of the girls we met at the girls' clubs. A few of the boys married the girls that they met at this time, the best example being my greatest friend Ginger (Albert Greenfield) who met his charming wife Dodie (Doris) when she was a very young girl. They have remained lifelong friends of my wife and myself and their friendship has been one of the most fortunate things of my life. It is very difficult for me to realise that it began over fifty years ago.

Another one of our boys, Joe Block, married a girl who became a dear friend of ours. Lily Block sadly did not survive beyond a few years after the war. Joe had since had many difficulties to face up to in life but, in the true club spirit, he is now the chairman of an organisation that gives medical help to people that have undergone a serious throat operation. (Joe's brother, Lou, unfortunately was the first member of the club killed during the war at the retreat at Dunkirk.)

Of the hundred or so boys that were members of the club, it is surprising how many have had what could be considered successful lives. One of them is now a judge, two or three are surgeons, three or four are eminent scientists, several are very successful business men and others entered a collection of other trades and professions that any society would be proud to count amongst its members. I have met old 'Vics' all over the world.

The most wonderful aspect of the club was the large number of friends that I made. Irrespective of differences in age, background and personality everyone was considered to be a friend. Naturally some were closer to me than others. Some shared certain activities and others did not. The friends that I shared all activities with were primarily Albert Greenfield, Monty Chaplin, my cousin Johnny, Manny Grossman, Mark Rosenfeld and Alfie Kershberg.

Monty, a tall skinny fellow, joined the RAF and immediately after the war he emigrated to Canada and we unfortunately lost contact with him. Johnny married a charming girl called Freda, and Manny still remains a friend of ours to this day. He was in the artillery during the war, and married Bertha whom we knew as young boys but who sadly died some years ago.

I probably played with Mark in my cot as he lived in Turner Street. He married a girl called Evelyn, and I occasionally meet him to talk about old times. He was another artillery man and I have several letters from him that I received during the war when he was in North Africa.

Then there was Sid Levy, my vice-captain when I was captain of the club. I knew him from *cheder* and he had two wonderful elder brothers, Dave and Charles. During the war, as a soldier, Sid was sent on a chiropody course which astounded him because he had no medical training whatsoever. When he finished this course he was sent to Liverpool, and apparently spent the rest of the war meeting soldiers at Lime Street Station and marching them across the city to the billeting area. He said that he was never called upon for anything remotely connected with being a chiropodist.

Jackie Caplan spoke with a lisp and was a very popular boy. The thing that astounded us was that when he entered a 'Do As You Please' competition on the pier at Ryde, Isle of Wight, he sang beautifully without the slightest trace of any speech impediment and won first prize. Jackie (we used to call him Chookie) was a regular contributor to our concert party.

I was also friendly with Colman Greenberg – co-secretary of the intermediate club – and his brother Ben. Maurice Finn was a wonderful bowler and finished up as a prisoner of war in Italy from where he wrote to me. Tommy Kleinman and Lou Kutzo were young managers and a few years older than me. Tommy was a cook with the Royal Fusiliers and Lou was a real character. Each year when we went on our ramble at Pesach, he would invariably refuse to carry a small haversack or knapsack but would always use a Bonn's *matzo* box to proudly carry his food for everybody to see.

We often used the home of Lionel and Gerry Rutman to play solo in. (Their father was one of the boys present at the opening night of the club in 1901.) Gerry went to South Africa, we occasionally hear from him there, and Lionel married an Oxford and St George's Club girl called Lily. The other venue used for playing solo was Manny Grossman's home. During the evening we used to cut cards as to who would be sent to the salt beef shop for saveloy sandwiches – all we could afford – although it was a standing joke amongst us that we twisted the cards so that Ginger would be the one to lose and do the errand. He took this all in good faith, knowing full well that he was being cheated.

I met Billy Raven in Italy, when he was in the Reconnaissance Corps and to my amazement, when I was in hospital in Naples, Len Mellows walked into the ward to visit a friend of his brother.

Sid Cohen was our resident pianist, whose services we called on for every concert we gave. Benny Reisman was built like a gorilla so much so that we nicknamed him Mock after a famous gorilla in London zoo called by this name. Jud Goldstein was also a tough character. The amazing part about a lot of these boys is that they were very tough, rough and somewhat undisciplined characters during their youth but almost without exception they turned into wonderful gentle people in their adult life. I like to think that the Club had a lot to do with it.

Chuck and Henry Saunders were members of the Club, Chuck sat next to me at Mile End Central School, went to Canada soon after the war but is occasionally heard of through mutual acquaintances.

Tabor Winecor was one of our really popular boys, as popular as he was short; Mo Reeback who was as tall as Tabor was short, was by far the tallest boy in the club. Umi and Sid Lipfriend, (Umi is a court judge) Len and Sam Rolnick, the Plotzker Brothers, Zulu Lewis, Wally Gordon, Morry Koslover, Henry (Boxer) Roffman, Lou

Sugarman, Dave Taylor, Albert Phillips, Harry Ternovsky, Harry Shulman, Doodie Samuels, Archie Lewis and Peskovitch, the Goldfarb brothers, the inimitable Bunky Cohen, the Hart brothers, three Scoblow brothers, Normie Gleek, Sid Bloom, the Berger brothers, Ronnie Marks (called 'Clark Gable' because of his good looks), Dick Morris, Alf Richman, Harry Merkin and many, many others who, after all these years I just cannot remember. They were all great fellows, united, friendly, imbibing some of that club spirit, that mythical, ethereal, magical spirit that every boy irrespective of background, intelligence or education found in the club.

The various managers had a lot to do with the fostering of this spirit, Reggie Flatau, Dick Rossiter, Charlie Jones, the Nabarro brothers, Eric Felix and the not-to-be-forgotten Alan Nabarro. Then there was Maurice Holt, the well loved Jack London, the Sebag Montefiore brothers, the Waley Cohen brothers, Lou Domb (brother of the scoutmaster that I had when I was in Harlands own troop). Everybody united to achieve what they could, all proud and still proud to this day of our association with the Victoria Club.

I have not mentioned in the list of friends of mine one particular name which certainly deserves a special mention of its own in any story of my life. I am referring to my old friend and later business partner, Nat Stein. I met Nat at the club and found that he too was a Hatton Garden apprentice. He worked at Stellman which was two doors away from my workshop. I got to know him and his family very well. His mother and father were truly gentle people who together with his two sisters and his younger brother formed a close-knit family. I am delighted to have been associated with the Stein family all my life.

Later on you will read about how Nat and I joined the Territorial Army, became separated during the war when Nat was sent to Canada but formed a jewellery business together after we were demobbed. We have been together as partners for something over forty years now. We have never, in all our years together, had the slightest disagreement or anything that can be called an argument and, as I always say, the credit for this has to go to Nat. His temperament is such that he has the ability to get on and work with anybody and he fully deserves all the praise for our long, peaceful and successful partnership.

During the war he met and married Venie with whom he shared many happy years until she passed away some years ago. We were all delighted, when he met his second wife, Joyce, to take part in their marriage ceremony and to continue our close friendship.

I was looking at a photograph recently of the 1938 camp (reproduced in this book). To my certain knowledge of the seventy boys in the photograph, over sixty were in the armed forces. We were the first generation who were taught to stand up and fight for ourselves. Our parents and families in Eastern Europe had to learn that it was wiser to bend with the wind in order to survive. We were the first generation brought up in a free society, instilled with the English traditions and spirit which formed our characters.

This was most severely tested during the period of Oswald Mosley and his blackshirt thugs in the East End of London. We resolved that under no circumstances would we allow Fascists and their propaganda, together with their insults and attacks, to come along to our community where our people were living and working in peace. It was very difficult at times because Mosley tried officially, with the permission of the authorities, to march several hundred strong with his blackshirts along the Whitechapel Road and Commercial Road in order to deliberately incite and frighten the Jewish Community. Whenever he tried this, the whole community turned out and Mosley was unable to proceed. The famous Cable Street riots took place where there were masses of people in the streets, standing firm in the face of baton charges by the police to clear the way, and in the face of mounted police charges. We were adamant that we were going to stand and fight – and we succeeded.

We had a system within the clubs whereby at any time, several of the boys were ready to run out to any given spot where Mosley supporters would congregate. A lorry would suddenly appear and twenty of the blackshirts would get out, stand on a platform, start insulting the population and try to have a speakers' meeting on the spot. Whenever this happened the word would go out and within minutes our fellows would be there and battle would take place. After a few attempts at this type of activity, the Fascists stopped and we at least had peace in our own district.

I remember standing in an enormous crowd at Gardiner's corner talking to a non-Jewish chap next to me. Gardiner's was a naval outfitters and the blackshirts were scheduled to march past in about half an hour's time. There were thousands of people there, not only Jews but all sorts of sympathisers including non-Jewish friends, dockers, socialists and communists – all determined to stop the Fascists from marching. When I spoke to this chap, he said that he was not interested in the march but that he intended to get his revenge on Gardiner's. I looked at him in amazement as, amongst this enormous crowd of people milling and shouting slogans, he calmly stood with a brick in his hand. Sure enough, when the police were charging, he threw the brick through Gardiner's window and walked off quite peacefully. He said that he had worked for them previously and was determined to get his own back for some imagined slight.

There was little fun in these battles for to most of us the principle was one of life and death and, not for the first time, I learned that one must not be afraid in life. As Roosevelt said, 'The thing to fear is fear itself'. One has to stand up and be counted when the time comes.

4
Soldier

It was patently obvious to anyone politically aware that after Prime Minister Chamberlain's return to England, after the Munich agreement in 1938, waving his piece of paper and proclaiming 'Peace for our time', full scale war was inevitable.

After some thought to my situation, now an eighteen-year-old with still a year remaining of my apprenticeship, I decided to join one of the voluntary services to be ready to play my part in the war when it came. Many of my contemporaries thought along the same lines and the first one or two club members to enlist gradually increased to ten or fifteen.

My workshop and club lives continued as before. My teacher at Glick's, Horace Craddock, was about four years older than me, and I owed a great deal to him. When he decided to join the Royal Naval Volunteer Reserve, which had a training ship on the Embankment, I thought I'd follow on. I am sure that it must have been his idea, for it would never have occurred to me to join the Navy since I had never sailed and had hardly ever seen the sea except for my holidays on the Isle of Wight and Southend. Nevertheless one evening at the beginning of 1939 we attempted to enrol. At first the recruiting officer was very welcoming but when he discovered that my parents were foreign-born he informed me that unfortunately only men who were both British-born and of British-born parents could be eligible for the Navy. He was extremely regretful but added that the Territorial Army and the RAF Reserves had different regulations and advised me to approach one of these services. Horace decided that although his family were most probably for countless generations British, he would forgo the Navy. By the time war had broken out, I discovered that this rule had been waived with many people of foreign extraction being both accepted and called up into the Navy.

After this setback I waited a few weeks until one day a letter arrived from the Jewellers' Union (of which I was a member of the apprentice section) informing me that there was a Territorial Army Unit in Leyton, which would welcome jewellers into its ranks as it was a workshop of the Ordnance Corps. Jewellers were classified as capable of passing their trade tests as either general fitters or instrument mechanics. In the early part of 1939, I discussed this with my close friend Nat Stein and, as he too was keen to join one of the services, we decided to go to Leyton where we were indeed made very welcome. We assumed that we would be suitable as instrument mechanics but apparently the unit had its quota of these, so we were termed 'general fitters unclassified' – whatever that meant! We were unable to be sworn in immediately as firstly we had to have a medical examination and secondly, as our parents were foreign-born, checks had to be made. This did not interfere with our initial training, however. Each Wednesday straight from work at 6 p.m., Nat and I caught the bus to Leyton where we spent the evening playing at soldiers. We gradually discovered the basic rudiments of being a private soldier in the British army. I was issued with a uniform and all the small kit that a soldier required plus a rifle that stayed with me right throughout the war; the number was Y987 – indelibly printed in my memory. The discipline was as strict as we had expected and we respected all the regulations that we were told about, simply doing as we were told.

We became very friendly with a small group in similar positions to ours and gradually became acquainted with the three or four hundred men belonging to our unit. We, at Leyton, were one of three sections; the other two were based at the Ford Works, Dagenham and the Ordnance Depot in Colchester.

Nat and I were the only two Jews in the regiment, having been specially sworn in just before my nineteenth birthday by one of our officers, Captain McKeegan. He was not quite sure as to how one swore in Jewish soldiers but he got hold of an Old Testament and we had worn our hats taking the Loyalty oath to the King exactly the same as everybody else.

In July 1939 we went to Beaulieu, Hampshire, for the annual fortnight training camp under canvas. After a few days' torrential rain which flooded out the whole camp, we were moved into billets in the Masonic hall at Beaulieu, where we did a certain amount of military training and began to become aware of what it was like to be a soldier. In our particular tent, we became friendly with some tremendous comrades including Eddie Ainsley, Johnny Carpenter, Johnny King and especially Jack Lister who had a terrific sense of humour. These fourteen days took the place of our club holiday, but Nat and I considered this a necessary sacrifice.

After the conclusion of the TA camp at the beginning of August we were not due to restart our weekly training until the first week of September. However, immediately we returned home it was obvious that the war clouds were gathering. The crisis situation continued until Friday, 1st September at about 11 a.m. when Mr Glick came into the workshop to inform me that my brother was on the telephone. Manny told me that the radio had just announced that a state of emergency was now in operation and all reservists, including the TA had to report immediately to their units.

Three others in the workshop had by then joined other units – Horace (the Ordnance at Chelsea), Bill MacDougall and Eddie Sayer (an RAMC TA Unit) – and we all decided to work until 1 p.m. before going our various ways. I telephoned Nat, arranging to meet him outside his office building, and the four of us at Glick's packed away and said goodbye to each other for we did not know what was going to happen. Thus the life that we had known up to that moment suddenly ceased and a new one was to begin.

Times were financially difficult. I was earning £1 10s 0d for a five and a half day week but, as I finished at Friday lunchtime I had thus only completed nine-elevenths of £1 10s 0d, less whatever national insurance deductions applicable. It wasn't until a long time after that I realised what a hard world we had lived in as I never thought anything odd about this loss of salary despite it being no fault of my own that I was not going to work – I was answering the call of the government and about to enter the service which had to play a large part in protecting us all. Yet neither I, nor the governor thought anything strange about docking a portion of my meagre wages. What a sign of the times!

Nat and I decided to go home to change into our uniforms before leaving at 4 p.m. from my house. The streets were unnaturally calm yet there was an air of tenseness like the moment before a storm. Warnings about air raids had previously been given and the whole civilian population had been issued with gas masks.

I packed my kit bag, including the first two books that I could lay my hands upon. One was a complete copy of the Works of Shakespeare, which I read and re-read many times as I did with the second book I happened to be reading. This was a novel about a young doctor at Edinburgh University called *The Wind and The Rain* by Merton Hodge. I retained both these books until some years later when my entire kit was lost.

Nat arrived to pick me up and we said cheerio to my family. My sister had come from Stoke Newington and together with my brother and my mother we received their blessings, were told to be careful and off we went. My mother was very good about it, considering that we had no idea when we would meet again.

This evening was the first of the black-out and there was chaos as people tried to operate within the constraints. Vehicles masked their headlights and it was all rather confusing as we took the bus to Leyton. Nat and I were quite happy, realising that an adventure was about to begin, although we felt it probable that we would be home after a few days. Whatever was to happen we at least had the satisfaction of knowing we had volunteered having only ourselves to blame.

There was turmoil as we registered at the drill hall where we were given our rifles, told to park ourselves and wait. To a certain extent it was a happy reunion for us because we met our friends from camp and we were all excited. At about 11 p.m. we were told that all the men who lived within walking distance could go home but those of us that lived further had to remain. Jack Lister who lived just round the corner invited me to stay with him that night.

We reported back to the drill hall at 7 a.m. prompt the next morning, were issued with shovels and spades and began to dig slit trenches in the field behind the drill hall where previously we had trained. We spent all day Saturday digging, stayed that night again at Jack's and returned the Sunday morning. There was an immense amount of activity going on but it was confined to the office with the NCOs and officers, having nothing to do with us privates. At 10.30 we were paraded and at exactly 11.15 a.m. Major Robson, our commanding officer, spoke to us. He said that it was his duty to read a statement which said that a state of war now existed between Great Britain and Germany. He added that as we were all volunteers presumably we all knew exactly to what we had committed ourselves when we joined the forces. We were now regular soldiers and he wished us the best of luck for the future in whatever events took place.

As he finished speaking, the air raid siren went for the very first time. The Major added that as we were the only troops in a radius of some three or four miles, if there were air raids we would be called upon to assist in whichever way was possible. If there was panic we would have to do exactly what our NCOs and officers ordered to assist the population. He was sure that we would do our duty.

We promptly filed into the slit trenches. Fortunately nothing happened and, after the 'all clear', we carried on digging just as we had been doing the past couple of days. We were excited of course, but the advent of war made no difference whatsoever to our lives for the moment. Before the war broke out we were digging trenches – after the declaration of war we were still digging trenches. I soon discovered that this was typical and few happenings made much difference to the worm's eye view of world events of the private soldier.

At 3 p.m. that afternoon we were paraded again and it was announced that we were going on a train journey. None of us was aware of the destination as we marched out of the drill hall where a crowd of civilians milled outside the gate. These were local residents, mostly the families of the men going off to war and for a few minutes it took my mind back to the various scenes I remembered of films about the First World War with units marching, flags flying etc. I think that any resemblance between the First and Second World Wars ceased there for things were very different from then on.

We boarded the train, eventually arriving at Colchester where we were taken by lorries to a small place called Wivenhoe. This is now the site of Essex University but at that time it was just a very rural part of England with many acres of countryside in which we could commence our military training. For the first few days we were busy setting up camp, erecting tents, marquees, toilet facilities and everything that was necessary for life to function even at the primitive level of soldiers in a training camp.

Once the camp was more or less shipshape we began our serious training to become professional soldiers rather than the amateur ones that we had previously been. Within a few days a great many of the older men had been shipped out to the British Expeditionary Force in France to fill in gaps in regular units. As we were under twenty, this did not include us and a large portion of the remaining men were of our own age. A collection of reservist NCOs arrived to give us our military training. They had been recalled to the colours and mostly retained the ranks that they had held when they had been with their regular units. They were all infantrymen, because the one thing that was made very clear to us was that we were in the army and our primary aim was to learn to be soldiers. Later we might be transferred to the type of occupation that we had been trained for in civvy street but for the immediate future we had to concentrate on our basic training.

Although generally speaking it was a very tough course, Nat and I took to it quite easily since living under canvas was second nature to us after having experienced several club camps. Fortunately in those first weeks of the war the weather was beautiful. We very quickly became expert with our weapons, learnt our drill, did plenty of route marching and the toughening up process made us as fit as we were ever going to be. We were isolated from the rest of the world being a few miles from Colchester. We were allowed out one afternoon a week when a lorry took us into the town where there was very little to do except visit the pubs and mooch around.

The food was one of my big problems because having never before eaten anything non-kosher I found that it took me several months before I could bring myself to consume some of the meals. The ingredients were usually of good quality although invariably badly cooked with the army cooks specialising in stews. I eventually learned that by putting on very liberal helpings of HP sauce I could manage to get it down!

There was a wonderful spirit in the camp – despite the usual moaning, groaning and swearing – but behind it all there was a marvellous sense of comradeship. Although we had our basic uniforms and boots we still had to be issued with other kit items since we still used our own underwear, socks, towels and other things of that nature. It took quite a while for the stocks that had been built up in the country to be distributed and we seemed to

ARMAMENT. SERGEANT, MAJOR
Name LEONARD SANITSKY

No. 7600752

Next of Kin MOTHER

Home Address 41 TURNER ST
COMMERCIAL. RO.
LONDON.
E.1.

יְיָ יִשְׁמָר צֵאתְךָ וּבוֹאֶךָ מֵעַתָּה וְעַד עוֹלָם

"May the Lord guard thy going out and thy coming
in, from this time and for evermore."

spend an enormous amount of time waiting. On one occasion we
queued for over two hours to receive a pair of socks and another
time I remember queuing just as long for a toothbrush. After
several weeks had gone by, it became extremely cold and we were
temporarily issued with old greatcoats that had been stored after
the First World War. Mine was a short green garment that had once
belonged to a cavalryman and it barely reached my knees. I looked
very odd, as did many of the others, but since we were rarely
allowed out it didn't matter much.

Our training days were so exhausting that each night we slept
like tops until we were woken at 5.30 with a thing called 'gunfire'.
'Gunfire' was an early morning cup of tea brought around by the
sentries at reveille and I thought it was highly civilised for the army
to recognise that at such an hour it is pleasant to wake to a cup of
tea.

When Rosh Hashanah approached at the end of September, Nat
and I asked to see the RSM (Regimental Sergeant Major) in order to
ask for permission to go home. Official leave had not yet started
although the local men were able to go home at night, but we
Londoners were certainly not yet allowed leave. We were taken to
see the RSM who, to us, was just above a god. He was the man who
seemed to do all the shouting at us and we were all terrified of him,
hating his guts although not really knowing him. RSM Tratt had
been in the Rifle Brigade and was, to put it mildly, a short peppery
individual. Yet, to our complete astonishment, he proved to be an

FROM
RABBI DAYAN M. GOLLOP, B.A.

SENIOR JEWISH CHAPLAIN
TO H.M. FORCES

IN CONJUNCTION WITH THE
VISITATION COMMITTEE
(REPRESENTING THE LONDON
JEWISH COMMUNITY).

TELEPHONE : HAMPSTEAD 0620.

13, FAWLEY ROAD,
WEST HAMPSTEAD,
LONDON, N.W.6.

26 Sept. 1939.

Dear Sandlsky,

     I have just learned from an official return that you are now a member of H.M. Forces, and should like to extend to you a hearty welcome.

     In these days of difficulty and stress, when human liberty is at stake, it is of the utmost importance for our fellow Jews to show their public spirit and take their full share in the defence of a country to which her Jewish sons owe a special debt of gratitude. I consider, therefore, that you can render great service, not only to the country, but also to the Jewish Community, by being a good soldier and a worthy Jew.

     It is hoped that in the near future a Jewish Minister will be appointed to visit your area and keep in touch with all Jews in local Units. Until you are aware that such an appointment has been made, will you, if you need any ministerial guidance or advice, please write to me. I shall be happy to help you in any way possible.

     In order to complete my records, I enclose herewith a postcard, which I shall be pleased if you will fill in and return to me at your early convenience.

     With all good wishes,

          Yours sincerely,

          Senior Jewish Chaplain
          to H.M. Forces.

extremely kind, intelligent man totally different off parade. This was the first time that I realised that in the army people had two sides to them. I also realised that the only way to deal with a large group of men is to shout very loudly to enable them to hear what order they were supposed to carry out. Unfortunately though, I always seemed to be in the front rank of any large group so the RSM and other officers invariably seemed to be shouting with their face about a foot in front of mine; their bellows almost sufficient to knock me over.

RSM Tratt listened to our request and said, 'Now look here you two, you are not going to get every Jewish holiday in the book with which I am quite familiar having been brought up in Bow, but I know how important Rosh Hashanah and Yom Kippur are to you. So you,' he pointed at me, 'can go home for Rosh Hashanah and you,' he pointed at Nat, 'can go home for Yom Kippur.' We thanked him profusely and disappeared as fast as we could.

Accordingly, for the very first time as a regular soldier, I went home on leave. I noticed that things had not changed very much. Everyone was highly expectant but life carried on in the same old way. The only exception was that there were a small number of families who had menfolk in the services and my family was one of these. In the East End Jewish community it was not the norm to enter the services so I was quite a novelty and people used to stop me in the street. However within a very short time my uniform became less of an exception and I received less attention.

I was delighted to be home, to eat my mother's *lockshen* soup, to see all my family and to show off to all my friends what a great military figure I had become as I explained to anyone who would listen how we were going to win the war.

I went with Ginger (who was still a civilian at this time) to the Holborn Empire to see a show called *The Little Dog Laughed* starring Flanagan and Allan. It was a very patriotic show reflecting the current feeling and was very popular for so far nobody had encountered any of the dramatic disadvantages of war. In a sense there was a feeling of relief that, after what had been happening in Europe, at last a decision had been taken. There were several well-known songs in this show, such as 'Run Rabbit Run' and 'The Umbrella Man' based upon Chamberlain's famous umbrella. I thoroughly enjoyed the show and all aspects of my few days of leave.

Back at Wivenhoe the weather gradually worsened, becoming extremely cold, yet we remained under canvas until the end of November when we were moved into Colchester. Here we took over an empty building and we now at least had the advantage of having some protection from the weather. We were now in the middle of the Phoney War, as it later became known, with a vengeance but there was nothing phoney about our existence. Unfortunately the first winter of the war was apparently one of the coldest on record so our main occupation was trying to keep warm, for our billets had no heating and we slept on the floor. I suppose that as the objective of the authorities was to toughen us up they succeeded in acclimatising us to difficult conditions – albeit nearly killing us in the process.

We had requisitioned the Corona Drinks Factory for our mess which was two miles down the hill from our billet. This meant that at 6 a.m. Nat and I had a two-mile trek just to consume a congealed fried egg upon a metal plate, fried bread and a cup of tea. The prospect of that uphill walk back was so unappealing that many a morning we decided to forgo our breakfast.

On the military side, our training continued and each day more and more men were being drafted to units that were going overseas to France. Still too young we settled as best as we could into the routine of being soldiers in Colchester. There was nothing new about that for Colchester was a very interesting city, having been a garrison town since Roman days, and apart from superficial grumblings, we adapted into the routine of army life. We became more expert with all sorts of weapons and learnt basic infantry training, all the time appreciating the good comradeship and the feeling that we had volunteered which made the whole thing both possible and almost worthwhile.

The cold winter continued, the river froze and we were able to indulge in some skating, making slides on the ice. Nat had to do that bit extra and promptly came a cropper necessitating several stitches in his chin, the scar from which is still visible today. Although half the unit went home for Christmas, Nat and I remained to allow two non-Jewish soldiers to take leave. Christmas Day was very traditional and we were awakened in the morning by the RSM, the warrant officers and the sergeants who came round to bring us our morning gunfire. The day was spent as a holiday with an enormous dinner and volunteer entertainment. The cooks excelled themselves and a first class time was had by everybody. Nat was dragged into the entertaining, singing his famous song of which he was most proud at that time, Richard Tauber's 'Vienna, City of My Dreams'. Now you might think it is odd that as we were at war with Germany, Nat chose a Viennese song of all songs, but nobody seemed to think anything peculiar about it at the time. On reflection, probably most did not realise it was a German song so everybody had a great time. I was on guard duty for part of that Christmas Day and it was very cold indeed but once I was relieved I entered into the spirit of the festivities and entertainment.

Guard Duty was one of the worst things, two hours on and four hours off over a twenty-four hour period. I found it very hard standing for hours in the freezing cold. However, all these things gradually passed and undoubtedly those men that were left of our original regiment were by this time highly trained soldiers, extremely fit and completely adjusted to the methods of army life. It says a great deal for the army system of training that it was able to take a group of mostly civilian men and in a few months knock them into shape.

5
On my Way

Concerning our training as tradesmen, some time during the autumn the wheat had been sorted from the chaff by the taking of the first trade test. It seemed very simple to Nat and me because we were able to do it but to my astonishment quite a few of the men were unable to pass. These men were re-mustered, no longer classified as fitters but were mostly used for cookhouse duties and other ancillary works that were needed in an army unit.

Nat and I, having passed our first trade test, were now classified as 'fitters class 3'. This enormous jump from being unclassified tradesmen raised our 2s a day army pay to 3s 9d (18½p) a day; a large increase if a small amount of money but meaning a great deal to us. I was already sending part of my daily pay home to my mother which enabled her to get an allowance from the army and when my money went up, I was able to increase her share which made life much easier for us both.

As tradesmen we held a special position in the army because there was a terrific shortage of all types of skilled people. The army knew that before long they were not going to be able to call up many of us because all the services required skilled tradesmen, as did the rapidly growing munitions industry. Most tradesmen would become exempt from call up to work in munitions factories so those that were available would be in great demand by the vastly expanding air force, navy and other army services. Although I never realised it at the time, we were being earmarked for even higher classifications as fitters and then possibly as NCOs.

In early 1940 Nat and I were chosen to be sent to the Colchester Technical College where we had to undergo our second-class trade test. This was a little more difficult. I recall that we were given a blueprint instructing us to make a piece of metal about six inches square and to fit a one-inch cube into the centre. The cube had to fit perfectly in each direction, quite a tricky procedure since the allowance of tolerance of light allowed was very small. The whole block itself, both in its length, breadth and thickness had to be perfectly filed and cleaned. However, if there was one thing that we jewellers were good at, it was accurate filing and we had very little trouble with this task.

The shake-out was now continuing. Of the original 100 fitters that entered the third class test, about sixty had passed and of this sixty taking the second class test only about half passed – including Nat and I.

As Class 2 Fitters, Nat and I were taken to the Colchester ordnance workshops and were set to work on the guns. We were given as assistants to a civilian fitter with the task of completely overhauling a First World War 18-pounder gun. We had to completely recondition it, including the fitting of the Martin Parry adaptor which modernised it from a horse-drawn gun into a motor drawn-gun. We found it very interesting working in the workshops with the civilians. Many practices had been developed between the two wars to drag out the job as long as possible to keep the men employed and they simply could not understand that now there was a war on totally different conditions prevailed. When army fitters were given jobs to overhaul we did them in a fraction of the time but at that time the civilian workers found it very difficult to adapt – may be later they did.

In June 1940 we took our next trade test. This time we had to make a much more complicated article with knuckle joints, but nevertheless we managed it satisfactorily. A fitter class 1 was considered the most highly skilled tradesman in the service and our pay had correspondingly risen to 5s 0d (25p) a day. Again only about half of the men that took this test passed and Nat and I were among the successful fifteen.

Entertainment facilities were sparse and, apart from the odd canteen, Colchester was a very dreary place with little to do in the evenings. Naturally I joined the local library and one of our haunts used to be St Mary's Church canteen where I became acquainted with the vicar. He knew that Nat and I were Jewish but we became very friendly with him, popping in for cups of tea and a wad, and spending a lot of our free time at the social club. Here we would play darts and spend a lot of time singing whenever somebody struck up a tune on the piano. We often went to bed very early after many a tough, exhausting day and I remember that on a few very cold Sundays we were so fatigued from the week that we would return to bed at about 3 p.m. and stay there until reveille the next morning at 6 a.m. (Our beds consisted of blankets on the floor.)

During this period when I went home on leave, I noticed that more and more men had been called up, and many of my friends were now in uniform. Otherwise little had changed. One afternoon AQMS 'Herb' Wilkins brought a telegram whilst I was working in the workshops expecting it to contain bad news but I was delighted to discover that my sister had given birth to a son, Ivor, and I had now reached the important rank of Uncle. In early May the German army quickly overran the Dutch and Belgians, and pushed forward into France. We watched these events very closely from Colchester because the main bulk of the British Expeditionary Force was in France. Within a few weeks the Wehrmacht with their Blitzkrieg had defeated the Allied armies but by the miracle of Dunkirk a great many of the BEF managed to escape from France – about 300,000 men. They had to leave behind all the heavy and most of the medium type of equipment with a large proportion only escaping with what they stood up in – some even having to abandon their rifles.

Now there was a very new situation with the German army just across the Channel from us. We were expecting an invasion immediately so instead of being a reserve army, training and waiting to join the BEF whenever required, suddenly we were the main army which had to defend Britain. Despite the RAF and the Navy, there seemed to be no real good reason why the Germans couldn't land plenty of men by a variety of methods either by air or from the sea. They had parachute divisions which they had very successfully utilised previously. As far as we were concerned, there was an entirely different attitude now to our position – we were being keyed up to take the role of an active service unit expecting conflict at any moment.

We had to carry our arms with us at all times, having to take our rifles literally everywhere. At bedtime our rifles lay beside us so they could be picked up immediately. This is no exaggeration because parachutists could arrive at any time and no matter what a soldier was doing he had to be prepared for any contingency. Fifty per cent of the unit had to be standing by day and night for any emergency so we started instituting rotas whereby one couldn't leave the billet without informing the NCO in charge. Everybody remained in good spirits, confident that if there was an invasion we would certainly knock the Germans back into the sea.

In June 1940 we moved into a new defence position at Newmarket in Suffolk. When we left Colchester I was rather touched because the vicar of St Mary's said he would include Nat and me in his list of names of soldiers to be prayed for at the next Sunday morning church service. At the time, I suppose we thought that good wishes from any source would be very useful.

In Newmarket we opened the first military-only run command workshop. We were now a unit in the field, our job being to cover a large area of Suffolk with all the recovery, maintenance and repair systems required by the army that was rapidly being moved to cover the coast ready for the invasion. We had to improvise whatever weapons we could as there was a desperate shortage due to the rekitting of the men who had returned from France and the need to bring other units in England up to combat strength. The new civilian Local Defence Volunteers, later the Home Guard were now making an appearance and also had to have some sort of weapons with which to carry out their role. At first we were making cudgels and coshes of all kinds which might sound a bit silly today but soldiers, particularly men from the civilian units, actually did night patrol and sentry duty around many of our supply stores armed merely with home-made truncheons. Fortunately they were rarely called upon to use them. We specialised in cudgels made from a length of steel rod on the end of which we welded part of the gear of a differential from one of the scrap vehicles. This gave a hefty chunk of irregular metal at the point that would hopefully make contact with the enemy.

The other part of our extremely important work was that we had to resuscitate a huge variety of guns that had been taken out of mothballs, having been discovered in all sorts of military establishments. Many were really museum pieces. Some were guns that had previously been considered too old to be used even in the First World War and we actually had some Boer War 13-pounders to resurrect. These guns were packed solid with grease so it was our task to de-grease them, clean them, check them over and put them back into firing condition before they were issued to various units. Once, when Nat was working on an 18-pounder, he opened the breech and out fell a shell which he deftly caught. After examining it carefully we realised that the shell was still live and had probably lain dormant in the gun for over twenty years.

So desperate were we to use any ancient gun that on one occasion a few of us went to a unit that was stationed by the coast where a fixed static 6-inch gun had recently been discovered. We managed to put it back into working order, but as only six rounds of ammunition had been found we couldn't fire the gun to test it because we didn't want to waste the little ammunition available. We checked it as best we could, simply telling the gunners, the sergeant and his crew, that in the event of an invasion they should point the gun at the enemy and hope for the best!

There were many incidents of this kind. We were also repairing some of the French 75s that the part of the French army that had escaped with the BEF at Dunkirk had brought with them. In England there was no method of repairing this gun, especially its recoil system which was sealed. However, we had to do the best we could and eventually became quite expert at these weapons. We improvised, repaired and cannibalised small arms of every description, working day and night in the attempt to gather as many arms as we could. We weren't alone, for everybody in the country was desperately short of weapons and every method of supplying the forces was tried.

Whilst this was going on, the Battle of Britain took place with the RAF and the Luftwaffe really fighting to the death throughout the summer. The Germans realised that to invade they had to get control of the sky but fortunately Dowding, the Head of Fighter Command, had retained some of our fighter squadrons in England for this very emergency. Often we would see individual combat; it was almost like the knights of old. We would see a fighter – a Spitfire or Hurricane – actually battling with an enemy plane and many times one of them would be shot down. As we watched these deaths in the skies, it felt odd to be safe on the ground as spectators. Altogether it was a very odd time as on many nights the code signal for the invasion came over and we all scrambled to our stations but fortunately one was a false alarm and the others practices.

As autumn approached, the RAF continued to contain the Luftwaffe and, although we did not know this at the time, Hitler had decided to attack first in the East, leaving Britain until he had taken care of Russia.

On 10th June an event had taken place which had meant very little at the time to me, for this was the day Italy officially declared war on us. As a result of that declaration, the 7th Armoured Division, which was a hotchpotch of various units put together in Egypt, moved into what became known as the Western Desert from where they were stationed around Alexandria and Cairo. They began making their way to confront the Italian forces in Libya. We began to hear names like El Alamein, Mersa Matruh, Sidi Barrani, Bukbuk, Halfaya Pass, Sollum, Bardia, Fort Capuzzo, Tobruk and Benghazi over the next year as the British, Italian and afterwards the German armies began fighting in the Western Desert. Little did I know that I would be taking a very active part in the desert by the end of the following year with all these exotic-sounding places becoming more than just merely names with which to conjure.

The next event of importance was that in the autumn of 1940 I was suddenly sent on an advance party to a place called Buntingford in Hertfordshire, which was to play a very important part in my military service. There were only about ten of us in this party, and we arrived at a huge hangar-like building stocked with reserve foods such as sacks of sugar and crates of tea. We were told that this warehouse was to be turned into the Eastern Command workshops for the growing army which was rapidly being mobilised. We began preparing the site and after a short time the rest of our unit joined us. We had prepared the ground for accommodation in Nissen huts and and all the necessary equipment was in place to begin building a permanent military base.

Nat and I were both promoted to lance-corporals here, and within a few months we received our second stripes earning us the rank of full corporals. As NCOs we experienced a vast change in status since many conscripts had now arrived. In a certain sense, we had now become the 'old' soldiers, and we began to feel more confident. We knew our way around, having been in the army quite a while, so we trained the newcomers and gradually incorporated them into the structure of a complete command workshop.

Our role was to do everything that was required by the army in

Eastern Command in order to maintain, repair and look after all its equipment. As a result of this all types of craftsmen were utilised including electricians, radio repairers, heavy motor vehicle mechanics, motor transport fitters, carpenters, welders and blacksmiths. There was an enormous variety of machine tools, which we rapidly had to learn to handle. Amongst these machines were lathes, millers, shapers and precision-grinding instruments so it was a fantastic challenge for Nat and me. We primarily worked on artillery in which we had most experience, the 25-pounders had begun to be distributed to units with every type of gun coming under our section for repair and maintenance.

When they were short-handed, I did a stint in the instrument mechanics workshop where they repaired instruments such as binoculars, range finders, speedometers. Anything, in fact, that could be classified as an instrument came here – and we tackled it. This even included typewriters and occasionally bicycles!

As far as Nat and I were concerned, the main advantage of being stationed at Buntingford was that we were now only twenty miles from home. Consequently we were able to get lifts into London on the thousands of vehicles that motored backwards and forwards throughout the week. At that period of the war hitch-hiking for soldiers was very easy and far quicker than the regular train service. Our visits to our families during the autumn of 1940 coincided with the first blitz attacks on London.

Such was the intensity of this blitz, mainly focused upon the docks that we were able to stand safely outside our Nissen huts in Buntingford at night and actually watch the sky light up with flames over London. The blitz continued for a long time with its terrible effects bringing the war home to all the civilians in a way that nothing else was ever likely to. Ironically, we were safer in Buntingford than the people in London and whenever we saw the sky filled with German bombers, we would look up in trepidation fully aware that they were aiming for the vicinity of our homes. Many of us were Londoners and we could only hope that none of our families, friends and loved ones would be killed or wounded by this brutal onslaught.

During our visits home we had to join with our families in all the precautions. We congregated in the air raid shelters, we often slept down in the tube stations; on several occasions we took part in helping to dig people out of bombed buildings and we assisted in putting out fires with stirrup pumps. It was a very grim period and whenever I turned down into Turner Street from Whitechapel Road by the London Hospital, I was apprehensive as to whether our home would still be standing. The shop survived the war although its roof was once demolished by a flying chunk of metal crashing through the ceiling into the upper bedroom where my brother Manny was sleeping. At first my mother, in conjunction with many others, had been evacuated and the shop closed but the moment the blitz seemed to die down, the people returned, attempting to re-start their lives until once again the bombing became serious and they had to leave again.

My sister Dinah and my nephew Ivor were first evacuated to Reading and then to Oswestry where Manny and Mick were occupied on some war work. Several of my cousins also went to Oswestry along with many others from my neighbourhood so there was quite a community there. A number were evacuated to the Buntingford area and, on one amazing day, when Nat and I were in the back of a three-ton lorry, we were suddenly delighted to see our friend Dodie walking along the country road. We shouted and stopped the lorry. She informed us that she, together with Ginger's brother Alf, his wife and Ginger's father had taken a small cottage nearby; Ginger was now in the services. Alf and Mr Greenfield were still travelling into town each day to carry on with their uniform-manufacturing business so we were therefore able to get a lift home whenever we wanted. This was a most peculiar method of travelling as Mr Greenfield had only just learned to drive his little Morris 8, so the whole journey consisted of cross-talk between him and Alf – who was attempting to instruct his father – and they did not stop arguing from the moment we set off to the moment we arrived.

For some weeks my brother Manny had been engaged to Mick's sister Freda, and I was overjoyed to receive a letter saying that they were to be married in Reading. Nat and I hitched a lift on the back of a coal lorry, finally arriving in Reading looking extremely grimy but happy to partake in the service. The odd thing was that we had no idea where in the town the synagogue was situated but, by a remarkable coincidence, as we dismounted from this coal lorry we stopped the first man walking towards us who said that he too was going to the synagogue and promptly showed us the way.

We tried to keep in touch with all our various friends who were now beginning to be spread all over the world instead of living in the very confined, small area of London's East End. Although today, when I think of it, twenty miles is a very short distance commuted by many workers, during the war twenty miles into the countryside was quite a phenomenon.

When on leave we spent our time with friends who were either waiting for their call-up or were also on leave from their units. During the phoney war period, many of the club activities continued, including dances and other social events that we shared with the girls' clubs. Dances still took place at our local favoured venues such as the Palais de Danses at Tottenham and the Paramount in Tottenham Court Road. During the blitz socialising became much more difficult but there was always a group of boys and girls that met at the clubs and dance halls so some sort of social activities continued even during the most difficult times.

Now that I was in charge of a section of men I regularly had to march them backwards and forwards, as well as practising how to be a NCO myself, from both the administrative and the disciplinary point of view. I had to reconsider my ideas and rapidly began to realise how very clever and efficient our training systems had been. Considerable skills were needed to organise such large groups of men, vehicles and equipment, bearing in mind that the raw material in most cases was of limited intelligence with a general lack of willingness to take on any form of responsibility.

I was put on the recovery team, which was very enjoyable in fine weather but not so pleasant in the middle of the night when the weather was foul. We had to have at least one breakdown lorry ready to go out at any time of the day or night to retrieve any vehicles that had broken down or had an accident, including Bren gun carriers, tanks, armoured cars and other transporters. I enjoyed our independence and being able to use my own initiative, because on most occasions I was the senior NCO in charge of the breakdown lorry. As we were anything up to sixty miles away from our unit, it gave me quite a bit of authority over the group of six men, with the opportunity to use my discretion about such things as refreshment breaks.

The other pleasing facet was that I was also a member of the workshop fire brigade which meant that I slept in the one Nissen hut that was attached to the main workshops, saving me an enormous amount of walking about! Although we had Sergeant Palmer, the chief carpenter, in charge, I had some responsibilities for the small group of us thus separated from the rest of the camp. There were two corporals in our hut, myself and Doug Shannon. Doug had been a supplementary reservist before the war and was quite different to any other man I have ever met. He was older than the rest of us and carried an air of authority about him that even showed itself when he was talking to senior officers. Everybody seemed to listen to his opinions and he was greatly respected. He came from Dumfries and, being the secretary of the Burns Society, was forever quoting Rabbie Burns. I was made an honorary member of the Burns Society which obligated me to learn by heart several of his poems. It took me a long time to understand these and I even gleaned what 'Auld Lang Syne' meant.

By coincidence most of the twenty men in our fire brigade were Scotsmen who became very good friends of mine. I found that without exception I got on very well with every Scot I ever met in the army, and many of my other close pals were Scots including Dougie Forsyth and Jock Keil. It took me a little while to get used to the idea that not only did the English chaps call them all 'Jock' but the Scots referred to each other as 'Jocks' as well. They were a wonderful set of fellows, contributing greatly to making a very difficult part of my life a lot easier and happier for me. I felt very privileged to be the only non-Scot invited to the Burns Night celebration which I took part in including the eating of a haggis that had arrived from Dumfries for the occasion.

It was about this time too, during the winter of 1940, that I was taken into hospital and detained there for three weeks with lumbar fibrositis. Fortunately this was nothing serious and I thoroughly enjoyed the rest, courtesy of the army's bureaucracy.

The war itself was going very badly and when we really thought about it – which was not very often – we could not see any happy ending to it at all. We were very young, had become accustomed to army life and our civilian roles had faded into the background. We were kept very busy so we tended not to think about the future but just lived from day to day. The funny part about it was that life was not anywhere as serious as it sounds here on paper. Most of my companions were very high-spirited with a youthful disregard for the future. I began to realise that I would never again be a jeweller and that I should start to take seriously my thoughts as towards what type of engineering I should progress. As a result when I saw an advertisement for a postal course which ultimately would lead to the AMIME Degree to become an associate member of the Institute of Mechanical Engineering, I wrote to this company and began a correspondence course. Fortunately a good friend of mine, a schoolteacher at Southend Technical College, spent a couple of nights a week teaching me mathematics – especially applied maths at which I was very poor. His teaching enabled me to think ahead and was most interesting.

Some time in the beginning of 1941 I was sent on a three-week course at Arborfield on the power traverse of tank turrets. It was a simple course about a very complicated subject. Most turrets were hydraulically operated which meant that the electricians couldn't attend to them while the fitters had no experience of overhauling them. I worked very hard, passed quite easily and achieved an extra notch in my army standing. It also taught me a great deal about hydraulics and later, when I went on to an armament artificers course at the Military College of Science, my knowledge both of the mathematics that I had learned from my teacher-friend and the hydraulic knowledge that I obtained from the power traverse course, stood me in very good stead.

In early 1941 we suddenly received a contingent of Jewish soldiers who were in the Czech army. They were tradesmen of different kinds and were now attached to our command workshops because, as I have previously said, a concerted effort had been made to collate all the tradesmen available. The senior NCO of this group, Sergeant Louis, spoke a little English but most of the others did not, so Nat and I found ourselves in the very odd position of suddenly becoming interpreters since a great many of these chaps spoke Yiddish. We also took them under our wing from the religious point of view – which was not very much I must admit – resulting in that every few weeks we would travel to Chelmsford for a service.

Once, when our normal driver was unwell, Nat volunteered to drive us into Chelmsford. Although I knew that Nat could not actually drive, I found myself sitting next to him in the front of the 15-cwt truck with about ten of the Czech boys in the back. Well, Nat was determined to learn how to drive so off we went. At first we crawled along at about ten miles an hour while Nat got the hang of it but, after travelling for a further three or four miles on an absolutely straight road, for no good reason that I have ever been able to ascertain, Nat did a peculiar twist on the steering wheel and before we knew where we were, the vehicle was overturned. To this day, Nat vehemently maintains that the road was twisted (now turning it into a something akin to a hazardous mountain pass whenever we talk about it) but, believe me, it was a very straight and very flat road. As we had been going so very slowly fortunately nobody was hurt. We all got out, told Nat in no uncertain terms what we thought of him, and he made the first of millions of excuses which have been increasing over the years. As the area was deserted we all put our shoulders to one side of the truck and, with a concerted heave, got it back on to its wheels, setting off again. This journey, which usually took about half an hour, lasted five times as long but we all survived intact. Our good humour returned as we still had a few hours remaining in which to roam around Chelmsford, free from army discipline.

Most evenings we remained in our Nissen hut, exchanged stories, discussing the war, going on leave and all the usual topics that young men talk about. The sense of comradeship remained very high indeed as we got on with the simple business of being healthy young men trying to make the most of our lives.

Once the winter was over our lot improved tremendously for the difference that weather makes to the quality of life for soldiers is immense. We were able to indulge in a great variety of sporting activities with Doug, Jock and myself being very keen on cross-country running. Most evenings we would don our shorts and vests, going for runs over the beautiful countryside. We would stop at various farmhouses where we soon became acquainted with the locals who would often offer us a cup of tea or a glass of milk as we paused in our runs.

On 22nd June 1941 the course of the war altered when Germany invaded Russia. My 21st birthday was on 30th June 1941 – I had now been a soldier for nearly two years. At about this time the authorities were seeking glider pilots and as Nat and I were beginning to feel like fixtures with our unit we decided to volunteer for this exciting scheme. We were then summoned to the RSM and given short shrift concerning this idea. He told us that the army hadn't wasted its time training us to the point we had reached just to waste all this on the piloting of gliders; our course had been mapped out in an entirely different direction. This was the first time that we realised that there was any long term plan concerning us and this was also when we were told that we were earmarked to go on an armament artificers' course to the Military College of Science.

This was quite a shock to us because until fairly recently this course, which in peacetime lasted three years, had been confined only to regular soldiers. Thus we carried on with our duties and in August we were told that the regiment's application had been approved. We were destined to go on the thirteenth course in Stoke-on-Trent. We owed our inclusion to the efforts of Major Robson (later promoted to colonel) and to Major Bonallack who replaced him as our commanding officer. Three of us had been selected: Nat, myself and Pete Brechist. Pete had also come via Leyton so we had known him a long time. He was the son of an English mother and a Spanish father. Unfortunately his father, a merchant navy seaman, had drowned when his ship had been torpedoed.

There was a terrific party at the local pub the day before we left with all our good friends popping in to wish us luck. This was one of the very few occasions in my life that I had so much to drink that I had to be carried home. After two years' regular service with the regiment I said cheerio with a splitting headache and feeling terrible.

In peacetime the Military College of Science provided all army mechanical and electrical requirements. Here projects were discussed, decided upon and in some cases constructed often in conjunction with the manufacturing civil firms or ordnance depots. Our course was primarily for the training of the army personnel that were to use and maintain this equipment which ranged from tanks down to the smallest of metal objects and instruments.

Two categories of people were admitted to the college. The first was at officer level already having a civil, mechanical or electrical engineering degree obtained either from normal higher education establishments or Sandhurst. These officers were termed EMEs. In the other ranks the equivalent to the EME was called an armament artificer of which there was a number of different types. We were going to be trained as armament artificers (field artillery). In peacetime these would have been either civilians who had completed a civilian apprenticeship before entering the army or men who had been trained within the army system at the boys training school at Arborfield.

The idea was that the whole system revolved around the officer EME and the other rank armament artificer. The amount of

NOTES ON ARTILLERY EQUIPMENTS.

Artillery Equipments can be divided into three types :-

1. Carriages - Equipments which travel on wheels and fire off them.
2. Mobile Mountings - Equipments which travel on wheels, but normally do not fire off them.
3. Fixed Mountings - Equipments which only fire from fixed emplacements. (Note that some Fixed Mountings are provided with special Transporters, so that they can be moved from one fixed emplacement to another).

Each type is designed to provide a stable, unmoving support to the gun in action, and to control the three movements of the gun viz-

Swinging movement in the horizontal plane i.e. Traverse
Swinging movement in the vertical plane i.e. Elevation
Backward and forward movement after firing i.e.Recoil and Run-out respectively.

In general, the principles of construction for all types are the same.
Each has **Basic Structure**
i.e. that part of the equipment which does not move if the Traversing Gear is operated. It is the main support of the gun in action.
Each has a **Super-Structure** consisting mainly of Carriage Body,Cradle,Recoil-system, Sights and Gears.

1. The Carriage body traverses on the Basic Structure, to which it is connected through the medium of the Traversing Gear, and some form of holding-down arrangement. (An anti-friction device is invariably interposed between the Carriage Body and Basic Structure).
II The Cradle elevates in the Carriage Body, to which it is connected through the medium of the Elevating Gear, and by some form of holding arrangement at the trunnions.
III.The Recoil system consists of Buffer (or Hydraulic Brake) and Recuperator (some form of compressed spring)
IV.Sights are required so that fire may be directed accurately and quickly on to the target.
V. **Gears**

Traversing Gear Moves the gun and sights together horizontally. May produce unlimited traverse (i.e. "All-round traverse") or else a limited amount of traverse (i.e. "Top traverse" or "Cross-axle" traverse).
NOTE: Mobile carriages can also be traversed bodily on their wheels.
Elevating Gear. Moves the gun and sights together in a vertical plane.

Brake Gear is provided on mobile carriages for use when travelling and sometimes when firing; and on Mobile mountings for use when travelling.

equipment was so enormous that in each case there were sub-divisions. Even in artillery, the field artillery was separated from the anti-aircraft artillery. Anybody who passed through the course was immediately promoted, irrespective of his rank on entry and this was very important to us because if we survived the course we would be promoted to staff sergeant with the way open for further promotions.

In peacetime our course would have been based at Woolwich but during the war it had been transferred to the five towns, including Stoke-on-Trent. We arrived at Stoke-on-Trent at 4 p.m. and were told to be ready to start work at 8 a.m. the following morning. As the various parts of the course were scattered about the area we were informed that we were going to have to reside in something like six different billets during the length of the course, including some private billets with civilians, and we were expected to behave accordingly. Our behaviour would be monitored to see if we were suitable in all respects to achieve our desired promotions.

In Burslem, Nat, Peter and myself were billeted with a little old lady who, on our arrival, enquired if we would like black puddings for our tea. Never having tasted such a delicacy and trying to be very polite, we assured her that there was nothing that we would enjoy more. Accordingly, that evening there was a pile of black puddings awaiting us when we sat down for our meal. All I can say is that although the locals may have considered them to be delightful, as far as we Londoners were concerned the best way of disposing of these puddings was via a newspaper wrapping and throwing them in the dustbin! Of course, we told our landlady that we had thoroughly enjoyed our meal and promptly went to the local chippy for our supper. The only problem was that we must have been a little too enthusiastic in our gratitude because at all our meals black puddings appeared regularly every night for the entire week that we were there.

This very kind Burslem lady could never understand my extraordinary surname of Sanitsky and always referred to me in the double-barrelled way of 'Mr Sanit-Sky'!

The next morning the senior instructor gave us the gist of the course. He made it quite clear that half of us were doomed to fail and that the only chance we had of success would be to work like slaves. Each day a précis would be issued listing the things being taught that day, and after the formal day ended at 5 p.m. we were then expected to return to the billet to study what we had been taught. If we were not familiar with what had gone on the previous day we would be unable to understand any of the subsequent lessons. Therefore it was essential not to fall behind and each night to ensure that we were absolutely conversant with the work we had just learned.

We soon discovered that he wasn't exaggerating and most nights saw us staying up until the early hours of the morning absorbing our course. On Sundays we were free to do as we pleased – provided we studied the previous week's work, for on each Friday afternoon we would sit practical and written tests which would be marked and discussed over the weekend. Each Monday morning any member of the course who was considered not to have reached the necessary standard would automatically be sent back to his unit. This too was no joke for, sure enough, eventually half of the course were politely dismissed.

We had to learn everything there was to know about field artillery because we would be going to various parts of the world where it was quite probable that we would never see another armament artificer so we would be the end of the line. We ourselves would have to answer any questions arising in the field – the buck would stop with us. We had to cover something like twenty-five different guns ranging from the smallest, the 2lb anti-tank gun, to the largest, a 9.2-inch howitzer; and between these guns there was one hell of a range. There were old guns still in use: 13-pounders, 18-pounders, 4.5-howitzers plus the new field artillery weapon that everyone was putting their faith in, namely the 25-pounder. In addition there were other guns still in construction about which we had to learn as they gradually came into use.

The course was sub-divided into the various independent parts of any piece of artillery with sections on the pieces themselves: carriages, sights, ammunition, recuperator systems and so on. After we had absorbed all the technical and mechanical side of the course, we then moved to the part of the course based upon army methods. We were expected not only to have a very good idea of the organisation of the army concerning the maintenance of the field artillery but also, as we would probably be in charge of other equipment, such as MT vehicles and Bren gun carriers, we were expected to have an administrative idea of how to control others in our section with different trade ratings from our own. We would need to have all the general knowledge and field training of senior NCOs and warrant officers so we were also trained and examined in these subjects. It was made quite clear to us that if we were not considered suitable on the military side, however well we might have done on the mechanical side, we still would not pass the course.

We literally ate, lived, slept and thought about nothing but our work for the next four months, and out of the thirty of us starting, only about half of us finished with Pete, Nat and me amongst them. We had been told that at the end of the course we would be given a placing according to our final ratings and that the first six people would be sent to Light Aid Detachments. Here, if they succeeded, the rank for the person in charge of the LAD was the elevated one of armament sergeant major or class 1 warrant officer. Frankly we would have been only too pleased merely to pass the course but, to our astonishment, when we crowded round the examination results list, we were delighted to see that Pete had come first with myself and Nat in fifth and sixth positions respectively. We were now set for an LAD and would be in charge of our own detachments.

A note at the bottom of the list said: 'All trainees that have passed the course should apply to the stores immediately for rank badges.' We did just that, collecting two sets of three stripes and a crown for our two uniforms. We immediately sewed them on being very proud to sport these shiny white stripes. I was listed to be sent to the LAD attached to the 53rd Field Regiment of Royal Artillery which was stationed in Norfolk. Then we went out to the nearest pub to relax after all the strain of the course with a sing-song and general celebratory evening.

The following morning, however, would see Nat and me being separated after being together from the day we had joined the Territorial Army back in Leyton. From our point of view therefore, underneath the festivities was a sadness that our time together had come to an end. Nat was going to an LAD of another unit also in Norfolk but we determined to keep in touch. We had spoken about our future hopes on several occasions and I had always said that if ever the war ended I wanted to start up on my own as a jewellery manufacturer. Nat had always said that he would like to join me, so when we parted we resolved to survive the war and maybe one day join together in partnership in civilian life as successfully as we had done in our army life.

6
In Charge

While we had been cocooned in Stoke-on-Trent, there had been plenty of air activity over Britain and the war in Russia was progressing at an enormous pace. Vast armies were fighting it out, huge tank battles had taken place and enormous casualties had been sustained by both the Germans and the Russians, the latter observing 'their scorched earth' policy. Now that winter was upon them both of the armies were fighting in the most deplorable conditions. Then, on 7th December 1941, the news came that the Japanese had attacked Pearl Harbour virtually destroying the American fleet there. With America in the war we could finally see a way that the Allies might perhaps achieve victory.

My promotion to staff sergeant was backdated to 1st September 1941 so there was a considerable amount of back pay to collect. The Monday morning I left Stoke-on-Trent found me literally on my own for the first time since I had entered the army. I was given a train ticket, told to travel independently, in my own time and under my own responsibility to join my new unit in the small village of Holt in Norfolk. Most important of all, I was to take over what was the ambition of almost every senior military figure through history: namely my own command. I was actually listed on the travel documents as Staff Sergeant IC of the REME Light Aid Detachment attached to the 53rd Field Regiment Royal Artillery. The meaning of IC is very important: *In Charge!*

Whilst we were on the course, a change had come about and we had been transferred from the Royal Army Ordnance Corps to the new Royal Electrical and Mechanical Engineers. It had been obvious for a long time that with the growth of electrical and mechanical equipment in the services, a very important part of army personnel was going to have to be occupied with the maintenance of all this new equipment. The days of mass infantry where virtually only an armourer was needed for each regiment were gone. More and more trained, skilled craftsmen were to be required to service the new equipment in the new type of army. Therefore it was decided to set up a new corps to cover this situation called the REME formed from sections from the

Ordnance Corps, the Royal Engineers and the Royal Army Service Corps.

Now that I had completed the armament artificers course I really felt that I was on my way with my new responsibilities and my new status. I realised that after all my civilian and army training, I was about to be tested. I had had various bouts of some authority in my life such as when I had been club captain of the Victoria Boys' Club and even, at the tender age of ten, as a prefect in Rutland Street School I remember having some authority being allowed to give lines to even younger children who broke the disciplinary code of the school. Now another completely different situation was upon me for I was going to a combatant unit which was soon to be sent into battle overseas with all the consequences that one would expect. I knew that I was responsible for the detachment and I looked forward to the challenge.

After several hours of travelling I was met at Holt station by a driver in a utility vehicle. He was very polite to me, called me 'Staff' in response to everything I said to him, acting in just the way that I would have previously acted had I been detailed to collect a senior person. He introduced himself as REME Lance-Corporal Harry Beaumont, the storeman of my detachment. I behaved as though I was accustomed to this deferential sort of treatment and he drove me to the headquarters of the regiment. At the regimental office I introduced myself to Terry Lewis, the sergeant clerk. He was about my age and very friendly. He told me that the Colonel had been informed that I was coming, that I should be taken to the sergeants' mess, install my kit, make my first acquaintance with the members of the LAD detachment and that the Colonel would then be pleased to see me the next morning at 10 a.m.

Terry introduced me to RSM Burrows who was a regular soldier of perhaps twenty years' service and everything that one would expect a Regimental Sergeant Major to be. He was very smart, very precise in the manner he addressed you and expected to be addressed by everybody else. Terry then took me across to the sergeants' mess in the village, and it was then I began to realise that I was entering a completely different life. The mess was a large, modern house that had been commandeered and it was run on very regimental lines. Sleeping accommodation was allocated according to rank and I was the third ranking member of the sergeants' mess. RSM Burrows was the president of the mess and Regimental Quartermaster Bob McCall also in his forties, was the next senior. It was thus a considerable drop to me, aged twenty-one, being the next rank of staff sergeant. There were about a dozen other sergeants or lance-sergeants in the mess, in charge of the various sections of the regimental headquarters and they were all very friendly. We had our own cook and kitchen staff and in many ways it was a very comfortable type of life, quite a contrast to what I

81

had experienced previously particularly as I was completely independent to come and go as I pleased and to run my detachment virtually as I wished. I was to remain with the regiment for the next three years so that it became my home and I was very happy and proud to be in it.

The 53rd Field Regiment was a territorial army unit with a long history including a very good record in the First World War. Its home base was Bolton in Lancashire where it originally formed part of the 42nd Lancashire Division. It had served in France and had been evacuated at Dunkirk. Most of the regiment consisted of Bolton men whom I found to be a very good crowd, proud of both their regiment and their home town. Most of them had been workers in the cotton mills and in many ways it was very much a family regiment. The Colonel, Lieutenant-Colonel Robert Greenhalgh, was a mill owner as were the OCs, the majors of two of the batteries and several of the officers. Most of the sergeant-majors and senior sergeants of the regiment had been with the unit for many, many years. There were one or two in fact who were still left over from the First World War and I suppose 80% of the men in the unit were from Bolton and the old territorials.

The regiment consisted of about 850 men with the regimental headquarters, of which my detachment was part, being divided into two sections; the A echelon and the B echelon. The former varied in size depending upon the situation and it controlled the three batteries that actually had the guns. The B echelon was the administrative, supply, signal and REME section which normally in action would be placed about a mile or so behind the forward part of the A echelon. A doctor and a padre were attached to regimental headquarters. We had a section of the Royal Corps of Signals whose job was to be responsible for the line of communications from brigade or division to the regimental headquarters and then to supervise the internal communications within the regiment. This section comprised a captain, a lieutenant and forty men of the Royal Corps of Signals. Last but not least there was a detachment of REME.

The first thing I had to ascertain was what exactly my job was and what exactly was the role of the REME detachment. The latter was primarily to act as a link between the equipment and all the REME facilities in rear echelons to our own. In other words anything that had to be repaired beyond the capabilities of my own detachment, was also my responsibility. I had to make sure it was taken to the nearest workshop facility which would usually be the brigade workshops. If, as happened during our service, we were an independent regiment at times attached either to division, corps or army, it was then my job to make whatever arrangements I could to have any equipment repaired which was beyond the capability or time of the Light Aid Detachment.

The second responsibility was to carry out repairs within the laid-down schedules that we were given. In other words we were allowed to change an engine of a vehicle but not to overhaul it, as we didn't have the facilities to do so. We were allowed to carry out many jobs on the guns and instruments that were above the capability of the Royal Artillery fitter, as we had the special equipment to do so. The detachment also was responsible for the recovery of any vehicle that broke down en route. Where it was possible for us to repair it, to put it back into action, we had to do so and if that was not feasible it was our responsibility to ensure that the equipment was recovered and taken along to the nearest capable workshop company.

The third responsibility was to co-ordinate all the Royal Artillery fitters and to ensure that they were carrying out their maintenance and repair work correctly. There was a continuous amount of work to do in view of the fact that there were twenty-four 25-pounder guns in the regiment, forty-eight limbers and about 170 vehicles. Then there were all the associated equipment and instruments that were part of day to day life, including such items as mobile cookers and anything else that was repairable. I suppose the two important things, when one boiled it down, were firstly that the regiment had to get to wherever it was wanted; so our job was to see that it arrived because once we were on the move the responsibility really stopped at the LAD. Secondly having transported the regiment to where it was required we then had to ensure that as many of the guns as possible were in a serviceable condition and were able to fire. Everything else revolved around trying to achieve that purpose.

My particular job was that as I was the senior REME person in the regiment, I was expected to be conversant with all this equipment. I soon realised that nobody was interested in the fact that I was trained in anything specific so I had to be very nimble at times because although I considered my major training to be guns (knowing mechanically far more than anyone else in the regiment) I also had to cope with various vehicles including Bren carriers and once even a Honey Tank. I knew little about much of this sort of equipment although I had learned, unofficially, how to drive, so I spent most of my first evenings practising driving the various vehicles around. Thus I was In Charge – responsible for all this equipment and making sure that it functioned well. There were laid-down methods, times of inspection, testing and training members of the Royal Artillery, taking them and training them to drive and giving them a short course on vehicles.

To assist me I had a detachment which at first incorporated a sergeant, a corporal, two lance-corporals and ten or so men. Two of these were storemen, one a welder, one an electrician and the rest were either MT fitters or driver-mechanics. So we had a wide variety of skills with which to carry out a great many tasks.

Apart from the personnel a most essential part of our equipment was a Leyland breakdown lorry which was used for all breakdown purposes and recovery work; plus it also enabled us to lift engines out of vehicles or to lift the back or front of vehicles in order to change the axle. We had to maintain a permanent recovery stand-by service which meant that a team had to be on permanent duty even while based in England. I had two large eight and ten-wheel drive vehicles; One was a GMC and one an Austin. These were fitted out with bins on either side as mobile stores which, with our card index system of the spares, enabled us to carry with us most of the small articles required for repairing parts such as valves and gaskets. We also had a 15 cwt truck for general purposes and a utility car in which I used to travel to the various batteries. There was also a motorcycle used for messenger work and for keeping contact with other road vehicles. This detachment of five vehicles and a motorbike made us a convoy by ourselves.

Apart from the spares, we carried a considerable amount of equipment and a small mobile tent arrangement that we could erect in places where there was no shelter such as in the desert making us an extremely versatile small workshop unit.

Obviously some of the men were better craftsmen than others but everybody pitched in and the spirit of the detachment was first class. We had already taken over a civilian garage which was all very organised and comfortable. I had to get to know my way around the three batteries of the regiment very quickly. These were three independent batteries, which in effect were three separate units. The 209 and 210 Batteries were part of the original regiment but the 438 Battery had been set up when regiments became larger during wartime. A battery was divided as follows: the battery headquarters, then each battery had two troops of four guns. We called the batteries Pip, Queen and Robert and the troops were A, B, C, D, E and F with two troops to each battery. Each troop had four guns with a Royal Artillery fitter who looked after them. Of the six Royal Artillery fitters the senior was a staff sergeant, a soldier who had been with the regiment ever since the First War as a territorial. In peacetime he worked as a fitter in one of the mills and we became good friends. He was well experienced in army ways and clever enough to cruise along happily avoiding trouble.

There was also a bombardier fitter with one of the troops and a lance-bombardier fitter and three gunner-fitters. One of these was a boy-trained soldier about my age, who was quite good at the maintenance. Of the six, three were very good, one or two were poor and the other one was not too dreadful. I had to discover their capabilities very quickly so that I could keep my eye on the lesser trained. Each battery had three or four RA trained motor fitters of varying degrees of competence and I had to rapidly assess these men too since we worked very closely with them in the LAD. Over a period of time it was a question of knowing upon whom one could rely to do something and those whom one had to carefully supervise.

I was kept very busy because the guns were actually on the coast in anti-invasion positions covering a twenty-mile area. Each day we had to send returns, for any time a gun was out of action it had to be reported immediately to regimental headquarters. Should it be out of action for more than one hour it had to be reported through to division. This became extremely important when we were in action because obviously the number of guns that any senior officer could call upon in a particular area was vital. Likewise with transport we had to send a daily situation report showing the number of vehicles that were in service and the number that were out of action for various reasons.

Within a few days of going to the LAD I reported to Captain Davis, who was the divisional REME officer responsible for the LAD, so he knew all about it, having joined them at the beginning of the war as a lieutenant.

The new system that was now in operation was that the establishment was for a WO1, an ASM (Armament Sergeant-Major) to be in charge of the detachment instead of as previously a lieutenant or a captain.

We had quite a long discussion and he made sure that I was aware of what my responsibilities were. He told me that at that moment the regiment was not in a brigade formation, but was part of the defence forces for fighting against any invasion that the Germans might try. The regiment was at the coast and I was really on my own as far as having somebody supervising me. Instead of having a brigade near me or brigade workshops to rely upon there was nobody senior to me until I got to him at division. I could use any workshops I could find in the whole Eastern Command area to do any necessary jobs. The main workshops were at Thetford, where I happened to know the ASM in charge because he had been with us at Leyton. Should my requirements be greater than their abilities – surprise surprise, I had to take the equipment to my old workshop company Eastern Command in Buntingford.

Captain Davis told me that our first job was to act as an anti-invasion regiment, and for this purpose we were stationed at Holt in Norfolk which was a central position for the three batteries. In the event of any invasion, the regiment would give me instructions. I was to co-operate with the Colonel who would be tactically in charge of the detachment. The second role of the regiment was to train continually in preparation for overseas service as part of an expeditionary force. The regiment's guns, as I had already discovered, had only arrived two or three weeks earlier, so over the next three months I was to get the LAD equipment and personnel up to scratch. We would have a priority to obtain stores and personnel, so I had to check over the whole equipment as soon as I could and let Captain Davis know about anything that I thought to be unsuitable to go overseas. The same applied within my little detachment for if there were any men that I didn't consider suitable for any reason, he would do his best to change them for me. I came away from his office with a very clear idea of my immediate tasks.

My prime task concerned seeing to the guns and ensuring that the various modifications had been carried out, so that if we only had a few days' notice to leave England at least the guns would be in the condition we wanted them.

After two or three weeks I had absorbed an enormous amount of information and had completely settled into my new life being busy from first thing in the morning until last thing at night. I tried to become acquainted with as much of the personnel of the regiment as possible particularly those with whom I was going to have to be working. I spent part of each day with one of the batteries getting to know the fitters looking after the guns, those looking after the vehicles and the quartermasters. I met the officers commanding each battery and various officers who were in some way responsible to see that the equipment was in order and inspected.

I met the Colonel who seemed very pleased to welcome me for I realised that for a few months he virtually had not had an LAD since there were something like six men left from the old one and no new people had been sent until I arrived – with a few others arriving a week or so beforehand. A few weeks earlier he had been issued with twenty-four brand-new guns and he was most anxious that I had a look at them to check that the fitters knew what adjustments had to be made on this new equipment. I was able to reassure him on this subject and when he questioned me regarding my experience, he was delighted to know that as I had been a long time at the command workshops I was familiar with all the modifications required.

I was conversant with all the minor faults that these guns had which were partly due to the dilution of labour in the ordnance factories. The finish on some of the parts was not up to usual army standards so whenever we had received a new gun in Buntingford we had spent a day or two simply removing burrs and other minor things which made a big difference to the accuracy and the proper functioning of the weapon.

Most of the units stationed in Britain ran occasional dances to which all the local girls were invited and my units regularly organised these in Colchester, Buntingford and Norfolk. The usual problem was the relatively small number of girls and seemingly countless soldiers. Nevertheless my friends and I always looked forward to these breaks from routine and a good time was had by us all.

I attended my first sergeants' mess party a few days before Christmas 1941, prior to half of the regiment going on leave. The officers of the regimental headquarters were formally invited, so the mess was very smartly cleaned and decorated reminiscent of what one would imagine happened in the regular army messes in places like India. The junior officers came early and stayed late and the Colonel arrived with the Adjutant staying for about an hour.

Most of the party was spent drinking and telling stories with everybody enjoying themselves. There was excellent food served by the mess staff who were all very smartly attired. During the course of the evening, as things became livelier, I was introduced to a quaint custom of the mess which I later discovered was normal in most sergeants' messes. The RSM stood up and announced that it was time for the entertainment. The system was that he would point one by one to any person irrespective of rank. Whoever was selected would then have to sing, recite or show his bottom! The RSM pointed to one or two who stood up and did their party pieces. By this time my mind was beginning to function. One thing was certain: under no circumstances was I going to bare my behind. I dug deep into my memory and remembered that the only other time I had any connection whatsoever with entertaining was back in the boys' club when I was a junior member. In my enthusiasm I had joined the concert party run by Lou Kutsovitch. I had been capable of singing as long as I was in a chorus, but unfortunately I had no voice of my own so I felt unequal to performing a solo number. Then inspiration struck as I recalled the Victorian melodrama called *Little Nell*. Four people had performed the four roles, namely Little Nell, her old father, the village constable and the villain of the piece. It had lasted about fifteen minutes and I knew the entire piece by heart because I must have watched it over fifty times at various concerts and camps.

A couple of weeks previously I had seen a film starring the American comedian Jerry Lewis in which he was intending to do a sketch on stage with several others. At the last minute his co-actors had not arrived because their coach had overturned and Jerry Lewis had enacted the entire sketch by himself. What he did was to play all the parts wearing different hats. I decided that I would do *Little Nell* in the same way. Having prepared no specific headgear, I took a serviette plus one or two of the variety of hats lying around and did my best with them. I persuaded a pianist to play 'dum, dum dum dum dum, dum dum' whenever I gave the signal to do so since this had to be repeated throughout the performance. As an example it went something like this:

> Now it was a dark and stormy night
> When my little Nellie went away,
> The Rooster died and the hens won't lay,

So in this window I'll strike a light,
Forty below zero, gosh what a night!
DUM, DUM DUM DUM DUM, DUM DUM.
'Who's there a knocking at me door?'
'It's your little Nell, don't you know me any more?'
'Where's the rat, the guy that used to call ya honey?'
'Did he send you home when you hadn't any money?'
'He was a West End guy, he could lie with ease,
'And he had more money than a dog with fleas.
'He left me on the night I was most forlorn,
'The very very night little Dumbo was born.'

That's an example of what the piece was like and I suppose, because most people were three-quarters drunk, it created a sensation to put it mildly. I had arrived, was now a character, had my very own party piece and for the rest of my army service on perhaps ten different occasions when I was called upon to entertain I invariably performed *Little Nell*. I probably improved as time went by for it was always very successful.

I spoke informally to the Adjutant for the first time during that evening and discovered that he was one of the only two Jews in the regiment apart from myself. His name was Captain Stanley Drapkin and he was from the Drapkin family who were connected with the cigarette industry. He was a rather shy sort of man and, apart from briefly mentioning the other Jew in the regiment, Louis Sunderland, a gunner in one of the batteries from the North of England, he didn't talk to me about anything else. I made a point of speaking to Louis on one or two occasions over the next three or four months and I was able to do one or two small things to help him. However he left the regiment at the end of the year, after being wounded in the Western Desert. He had trodden on a mine, and lost his big toe.

A few days after Christmas I went out with the regiment and for the first time actually heard a 25-pounder shell being fired. This may sound odd but although I was an expert on the gun itself and its mechanisms it was not normal practice to test the weapon by actually firing it. We used to utilise a device known as the apparatus pullback which was to all intents and purposes meant to have the same effect as firing the gun. I was really surprised about one thing as I stood by each gun as it fired, for I had not realised what a loud noise it made. I understood very quickly why most of the veteran sergeants who were in charge of each gun were virtually stone deaf, since after one or two rounds had been fired you really could not hear what was being said. Earplugs were issued but mostly not worn unless there was going to be a larger programme of firing in which case they were compulsory.

During this test all the guns fired well and there were only one or two minor adjustments that I had to check out. Basically there were no problems and everyone seemed to be perfectly satisfied with my performance.

After a week or two we went on manoeuvres which were very different from the one day infantry training I had previously encountered. These manoeuvres lasted a few days, with a Red Army versus a Blue Army, and in every way it was tried to simulate conditions of action.

In this instance my duties concerning the guns were easy since these weapons weren't actually firing but I still had to get the regiment to its destination. A few vehicles broke down with minor faults that we were able to repair in situ, but one idiot in a 15 cwt truck had crashed into a ditch so we had to tow the vehicle and park it in a field from where we could retrieve it later. The only other point I remember was that while we were repairing those vehicles that had minor petrol or electrical troubles, we were about one hour behind the Quartermaster's vehicles. We took the wrong turning and couldn't find them. More by luck than by judgement and by going by a different route, we finally managed to attach ourselves to the end of the column, just as they were turning into the field in which we were going to spend the night.

The Quartermaster said to me, 'For one minute I thought you had got lost.'

I looked him straight in the eyes and replied, 'No, of course not. We were doing our repairs and knew exactly where we were.'

He seemed to believe it and that was the end of that.

Now that Christmas was over, the guns had been fired and we had had our first manoeuvres, I was kept very busy with preparations for overseas. New personnel and stores were arriving all the time and I got to know the ASM of the LAD infantry battalion about half a mile down the road. We became very friendly and helped each other out on REME matters where possible.

One morning I got a message from him to say that two storemen were going to arrive at Holt station that afternoon and he would arrange for a truck to pick them up since one was destined for his LAD and one for mine. I made all the necessary arrangements so that when I returned late that night from one of the batteries our new man had been officially documented on to our roll. I met him the next morning; his name was Billy Beal, and he was the oldest member of my detachment. He had just scraped into the age and health requirements. He was a married man from Leeds and was with me for the next three years.

Two or three days later I had occasion to call in on this ASM and to my astonishment I was greeted by an old friend of mine – Jackie Solomons. I had known him and his brother Harry in the days of my *cheder* in Baker Street where we had been taught by Rabbi

Rabinowitz when I was about six or seven years of age. It turned out that Jackie was the second storeman that had arrived. Billy had got into the truck after Jackie and when they had stopped at my LAD somebody said, 'One of you get out here.' Since Billy was the last one in the truck he dismounted and therefore he joined my unit, while Jackie had gone down the road to the other LAD. About two months later he was involved in a vehicle accident and very badly hurt. He was hospitalised for several months and then discharged from the army. It is another small incident that virtually affected, in this case, his life. I often was sorry that he didn't get out of the truck instead of Billy Beal for although Billy became a stalwart of our LAD it would have been nice to have Jackie as part of my detachment.

In the course of the following weeks I had to carry out all the modifications to the guns so it was arranged that I would go along to the REME workshops in Thetford where I could use their facilities. I stayed there for four weeks and found it very fortunate that the recently appointed ASM of the workshop was an old friend, Jack Brooks, from the territorial unit at Leyton. Jack's presence simplified things and made it much easier for me. The guns arrived and we carried out the modifications. I had to supervise the work not having to do it myself, since there were several competent fitters at Thetford. After I returned to the unit, I was congratulated by both the Colonel and Captain Davis who were very pleased that everything had gone well.

There was one important thing that I obtained from Thetford via my friend Jack. It was in connection with the fact that I knew from experience there was a pretty bad fault on the 25-pounder gun. This was a fault in the sight, for the gearing within it required modifications to it that only a new sight could do. Eventually this was done, but all the guns we already had in action had suspect sights. The spares to repair them were simply not available and I had had reports back from overseas that there were many guns out of action simply because the sights couldn't be repaired. I checked up and found that for the twenty-four guns we had in the unit we were only allowed, by the establishment, to have one spare sight. I decided, unofficially, to try to pick up a couple of extra sights that I could take with us, which I hoped might give us more time to replace the sights as they went wrong. I was able to acquire one sight from Jack, so with the one already on establishment, I had now doubled my number of spares.

I decided that my best chance of obtaining extra sights was to visit my old friends at Buntingford. I had wanted to see them anyway as I knew that there were various gun spares that I could get unofficially from the Quartermaster apart from sights. Thus I arranged for one gun that needed a major repair to be sent to Buntingford and I accompanied it to the command workshops for three days. During this stay I was able to pick up a variety of spares and to my delight I was actually able to acquire three complete sights which meant that now I had five sights, up my sleeve, so to speak, instead of the one that I was officially allowed. The significance and importance of this you will see later on.

I met many of my old friends at Buntingford. We went out and celebrated the fact that I was now a staff sergeant. They were delighted at my promotion although I took plenty of ribbing because I was now on the other side of the fence. It was odd staying in the sergeants' mess after being with the unit as a private and corporal for such a long time. Suddenly I was sitting next to the original RSM Tratt, ASM Doyle and others, whom earlier I had thought were pretty well up there with the gods.

Back at Pip, Battery 209, there were two sergeants, the brothers Jackson. They were both No 1's on the guns and were old members of the regiment having been with the unit from about ten years before the war. They were known and liked by everybody. One of them had allegedly committed an offence so a court of enquiry was held to investigate whether or not he should be court-martialled. As it revolved around a technical matter, I was called to give evidence as the senior REME person. It was a very formal occasion, and when it was my turn to give evidence, I was asked what I thought of what the sergeant had done. The breechblock of the 25-pounder gun is a solid piece of machine steel about 10 inches thick and an 18in x 10in rectangular block. This had to withstand the blast of the cartridge case when the gun was fired. In the centre of the block was the firing mechanism which was screwed into the block. Nobody was supposed to take the firing mechanism out of the block to unscrew it, except the fitter during maintenance.

Some of the sergeants who had been with the regiment a long time were quite familiar with these things so they used to exceed their official authority and do certain maintenance themselves which was perfectly allowable. However, strictly to the rule book the firing mechanism shouldn't be removed. Jackson had taken out the firing mechanism, cleaned it but when he put it back he cross-threaded the screw so the block was rendered useless as was the firing mechanism. The gun was out of action which as the cost of the block and firing mechanism was probably about £450 and they were not readily available.

Not knowing much about this sergeant, I was not aware that he was very popular and nobody wanted to lose a good sergeant. However, when I was asked for my opinion, after I had examined the mechanism, I was able to say that in my experience I had come across this before. Some of the people working in the ordnance factories making these weapons were diluted labour and when the firing mechanism was originally screwed it was sometimes then cross-threaded. Consequently when it was taken out by anyone

91

however senior, it would still have been useless. So, in my view, although in theory the sergeant was not supposed to do it, it would not have made any difference and therefore he was not at fault.

Everybody was delighted and the sergeant was cleared. From then on I was very popular in 209 battery from the Major downwards and certainly with Sergeant Jackson, his brother and friends. This was another example of how one's luck has to hold. In this situation there were many things I did not know and it would have been very easy to say or do the wrong thing and become very unpopular in the regiment which was a close family unit. You had to really prove yourself before you would be accepted but once you were accepted it was a wonderful regiment to be part of.

About this time I received a letter from Nat, who was no longer with the regiment he had been originally posted to, because on arrival he realised it was an ack-ack regiment not Field Artillery. A mistake had occurred but, as always with the army, once he was out of step and something had gone wrong with the system, nobody knew what to do with him. He was thus awaiting reposting.

The war continued and many world-shattering events were happening. I was busy in my own small world trying to mind my own business. By the end of April, I was well established in the regiment and, to the best of my knowledge, I had been accepted, indeed was considered to be an asset to both the mechanical and social side of the regiment. As a REME staff sergeant I was in a position not to have to bear down too heavily on the disciplinary side. I could afford to be much friendlier with people of any rank than for example the equivalent NCO or warrant officer could in the Royal Artillery.

As things were now shaping up with the LAD it was decided that I should go to Arborfield on a three weeks' tank recovery course. From the reports coming in from the Western Desert, virtually the only part of the world in which the British were fighting, a new approach was required with regard to the recovery and repair of tanks. All sorts of things were forever going wrong with them since they were very complicated bits of machinery, and technological advances meant that many repairs were beyond the capability of the fitters attached to the tank regiment. Instead of various lines where the tanks were forward and the first workshops were automatically a few miles behind with the major workshops several miles behind that, it was realised that a much more important part of the repair system had to right up there with the tanks.

Rommel had a fantastic system in the Afrika Korps. If a tank was out of action, recovery services were there virtually within minutes, taking it back two or three miles, if they couldn't fix it on the spot. Our tanks were working on the old system. If a tank went out of action it often took a couple of days before it was even recovered from the battlefield. It then had to go back a much further distance so that the time involved in putting it back into action was far greater than the enemy's.

The bigger and more complicated the equipment and the more mechanised the army became, meant it was more and more necessary to have the REME services right in the forward areas carrying out their duties immediately. People like myself, in charge of Light Aid Detachments, were being sent on the tank recovery course whether or not we were with tank units because they were taking recovery units from all sorts of LAD's and using them in the desert to recover the tanks. They therefore wanted all the new people to be trained before they went out.

Fortunately in my previous experience I spent a lot of time as a member of the recovery teams although I did not know much about tank recovery which was a more complicated system with heavier equipment involved. On the Arborfield course there were about twenty staff sergeants drawn from all over the country. To our astonishment it was made very clear to us that we were now very much a part of the most forward units and in my cases there would be no troops whatsoever between us and the enemy. We would be the forward troops, involved in things where tank battles would probably be actually going on at the places we were at, especially if we were to go to the Western Desert. The old days of the front line with trenches and so on, were finished.

As a result of that, the first complete week of our tank recovery course was to be the exact opposite – a tank knock-out course. We were to learn how, with the weapons we would have available, to knock out enemy tanks. As an example, our breakdown lorries contained crowbars. These were about six foot long with a flattened sharp edge at one end angled to the main shaft for levering etc. It was made of mild or hardened steel perhaps two inches in diameter and thus quite a weapon. We were taught to hide in a ditch and to wait for a tank to come along the road putting, if possible, an obstacle in the road to stop or slow down the enemy tank. The idea was that from our position in the ditch we could thrust the crowbar between the spokes and the track where with luck it would jam, either dislodging the track from the tank or actually breaking part of the sprockets that were rotating, thus putting the tank out of action. To make us get the feel of this, as it sounded pretty difficult when we started, we had to go inside the tank and drive it. We realised that in a tank one's sight is very restricted. There is a slot through which one can look and whereas distance views are quite clear, the fact is that there is no view of the side of the tank.

We were also taught how to make Molotov cocktails quickly and other types of incendiary devices which, if we slowed the tank down, would then enable us to set it on fire. Fortunately I must say here and now that I was never actually called upon in my army career to attempt any of these heroics and I thank God for that!

A happy thing happened on the tank recovery course which surprised me somewhat. On the second day somebody said, 'Have you seen the regimental orders?'

'No, I haven't yet,' I replied.

I was told to have a look at them because I had been promoted to warrant officer class 2 armament quartermaster sergeant. I dashed over to the regimental office where to my astonishment my name and promotion were posted, dated 1st May 1942. Afterwards, when I returned to 53rd Field, I was told by Terry Lewis that five minutes after I had left for the course the promotion had come through. Rather than let me wait for three weeks he himself had posted it to Arborfield.

Warrant officer rank was another very different cup of tea from being a staff sergeant. There really is as much difference between a corporal and a staff sergeant as there is between the latter and a warrant officer. This was entering a new field. As a warrant officer I was now called 'Sir' in answer to any question I put to anybody. It was 'Yes, sir,' 'No, sir,' and 'Three bags full, sir'. Also, although this sounds a very small thing, I was entitled to wear a peak cap. The only difference in wartime between officers and other ranks was that officers were allowed to wear peak caps whilst other ranks had to don the forage cap; the battledress was the uniform we all wore. In this case the officers were classified as commissioned officers and warrant officers. So now I was a WO2, people referred to me as 'Q. Sanitsky'.

All the other nineteen were staff sergeants so I was the only warrant officer and thus the senior rank on the course. There were hundreds of NCOs at Arborfield in the various messes but there was only a handful of warrant officers so I was now entitled to use the warrant officers' mess. The other important thing was that as a WO I didn't have to book in and out when I came or went and most important of all, I was actually allowed a weekend pass for each of the three weekends I was on the course. I was able to return home to see my family and friends all of whom thought I was doing extremely well.

By my return to the unit, our efforts were beginning to come to a climax. It was not official that we were going overseas but it was expected at any time. We were as ready as we were ever going to be.

7
Desert, Here I Come!

At the end of May I was given a ten-day leave, so I returned home to Turner Street where I saw my family and many of my friends who were also on leave. I had a very enjoyable time despite the continuing air raids; the war had already changed the whole of the Jewish East End enormously.

On my second day home I received a telegram informing me that this leave was an embarkation leave and had thus been extended by a few days. I had previously prepared my mother and family for this news, and I tried to make it easier for them by telling them that I would be nowhere near any fighting or action. I told them that in actual fact life would be much safer for me overseas in some out of the way post thousands of miles from any fighting than it would be if I was in London or evacuated somewhere in England as a civilian. My family, and my mother in particular, had got used to the idea that I did not live at home any longer and that I was perfectly capable of looking after myself. They were delighted to see me whenever possible but had accepted that I was in the service and could only visit on odd occasions.

I was always very careful to send my mother one letter each week whatever the circumstances and in the whole of the six and a half years that I was away (six years, six months and two weeks to be exact) I never failed to write to her. I must admit that many of the letters were very short and very stretched out but in each of them I would reassure her that I was well and thinking of her, my brother, my sister and the rest of the family.

I eventually returned to what then was my real life with the 53rd Regiment at Holt. The place bustled with men coming and going from leave as the regiment was keyed up for the imminent departure to a new venture, a new way of life and all that we had been training for. We were to go overseas and nobody knew when or if we would ever return.

The last important thing we had to do was to go out with the guns, fire them and calibrate each gun. During this firing period a lot of the work I had performed on the guns would be tested as would some of the modifications which we had carried out. Fortunately everything functioned correctly so I was satisfied that from a REME point of view we had done everything that was expected of us. Thus I had passed what I considered to be my first big test concerning preparation. My ability in action was the next great test I should have to face.

My responsibilities were to become very different. If we were in a battle area it would mean that every time I issued an order to one of my men he would be at risk. If I had to send somebody to do a task somewhere, the person that I had chosen would be in danger whilst the one who had not been chosen at that time would be comparatively safer. Every one of my decisions was important with real people's lives being at stake. That same situation would occur with the guns, for if a gun fired correctly lives would be saved and the infantry would be protected. Should a gun fire incorrectly then our own men would be at risk for a gun could explode injuring our own troops. Accidents could happen should I fail to perform correct maintenance and repair procedures. In the same way vehicle and instrument functioning were vitally important so that food and other supplies would efficiently reach their destinations. Yet I did now have a certain amount of experience plus my confidence in my own abilities had been growing during the whole period that I had been with the regiment.

We were issued with tropical kit so we presumed that we were destined for the Middle East. Some said that this didn't mean anything at all because some units issued with tropical kit had found themselves stationed in Iceland where the kit had promptly been taken away from them! Yet, to anyone looking at the war as a whole, it was obvious that it was going to take a considerable amount of time for the necessary build-up in Britain for an Allied expeditionary force to be able to invade mainland Europe, where the war had to be won. Meanwhile most of the British army that was active would be fighting in the Western Desert, for it was vital to try to throw Rommel out of North Africa. At this time our position in Africa was looking very precarious. It was impossible for any of our ships to traverse the closed Mediterranean and the only way we serviced and supplied men and equipment to Egypt and North Africa was the terrible long route round South Africa up through the Straits of Madagascar and through the Suez Canal.

I was twenty-two years old on 30th June 1942 and about that time I was sent on an advance party of the first few vehicles to go to the port of Gourock in Scotland. I had to be on board the ship before the regiment arrived, so that I would be able to answer any questions from a REME point of view. At Gourock I was informed that we were to sail on the *Duchess of Atholl*, a Canadian Pacific luxury liner, which was to house about 2,000 troops. I introduced

The author as a REME Armament Sergeant-Major in Egypt.

Me, aged 3, third from right, back row, at
Baker Street School, Stepney.

Aged 8, in the yard at Turner Street.

On 12th May, 1942, all the Jews of Gombin were sent to the death camp at
Chelmno. Among the very numerous members of my family who perished were
my uncle, aunt and entire family in this photograph.

At weekend camp in 1934 at Broxbourne. Myself (left, rear), Chuck Saunders, Alan Nabarro, Tommy Kleinman.

Summer camp, 1938, in the Isle of Wight. *Left to right:* Chuck, Johnny, myself.

1938 summer camp: the winning tent. (I am far left.)

1938 summer camp: I am fourth from the right, second row, next to Johnny.

In the yard at Turner Street.

Day trip to Westcliffe-on-Sea, aged 18. *Left to right:*
Ginger, myself, Monty.

Me – a few weeks after war broke out.

With Ronnie Muir and Jack Lister. I am
on the left.

Nat and myself, newly promoted to staff sergeant.

In Port Suez: *left to right:* Battery Sergeant-Major Jimmy Light, DCM (later killed in action), myself, Sergeant Gordon Emery.

Back row, left to right: Spiff Binks, Pete Adams, myself; *front:* Unknown, Bert France (later killed in action), Len Flynn, Jack Wragg, Harry Beaumont.

Sergeants' mess at Beni Yussef.

25-pounder gun in action in the Western Desert. *Imperial War Museum.*

Me in Egypt just before entering the
Blue.

LAD in action at El Alamein. Our workshop tent with oxyacetylene welding
plant on left, myself centre, and two of us, Unsworth and Flynn, on the bench.

Quad towing 25-pounder gun and limber advancing along coast road to Tobruk. *Imperial War Museum.*

Entering Tobruk after the advance from Alamein.

With Tommy in South Italy.

LAD and QM section in Italy.

Leave in Cairo. *Left to right:* Cousin Johnny, me, Pete Adams, Tommy Sinclair, Bill Langley.

25-pounder gun in action in the mountains of Italy. *Imperial War Museum.*

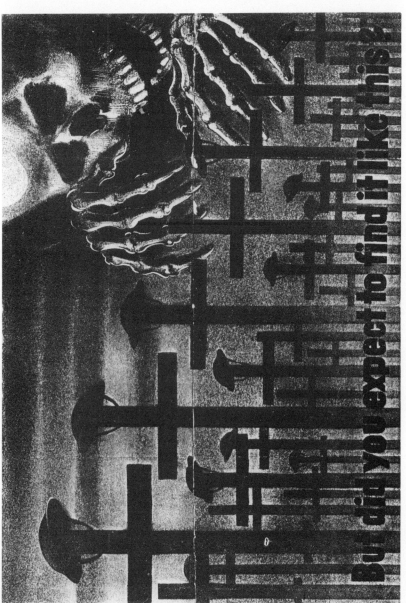

But did you expect to find it like this?

One side of a German propaganda leaflet for the British. The front showed an

Brigade Bren
gun carrier in action.

LAD repairs in the line.

LAD breakdown squad at work
on carrier during action.

LAD fitters after putting mined
carrier back into service.

Visit by Moisha Sharett who later became Prime Minister of Israel.

Bivouac, but Avni has managed to scrounge a chair.

LAD group on 'Gefilter Fish'.

Members of the Jewish Brigade from England with senior
chaplain Rabbi I. Brodie.

Jewish Brigade cemetery in Italy.

In Austria at last.

Here I am giving last minute instructions before crossing
the Alps en route to Holland.

myself to the ship's RSM who told me that I could join the warrant officers' mess, where I should wait for the rest of my unit to arrive. There were two officers' messes, one for those of field rank such as majors and above and a mess for junior officers. Then there was our mess which was the only time in my army career, except for Arborfield, that I had seen this. There were also two sergeants' messes and messing arrangements for the other ranks.

The warrant officers' mess was in a very luxurious part of the first class area of the *Duchess* and, as I was among the early arrivals, I settled myself comfortably in a cabin which I shared with another warrant officer. The mess was still run on similar lines to its civilian glory and I was astonished to find that a menu was actually printed each day showing the different meals available. These meals were the biggest surprise of all because the *Duchess* replenished its food supply in South Africa, a land remote from the war, where every commodity was bountiful. It took us several days of gorging ourselves on a superb variety of food before we got used to it.

There was a library on board so for two or three days I happily read, slept in my luxury cabin, ate food that was in many respects better than that served in many top West End hotels today, and waited for my eighteen LAD chaps to arrive. I arranged permanent jobs for them during the voyage serving in the various messes and bars. They were overjoyed at my efforts on their behalf since these were very cushy jobs for, as you can imagine, those serving as barmen had as their only requirement the ability to remain standing up and those on officers' mess duties could partake of all the wonderful food available.

We were all happy and I was especially lucky as I was the only warrant officer on board who did not have one or two hundred men to look after and to see that they were occupied. I simply assigned my men to their pleasant duties and told them that I would see them at the end of the voyage making sure that should they need me they knew where I could be found.

We set sail on 17th July 1942. Just prior to this a brand new Bofors ack-ack gun plus crew had arrived. The gun was installed on the top deck as our anti-aircraft weapon. We were part of a very large convoy protected by various Royal Navy ships. The largest was a cruiser plus several destroyers and other small craft. The convoy was not just military for there were many merchant ships carrying goods to wherever we were destined.

The liner was known as 'The Rolling Duchess' because the way she was built gave her a rolling effect going through the water. Her top deck was reserved for those of the rank of general and above and it also accommodated the gun crew. The second deck was used for other senior officers, the third for junior and warrant officers and the bowels of the ship were jammed solid, crammed full with the

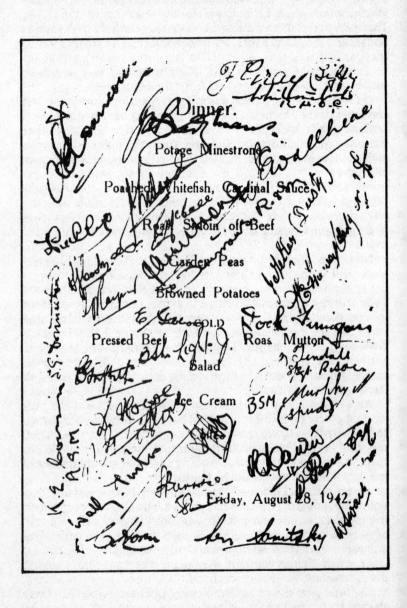

Duchess of Atholl dinner menu for 28 August 1942, signed by members of the
Warrant Officers' Mess.

2,000 troops. The conditions here were appalling. Men slept everywhere, some with hammocks and some simply sleeping on the floor. It was the middle of the war and an enormous amount of shipping had been lost so this convoy had to take as many troops as was possible.

There was no flag waving, no bands playing; all that happened was that the ship slipped its anchor and our journey began. The first few days on board were chaotic for everybody except me. All the other warrant officers, with the help of the various NCOs were chasing about with lists in their hands trying to organise where their men were going to sleep, seeing to it that their charges were all given positions and places in the very complicated system of eating.

Fortunately the weather was mild so most of us very quickly acquired our sea legs after a little bit of seasickness and queasiness. On the first day of the sailing I visited all my men in LAD, tucked them nicely up in their various jobs, wished them *Bon Voyage* and promptly retired to sit quietly in the library where I could mind my own business in the midst of this flurry of activity on board the ship.

On the first morning I went on deck, I was astounded to see a huge armada of shipping as far as the eye could see. The troop-ships were concentrated in the middle of the convoy and the cargo vessels were all around the outside. Presumably it was Hobson's choice which was the safest. The troop-ships were the bullseye – what the enemy was most interested in sinking – but being in the centre of the convoy were the most difficult target. On the other hand ships on the periphery were easier to sink, but were not the prime objective. You pays your money, you takes your choice. We were escorted by the Royal Air Force as far as it was possible but they disappeared after the first two or three days. The Royal Navy was continually circling in and out of the convoy, like a mother hen. All the ships were capable of speeds of different knots per hour and the destroyers were always hailing over the speakers to the smaller merchant ships which kept falling behind unable to keep up with the convoy. Everybody had to carry a life-jacket; you slept with a life-jacket, ate with it and were never without your life-jacket in your hand. At this period the shipping losses were horrific. The numerical strength of the U-boats was forever increasing.

We were informed that, at 11 a.m. on the first morning at sea, all the convoy's ack-ack guns would be tested. After that if we heard any gun fire it would automatically mean that the enemy was about and we were under attack; there were no two ways about that. At the time appointed, an unholy row broke out and the whole convoy was in complete bedlam – except for the silence on the top deck of the *Duchess of Atholl*. It appeared that the only gun that had failed to fire was the one we had on board.

Half an hour later I had retired to my comfortable chair in the library when a message reached me. I had gone to the kitchen to get a cup of tea and was told by the mess waiter that everybody was looking for me. Lieutenant-Colonel Greenhalgh, the colonel of the 53rd, wanted to see me urgently.

When I reported to him he said that as the ack-ack gun had not fired he had told the Commodore and the other senior officers that it was fortunate that he had a warrant officer aboard who was a great expert on all guns. He had thus volunteered me to repair the ack-ack gun. I could only keep my fingers crossed as it was pointless to explain to the Colonel that I was a field artillery expert and knew precious little about anti-aircraft guns. I put on the bravest face I could muster and began to prepare whatever excuses I could think of – such as the lack of spares or lack of repair facilities.

I tried to look as confident as possible for I had very quickly discovered that looking confident was one of the greatest assets you could have when asked to do something about which you know very little. The CO said that there was a ship's engineer workshop and all its facilities would be at my disposal. He was most confident that I could fix the gun and was looking forward to some kudos from the senior officers for being the one who had come up with the solution to their problem. If the gun could not be repaired the ship would be defenceless from enemy air attack.

I went to the top deck where I found the sergeant and crew sitting around doing nothing. The sergeant told me that he hadn't seen the gun before coming aboard. He was merely an ack-ack sergeant who happened to be travelling in the convoy and had been picked out completely at random together with a crew that he had never met before. He knew nothing about the Botors gun from a technical point of view.

I examined the gun which had been delivered on board straight from the Ordnance Depot. Beside it were some unopened boxes which nobody had bothered to investigate. I knew that the gun had to have been tested at the depot and I presumed that there were only going to be minor faults which hopefully I would be able to attend to. The most important item I needed was the handbook which would explain everything about the gun. Here each of the mechanisms would be shown with the drawings in an exploded position so that by looking at the handbook I would be able to tell what each part consisted of. I opened the boxes, which fortunately contained various spares, and, to my utmost delight, I discovered a brand-new handbook. I was more pleased to see this book than I would have been to find the Kohinoor Diamond! I sat down and studied both the book and the gun.

The main mechanical difference between a field and an ack-ack gun was very simple: it was the loading mechanism. A field gun was operated with a single loading shell – in other words the shells were put in one at a time physically by the gunner. Into the cartridge of a 25-pounder, for example, was put the type of powder required for the particular firing that was going on at that moment. The powder bags were red, white and blue representing the three different strengths and the gunner prepared the shell dependent upon the particular reason that the gun was going to fire. Thus on a field gun one had the shell and the cartridge containing the powder and each one was put in individually. After the gun was fired a new shell was inserted.

With an ack-ack gun there was a complete shell, like a rifle bullet. The process was that the gun would be loaded, a shell would be put into the breech, fired and then the cartridge would be ejected. The next shell would be automatically loaded, again fired and again ejected. On the Bofors it was normal to have clips of five shells, so it was a quick-firing gun enabling all five shells to be automatically fired rapidly one after the other. What had happened was that there was a fault in the loading mechanism and the shell simply hadn't slid into the breech.

It was immediately obvious to me that I was dealing with the old problem of diluted labour. In other words, everything was in perfect order but the final touches, the finesse, the final perfection required on the breech mechanism had not been carried out thoroughly. Since the gun was new it had not been to a REME workshop, it hadn't been put in order and this was what was required.

By this time I was now being watched with interest by the generals who had been walking around and sitting on the top deck. They were very friendly and they had a terrific faith in their own system of training and promoting people. I could see that they were thinking that here was a very young REME warrant officer busy with the gun, looking as though he knew exactly what he was doing. He therefore must be extremely good to have become a WO at such a young age and must have a terrific technical knowledge. The last thing I could tell them was that I had never before seen a firing mechanism of this type of gun. However, as I didn't want to get thrown into the water, I never mentioned my inexperience but pretended that if the gun was repairable I would be able to do it. I metaphorically kept my fingers and toes crossed for what was neither the first nor the last time in my army career.

I very carefully stripped the firing mechanism and, by looking at the exploded drawing in the handbook, had soon amassed fifty or sixty assorted pieces of metal. I laid these out on a blanket on the deck. To make sure that I knew what I was doing as I stripped each part, I drew a diagram on my notepad and very carefully wrote down exactly what I had done. Then, with a piece of chalk, I put a number on each piece since many of them looked very much alike. Now that I had all the components laid out neatly in front of me, I could see that several had burrs on them preventing the smooth operation of various parts sliding into each other. After telling the sergeant that I was going down to the workshop in the bowels of the ship – warning him that if anybody touched my collection of parts in my absence I would personally throw them overboard – I went down to the ship's engineer who, like many of his profession at that time, was a Scot. He gave me free run in his workshop and provided me with an essential set of needle files. I was now back to doing the thing I was most expert at as a young jeweller! I returned to the top deck with the files and various grades of emery paper and meticulously removed the burrs on all affected parts. Whenever I removed a burr I carefully used emery paper to ensure that all the working parts were as smooth as though they had been polished.

Finally all of the working parts appeared satisfactory and were operating well when I slid them up and down each other where it appeared they should function. I carefully put a thin, light covering of fine oil on each part and reassembled the whole mechanism. Thank God there were no pieces left over for by this time it was late evening. I tried out the mechanism as far as possible without firing the gun and everything seemed to operate very well so I reported to the senior officer. After the ship's captain had received permission from the Commodore, it was decided that the gun would be re-tested at 11 a.m. the next day. The whole convoy had to be warned because of the previous declaration that any further firing would signal enemy action.

A crowd surrounded the gun just before the appointed firing time. It consisted of the gun's crew, the generals, all of whom looked very confident and happy with themselves, Lieutenant-Colonel Greenhalgh, who was not supposed to be on the top deck but intended to take some credit, and finally me. I stood just by the gun trying my best to look totally confident. I thought to myself, 'Well, Len, you've done everything you could; it's no use worrying about it.' I had made all the excuses I could, saying that if the gun didn't fire it was because the internal mechanism in the recuperator or breechblock was preventing it, thus demanding base workshop facilities which we didn't have on hand. My excuses fell a little flat and I preferred not to consider the consequences of the gun not firing.

Promptly at 11 a.m. with the crew sitting on the gun and the whole convoy waiting to hear a noise, the sergeant got the signal to fire. He pulled the firing lever. A sigh of relief came from me because there was a tremendous bang and the gun fired the shell beautifully.

I was suddenly a hero. I now tried to pretend that I knew all along it would be all right. My Colonel was delighted, proudly claiming that of course anybody in his regiment would naturally do the job that was required. Everybody was delighted. As a by product of all this, for the rest of the trip the top deck was no longer out of bounds to me. I was the chap who was mechanically in charge of the gun and so was at liberty to be up there whenever I desired. When we were in the hotter part of the world it was wonderful to sit on the top deck. I found myself a comfortable deckchair in a shady spot near the gun and spent some very pleasant times contemplating the sea! Fortunately, the ack-ack never had to be called into real action for the rest of the voyage.

As we continued our voyage to our still unknown destination the weather became hotter and hotter. We were heading south and after several days we made our first stop at the port of Freetown, Sierra Leone. This appeared to me to be right out of a Rudyard Kipling story. The moment the anchor had settled we were surrounded by 'bumboats' selling fruit and other goods. These little vessels were manned by the blackest people I have ever seen. I was told that the natives in that part of the world (also incidentally called the 'white man's graveyard' were so black that they were actually termed 'blue'. These natives busied themselves selling their wares and used an ingenious system of ferrying their merchandise by means of baskets hoisted to the troops crowding the rail. We told everybody to be careful about what they purchased because various stomach troubles were bound to ensue but, as there was such a variety of exotic fruits – including bananas – which either had never been seen before or hadn't been seen for years, it was difficult to prevent people from buying altogether.

Most of the convoy was anchored outside the port but we had actually docked in Freetown because we had a prisoner on board our ship, although we had not known about this previously. As I was the warrant officer who seemed to have nothing to do, I was detailed to take the prisoner ashore. He was a small Greek chap who only spoke a few words of English so, with him in handcuffs and accompanied by two guards, I boarded a small boat in order to deliver him to the dockside office of the military police. My whole stay in West Africa was no more than an hour and I think that this was the shortest time that I spent in any country during my travels. It was the first time in my life that I had stepped upon foreign soil and even this dockside was very different to anything I had ever experienced. It was also extremely hot.

After three or four further days of heading south, we were informed that our next port of call was to be Cape Town, South Africa. The whole convoy would spend five days in the harbour there and the troops would at last be allowed shore leave, under certain conditions and restrictions.

The political situation at that time in South Africa was immensely complicated. At this time South Africa was part of the Commonwealth with Jan Smuts being their pro-British Prime

103

Minister. However, most of the Afrikaaners, who were the majority of the whites, were anti-British. As only whites were allowed to vote, these Afrikaaners were numerically the largest group in the country and politically the most powerful, although it took a number of years after the war before they managed to get their majority in parliament and break away from the British connection. This group were thus pro-German, being aware that a German victory over Britain would automatically break the link between our two countries. A considerable part of the Afrikaaners were extremist, yet even they had a right wing which was known as the Brotherhood. They were completely pro-Nazi and naturally anti-Semitic. In fact they were anti all sorts of things, owing to the nature of the various groupings of people in South African society. There was a large Jewish population who sided with the British South Africans but at the time we arrived their morale was very low indeed. The war had gone badly for Britain up to that point and we had not yet won any victories for some time. The arrival of our convoy was therefore a terrific boost to their spirits.

Obviously Cape Town was full of spies and informers for the Germans so from the moment that we arrived there was no longer any cover of secrecy for us. It was therefore decided that a morale boosting march, through the main part of Cape Town, would take place by the entire contingent. Our troops were also in need of a morale boost since conditions on board had begun to deteriorate due to the overcrowding and the intense heat. At a special meeting between the CO and all the warrant officers, we were instructed that we should use the stay in Cape Town to get things back on an even keel. There had been many cases of insubordination and I was personally fortunate that I had not experienced any of this type of problem since all of my small group of LAD remained content with their lot.

Anyone not on duty was allowed to go ashore each day but all were warned to behave well and, in particular, instructed that the native quarter known as the No 6 district was absolutely out of bounds to any troops whatsoever. We were also informed that when we disembarked we would be greeted by representatives of the South African Women's Voluntary Services. All the troops were invited in pairs to visit the homes of these friendly families and, to facilitate this, three or four women stood at the gangplank directing troops to a long line of motor cars on the quayside. Troops who desired to do so simply entered the next car in line taking pot luck as to who was going to be their host. Many took advantage of this, but a number preferred to make straight for the local bars and other places of entertainment.

On the Saturday afternoon, I had to attend a 'Showing the Flag' march as did all the other troops in the convoy on one of the other afternoons. It was truly an impressive sight. All the troops wore khaki drill for the first time and two or three military bands had arrived from somewhere. Several thousand troops took part in this magnificent display. It was Rudyard Kipling and *Lives of a Bengal Lancer* all rolled into one with a vengeance, seeming to have nothing at all to do with wars and fighting but everything to do with *Boys' Own* stories; the mystique with which we had been brought up as youngsters. It epitomised the idea of the great British traditions of colonialism and the fighting qualities of our soldiers. It was certainly all good fun and no doubt it served a very good purpose because I must admit I was very impressed by the march. I am quite sure that the many pro-German sympathisers or spies watching us must have thought that there was still life in the old lion yet!

The most interesting facet of my stay in Cape Town was my patrol duty through the No. 6 district. Cape Town was divided into many areas, and a warrant officer with eight armed troops accompanied by a local policeman was to be in reach of the districts continuously patrolling in four hour shifts. Without this duty I would never have known such an area could exist; yet it began only fifty yards off the main street. Suddenly the wonderful modern buildings, the motor cars and the opulence of Cape Town abruptly ceased as though severed by a knife. I was accustomed to the slums of London, considering places like Old Montague Street and the back of Cable Street – with their old tenements, filthy streets and narrow roads – to be most run-down. However, to compare the No 6 district to Old Montague was like comparing Old Montague Street to the West End of London.

The No 6 district was a complete shanty-town. It was very hot and the number of people milling about it was astounding. The streets were so crowded that there was simply no possibility of any vehicle, other than perhaps a bicycle, traversing them. The stench was overwhelming and for the very first time I realised the difference between the life style of most of the Cape coloureds from that of the affluent white population. I was also assured that the coloureds lived in even better conditions than the blacks, but as I never had any dealings with Black South Africans and never saw their district, this was just hearsay.

The South African policeman spoke English and was quite an affable man although we did not touch on politics at all in our conversations. This was the first time that I had worn my revolver with any possibility of any serious intent but the police sergeant assured us that the Cape coloureds would be very friendly and there should be no problems whatsoever.

Our task was to ensure that there were no troops in the area and if we did find any they were to be arrested and taken back under escort. We marched as best as we could finding everybody to be very amicable indeed. The children followed us as novelty and every twenty minutes or so we would stop to have a five minute halt in view of the heat. During one of these breaks we stopped by a stall selling drinks and were offered refreshment by the stallholder. We asked the policeman if it was permissible to accept and he said it would be perfectly all right. It was a very sweet wet drink, reminding me of those I used to have as a small child when we simply poured some sherbet into a cup of water.

Everything remained very low key until the main object of the exercise had to be carried out. I was twenty-two years old and younger than most of the people I was in charge of on the squad, certainly considerably younger than the South African policeman. We had to visit several brothels and I did not know what to expect, this being completely out of my sphere of knowledge. We were taken to each of these apparently official brothels for the policeman knew exactly where they were to be found. In appearance they looked exactly the same as the rest of the shanty-town. We knocked at the first door, there was a red light outside, and after an interval of time a man opened the door. He was not surprised at all to see us and said 'Good afternoon, sergeant!' to the policeman whom he seemed to know quite well. We then went into this dilapidated two storey house and looked into each of the rooms in search of any troops. Everything was in a squalid condition and the women looked the same as any of the other women in that area. I thought that it was the most inefficient method of trying to catch any miscreants because in the interval after we had knocked at the door anybody who should not be in the place could simply exit by the wide open back door.

We toured about six brothels and only in one did we find a soldier. He was so drunk that he had made no attempt to escape. He was taken in tow and placed under arrest. The only other incident during the course of the rest of the afternoon was that we saw two soldiers who claimed to have got into the district by error. As they seemed quite respectable men to me, I said to the policeman, 'It's obviously a mistake, just let them go,' and they promptly left the district.

It was a fascinating afternoon. I learned more about life, and South African life specifically, in that one four-hour period than I could ever have learned in a year of study. I have never forgotten it; the scenes are as vivid to me today as they were over forty years ago.

After a wonderful party given by the Leveton family, who had given us great hospitality during our stay, we returned to the *Duchess* and soon the familiar throb of the engines was heard, heralding the next stage of our travels. This was the most dangerous part of the whole journey for ample time had passed since our arrival in Cape Town for every German submarine in the Atlantic to be alerted to the convoy's position. We knew that our route along the east coast of Africa was going to be a very tricky period for us.

106

We passed Port Elizabeth, East London and Durban, hugging the coast with protection from the air force which was based on land in various parts of South Africa. We then entered the Straits of Madagascar. It was here that some time during the night, after we had gone to sleep, we heard a violent explosion somewhere in our convoy. The sound of this was like nothing I had ever heard before and, in sheer terror, everybody snatched their life-jackets and rushed on to the decks. By the time we arrived there was absolutely nothing to be seen. Our ship continued its journey, zigzagging as usual, and we finally returned to bed although I imagine that very few actually slept that night. We discovered afterwards that one of the merchant ships had been torpedoed and sunk. The destroyers and naval ships had then chased round dropping depth charges all over the place; fortunately that was the only loss.

I stood on the top deck the next morning and thought to myself, as I looked down from that height into the sea, that if we were going to be unlucky and the *Duchess* should be torpedoed, I doubted whether I would bother to jump. It all seemed much too high. I was also thankful that my parents had been born in Poland because I remembered that that was the reason which had prevented my being accepted into the Royal Naval Volunteer Reserve. On reflection I decided that I was in no way a sailor; the sooner I got back on to dry land, the happier I would be.

From then onwards the rest of the journey was relatively uneventful. We sailed round the horn of Africa, past the port of Aden and into the relative safety of the Red Sea.

An important disciplinary problem arose during this part of the voyage. Because of the dreadful conditions on board fighting had broken out between two groups of men at one of the messes, in a clash over feeding arrangements. When the junior NCOs tried to stop it they were unable to do so and a near mutiny erupted. About 400 men were involved and it was a very serious breach of discipline which had to be ruthlessly stamped on because of the circumstances under which we were all living.

It was decided that instead of the lance-corporals or bombardiers who were stationed at the entrance to the mess decks stronger discipline was needed and that a warrant officer with sergeants should be dotted all around the area. Once again, as I was the only warrant officer who appeared to be unoccupied I was called to the ship's colonel and told that I had to deal with this situation in a very firm manner. I did not try to explain to anybody that REME warrant officers were simply not used to this sort of nonsense. We were used to dealing with small groups of more intelligent soldiers and could usually be quite reasonable in the way we dealt with our fellows.

I went down to the mess decks with about ten NCOs of various ranks and reconnoitred the situation. I instituted a firm system whereby the warring parties were all separated and the corridor where the dispute had originated was cleared out. This corridor was about twenty-five yards in length and had been jammed with a mass of troops. I stationed sergeants at each end with strict instructions that under no circumstances was anyone to be allowed into the corridor other than in single file as they approached the serving tables in the mess. Most of the trouble had occurred because various batmen to officers had tried to cut in on the queues. They expected priority because they claimed to be busy doing their duties and this was the only time they could come for a meal break. Since most of the others had to queue for an hour for their food there was a great deal of bad feeling concerning this queue-jumping. I stated that every man had to wait his turn irrespective of what job he had. This made various officers highly indignant and they still tried to get their batmen priority feeding. I simply refused and referred them to the ship's colonel. Notwithstanding this, many of these batmen tried to come through but my instruction to the sergeants was that anybody at all who stepped past the line into the corridor was to be put under arrest without any discussion whatsoever. I had a separate room large enough to accommodate anybody that was arrested.

Everything worked splendidly. The only slight hitch to this was that several people were arrested who, I discovered later, were patients in the ship's hospital. They needed to cross the corridor to reach the toilets. After an hour or two of my new regime, the medical orderly sergeant came rushing over to me indignantly stating that we had arrested half of his patients! Fortunately I soon sorted them out and they were released.

As a result of my new system and by adopting a very threatening attitude, the very sight of me frightened any prospective trouble-makers. As none of these troops knew me personally, they presumed that any man to have reached the rank of warrant officer at so young an age must be the biggest swine on God's earth! the mutiny had ceased and the Colonel congratulated me.

I had discovered another lesson, namely that the illusion of strength in most cases is quite sufficient to make people behave themselves. In this case, the illusion of my warrant officer rank and my youth was quite enough in itself to instill the discipline necessary without my having to do much in the way of punishing people; the threat was sufficient.

We finally reached the Red Sea and on one welcome bright day our voyage came to an end as we entered Port Taufiq in Egypt. Our naval escort left us and, as they passed by each ship, we gave them three rousing cheers for looking after us, before they returned home. We disembarked and said goodbye to the *Duchess*. We were absolutely delighted and I could have kissed the ground when I stepped ashore.

A long time later we heard that as the *Duchess* was returning home to England, carrying a consignment of Italian prisoners of war, and despite flying Red Cross flags, she had been torpedoed and sunk. We understood that most of the crew and some of the prisoners were saved but unfortunately many drowned. That was the end of the 'Rolling Duchess'.

The closure of the Mediterranean to Allied shipping resulted in Port Taufiq becoming a key factor in supplying the forces in Egypt and in the desert. It appeared to be a completely chaotic situation wherein this tiny, unimportant port suddenly had to become the main army administrative supply post. In the very short time that we were there it struck me as a totally dilapidated area. Most of the buildings were built of mud and plaster, and there were neither any greenery nor any flowers to be seen; just the occasional palm tree. Port Taufiq was a small, hot stinking place – the smell being the first thing we observed there and which remained with us until we shook it off once into the desert.

Yet the place fascinated us all. The streets were crowded with Arabs who seemed to be wearing bed sheets in such a tattered state that they resembled bundles of rags while the women were shrouded in black adorned by a variety of veils covering their faces.

To my absolute astonishment (and a feather in the cap for the army Post Office) there was mail waiting for us in Taufiq. I had several letters given to me which had been written over the past two months. This was my first introduction to the incredible system of air mail letter cards, which we would both send and receive. Letters would be written on standard-sized foolscap and would then be photographed, miniaturised and posted. At their destination the letters would be blown up again for delivery. One of the advantages to this method was that photographs could be pasted or pinned on to these letters and later also be reproduced.

My batch of letters informed me that everything was fine with my family but, in a letter from my sister Dinah, there was a piece of information that at first astonished me and then made me very happy. My mother had been introduced to a widower named Sam Mattey and she was contemplating marrying him. She wanted to know what I thought of this idea. My main anxiety about my family had concerned my mother. As my brother and sister were now married with their own families, my mother was on her own and living in extremely difficult circumstances. I immediately wrote home saying that I was delighted at this news and that a big worry had now been lifted from my head.

Sam Mattey had been brought by his parents, Yosef and Surah Riva, to England from a small town in Russia called Matteshev. His late wife had been a piano teacher Katie (Gital) who had also emigrated from Russia as a young child with her parents, Abraham and Basha Gold. Sam had opened a small tailoring workshop, which soon prospered, and he had then moved into retailing, first in Forest Gate and then in Ilford. He had a son called Leslie and four daughters. The eldest was Freda followed by Mary, Frances and then Sonia. I little realised at the time of receiving Dinah's letter that Sonia was going to become the most important person in my life.

It was decided that the drivers were to be left to bring on the vehicles once they were unloaded and that the rest of us were to go forward. I left Corporal France with four of my detachment drivers and the rest of us marched straight to the railway station. After the usual administrative delays we boarded a train reminiscent of Stephenson's Rocket with its open carriages and bare boards to sit upon. We were perfectly content about this as the novelty was enormous and we were all in good spirits, delighted to be back on terra firma. We were also still relieved to have survived the dangerous sea journey. The countryside that we travelled through appeared to be mostly semi-arid. There were women working in fields with what appeared to be tools straight out of the Bible and the villages that we passed were just a collection of mud huts. After various delays, moving very short distances at a snail's pace, we eventually detrained in what appeared to be a tented camp alongside a canal. This canal was called the Sweetwater Canal, which was a complete misnomer appearing anything but sweet. We were warned that under no circumstances were we to enter this canal and that if any individual should be unfortunate enough to fall into this multi-diseased water, then he must immediately report to the Medical Officer for a series of injections.

There must have been thousands of tents at the enormous camp – it could have housed an entire army – but we were the only troops there at first. I staked a claim for the LAD which would give us some hard-standing in anticipation of getting our trucks and starting to carry out repairs.

After a day or two everybody had settled in and we began to get the hang of conditions in the Middle East. Naturally we all wore the khaki drill that we had donned on board ship as soon as the weather had got warm enough, and our first duty was to listen to a number of lectures by the medical people on how to remain healthy in a hot climate. We were given very simple rules mainly about not drinking any water that had not been distributed by our own water tanks. One of the simple tips that we were given was that it was sensible to wrap a towel around our waists when we went to sleep at night. This, apparently, would prevent kidney problems. I found it a very comfortable thing and I religiously wound a towel around my waist every night. The most important factor, from a medical point of view, was the anti-malaria precautions. Malaria was a big problem throughout the whole period I was abroad and there had been many systems of different pills and treatments. Finally a simple system was adopted which involved taking a daily mepacrine pill and the use of anti-mosquito cream to be rubbed on to our exposed parts one hour before sunset. We strictly adhered to these regulations and I am quite sure it was greatly instrumental in keeping the disease in check.

I began to prepare for the arrival of the regiment's transport and guns. I contacted the base REME officer and obtained from him a list of all the modifications that were necessary for desert usage. Most of these adjustments were to do with air filters and water systems but we also had to have other equipment such as sand trays, spades, water cans, food boxes and sun compasses.

Food boxes were necessary because once we were in the desert each vehicle was responsible for feeding the men it contained. Feeding as a unit was finished so rations and water were issued individually to a vehicle, allocated according to the number of men travelling on that vehicle.

Each vehicle was issued with two sand trays which were metal ladders attached by the fitting of straps on to the sides of the vehicle. Whenever the vehicle got stuck in the sand the men would have to take the sand tray and dig under the wheel so, with everybody shoving, it could be moved out of the soft sand.

Ordinary compasses were in short supply but as most movement was during the day we managed with sun compasses. These resembled old-fashioned sundials and were fitted on to the front of the vehicles so that they could be viewed through the windscreen, and the degree we were travelling on could be more or less ascertained. At night we had to learn to recognise simple constellations of stars so that we could find our way when the sun was no longer visible. Although a few men, after having one or two beers too many, found it difficult to find their way from the canteen to their tents, we very quickly got in to the habit of looking up at the sky as soon as we came out of the tents. I became quite competent at this and used this system extensively whenever I had to travel in the desert at night time.

Before the guns and vehicles arrived, I was given a motorbike as a temporary method of getting around. I had never learned to ride a motorbike so Flynn, the detachment's electrician, drove for me and I sat pillion. He took me wherever necessary, although at times he appeared to imagine he was a speedway rider and whenever I got off the bike I considered how lucky I was to have remained in one piece!

At Tel-el-Kabir, which was about twenty miles away, there was a huge ordnance depot; almost a city of its own. Here I saw the RAOC major in charge and arranged with him to collect all the spare parts that I required. I needed two three tonners to collect them all. One of the things that surprised me about T.K., as it was known, was that there were a lot of Palestinian soldiers working in the depot.

111

This was the first occasion I came across Jewish soldiers from Palestine in the British Army. Flynn was astonished to hear me speaking Yiddish to them, being simply unable to make head nor tail of it. I became very friendly with these soldiers and was given absolutely royal treatment. I never had the slightest problem in obtaining any stores that I required from them.

Our LAD was now in business. We had a portable shelter into which we put our welding equipment and a small forge. We had our hard standing so we were perfectly happy to jack up our vehicles and do whatever was necessary. Most of the batteries were completely flat after our long journey so we were kept busy charging them up and checking them out. There were many minor faults that had occurred apart from the inevitable two or three vehicles that had had accidents either on the original journey to Gourock or during the journey from Port Taufiq to the camp. There were something like 160 vehicles that needed some sort of modification and it took us about two weeks to get the regiment into a condition fit for use in the desert.

Most of the modifications to the guns had been seen to when we were at Thetford but there were a couple left solely for the desert which we quickly carried out. Before leaving the UK I had changed my personal utility vehicle for a Humber 8 cwt truck which had four wheel drive. This was a great improvement for there were few jeeps around and we never had any in the regiment whilst we were in the blue.

We learned that nobody called the desert 'the desert' but it was referred to as 'the blue'. When you spoke of 'in the blue' it showed that you were a true desert campaigner. We had several lectures about what life was going to be like once we were 'in the blue' and 'in the line'. The desert war had had certain successes to date but plenty of retreats as well. It appeared to us that the army spent most of its time chasing across the desert – and then being chased back again. At this time, the front line was at a place called El Alamein. There was a railway station there about twenty-five miles from Alexandria along the coast, so we were informed that there was no further room to retreat. There was only one way to go – back across the desert. In an odd way we were looking forward to going into battle because it seemed exciting after having been in training for such a long time. In a sense it was all very romantic.

As a final desert training before going to the front we had a few days of exercises. These seemed to consist of getting our vehicles stuck into the sand and then digging our way out again. We very quickly realised that our Leyland breakdown lorry, which was excellent on roads, was pretty useless in the desert. We began to get into the habit of using any four-wheel-drive vehicles, that we had, to pull out those stuck too deeply in the sand or that had overturned or had any kind of accident. We tried to avoid using the

112

breakdown lorry as much as possible for recovery purposes but to confine its use to that of a mobile workshop. We had been told that we were only going to perform very minor repairs but in practice we tackled some very major ones. We changed major assemblies and would then simply send them back for overhaul. We became very adept in the open and, for example, we could change a complete engine on a Ford 3-ton lorry in four hours and, in the same amount of time, we could put a complete rear axle on a vehicle.

In a lighter vein, the LAD was given a small portable gramophone with a number of records. The gramophone was always left on the tailboard of the stores lorry and it became a ritual that anyone who happened to walk by would automatically wind up the gramophone and start playing a record. Gradually these records were broken or damaged in transit and by the time we left the Western Desert we only had one left which we looked after very carefully. This record had a song called 'Invitation to a Dance' on one side and 'Flowers for Madame' on the other. I don't remember who recorded it but we got to know every part of the record and, even today, the tunes still run through my head, since I must have heard these lovely melodies thousands of times.

We did not have any portable radios but there was an army issue radio for communication purposes and, every now and again, we would defy regulations, switch on and listen. Mostly we heard the German Afrika Korps – the easiest station to get – who were forever playing 'Lilli Marlene' – which seemed to go on and on and on. By the time we came out of the desert we knew many of the words of this German song and, in fact, this was the song that the 8th Army literally took over from the Afrika Korps, becoming as popular with us, no doubt, as it had been with them.

Finally we were ready for our move into the desert. It felt about time that we began to have some victories. The British Army had mainly been fighting in the Western Desert since the evacuation from Dunkirk and we were light-hearted, ready to play our parts and do whatever called upon to do. We had great pride in the regiment and great confidence in ourselves.

My detachment, my little band of men, consisted of a variety of interesting characters. Staff Sergeant Pete Adams was a wonderful fellow, a boy trained soldier who came from a military background. His father was a soldier and Pete had been brought up in India. He had joined the Boys' Service at the age of fourteen and had been trained in the Boys' College as an armourer. He was about my age and, to him, the war was a godsend. Had it not been for the war he would have probably remained a craftsman for years and could never have hoped to attain in peacetime any rank higher than sergeant. Here he was now a staff sergeant with the prospect of reaching ASM or even taking a commission.

113

Next in rank was Sergeant Frank Storey. He was a terrific motor fitter, without doubt the best we had in the regiment. His mother was Italian and so he was able to speak the language. He was a fantastic credit to our unit.

Corporal Bert France was a fitter who had been with the regiment from the beginning of the war. When we left Egypt he had had to remain behind in hospital suffering from malaria. He had then had a cushy job in the base workshops in Cairo where he could have remained for the rest of the war. However, he wanted to rejoin the regiment and he wrote to me asking me to arrange for him to be brought from the Middle East to Italy. After a great deal of time and trouble I arranged for this transfer and we were all delighted when he rejoined us.

Lance-Corporal Harry Beaumont was a perky storeman who kept all our stores and records in meticulous order, and Lance-Corporal Joe Allen took charge of the breakdown lorry always doing everything that was required of him.

We had various craftsmen, including the cheery Spiffy Binks and the well-experienced electrician Len Flynn who had been a regular soldier for about five years before the war. Len was not the greatest of electricians, but as long as we kept an eye on him he was an asset to the unit.

Jimmy Darrell, another fitter, was the youngest, and storeman Billy Beal was the oldest in the detachment. Billy was a tailor from Leeds who had worked with many Jewish people, had many Jewish friends and therefore knew a great deal about Jewish habits and customs. He was married with children, and we always felt a bit sorry for him.

The fitters consisted of Eddie Taylor from the Midlands, George Leigh from Yorkshire, Ollie Springitt – a slow moving but very sturdy man – from the South of England, Harry Green a typical Londoner from Bethnal Green and finally Bill Unsworth, a driver mechanic. Bill was a Northerner who, in civvy street, was an official of the National Association of Boys' Clubs so he and I had a great deal in common.

Jack Wragg was a welder who came from Birmingham, a typical Brummy. Jack and I were particularly good friends because when I became a WO1 I was entitled to have a batman and Jack volunteered for this job. He remained with me until about three years later when I left the regiment.

To my knowledge we all survived the war except for Bert who was killed by a 88mm shell, and Harry Green who died in action as a result of an accident. Eddie and Jimmy were in a jeep that drove over and triggered off an anti-personnel mine; both recovered although Eddie remained deaf in one ear.

Our final instructions concerned mines. Apparently the whole battlefield was littered with mines of all kinds including anti-personnel mines. We were warned to stay put as much as possible, not to pick up objects that were lying around as the Germans had attached explosives to almost everything one could think of, scattering them from the air and by other sorts of methods. From then on, mines became the biggest hazard we faced. Scarcely a day passed without someone in the unit being either killed or having a narrow escape from being maimed by a mine.

We were given three days' emergency rations with very strict instructions that they were not to be touched without the express order of the senior officer present. It was a court martial offence to open these rations without authorisation. It was obvious to everybody that there would be occasions when rations could not be delivered to us so we would have to fall back on the emergency rations and water in particular. Strict rationing of water was to take place. We, in the LAD, were a little more fortunate than most because we were actually allowed extra to replace water in the radiators of our vehicles that may be leaking or damaged in some way – quite a common fault all the time that we were in the desert.

We soon became accustomed to the 8th Army method of eating. Most of our rations were canned: we had tinned potatoes, tinned bacon, tinned stew and tinned bully beef. The Quartermaster did his best to bring us fresh vegetables and other fresh foods whenever possible. There were four water carts which provided a daily ration to each man. Our method of cooking was to cut a flimsy petrol tin in half, put a shovel full of sand into it and then some petrol. We set this alight and heated our tins on a grid placed on top of this can. It was a very fierce flame which usually heated up our meal in about two minutes flat. It was also a dangerous method and many men were burned as a result of cooking in this manner but it was the quickest and most efficient way of heating a meal. If it felt likely that we would not have the time to stop to cook, we would hang tins of bully beef or stew on to the engines of the vehicles. After a couple of hours of travelling at least we would then have a lukewarm meal to eat.

We were told that initially we were to be attached to 13 Corps. The regiment left the camp early one morning and I was informed that somewhere along the Cairo/Alexandria road we would be instructed on the route by cutting off into the blue to follow the regiment. We had one or two vehicles which were playing up and were also rather delayed because we had various breakdowns on the road. By tea time the rest of the regiment were several hours in front of me and had disappeared into the blue.

I had a small group by now which consisted of the LAD, a gun with its limbers, crew and quad towing it from R Battery – it had taken us two hours to fix it up as we had to take off the cylinder head – two 15 cwts from Q Battery and a three ton ammunition lorry from P Battery full of various stores. Thus I had quite a small convoy of my own with approximately fifty men for whom I, as the most senior person, was now responsible.

I made sure that we kept a tight convoy as we travelled slowly along the road looking out for some indication or message left for me to explain how I was to find 13 Corps. Finally I was flagged down by a military policeman on a motorbike. He informed me that an officer of the regiment had waited as long as possible to give me the instructions and had given this policeman a small piece of paper to pass on to me. This note said that Lieutenant-Colonel Greenhalgh had left instructions that we were to leave the road and to head into the desert for 25 miles on a bearing of approximately 245 degrees where we were to report to 13 Corps Report Centre, C Track, south of Hamman. I still have this piece of paper, which is why I am able to accurately recall this message. We used the sun compasses to get the required bearing and set off into the desert.

I was very green about deserts but necessity is the mother of invention and we all learned very quickly. I gave my convoy strict instructions to stay close to me and keep an eye out for enemy aircraft or other dangers. I impressed upon them that officially the regiment was in action and that although we were still quite a way from the front every yard took us nearer to the battle lines. I had to stop on several occasions because, however careful we were, there were still patches of very soft sand in the area and each time a vehicle became stuck I had to halt the whole convoy until the vehicle was freed.

About half an hour before daylight disappeared I decided that we must stop and laager (camp) in the desert. I instructed the sergeant in charge of the gun to arrange for two sentries to be posted on duty in turns throughout the night and, after we had eaten our meals, we went to sleep in order to make an early start the next morning. Although we were only a few miles into the desert there was one big advantage here, that was immediately apparent; namely the ability to eat a meal without millions of flies pestering us. The most inconvenient thing about any inhabited area in the Middle East was that one had to perpetually have a fly whisk at the ready. Once out into the desert it was fly free and wonderful.

8
In the Blue

At daybreak the next morning we breakfasted and then continued on with our journey through the desert. I tried to keep to the hard sand and was fairly successful but we still had to halt a number of times over the next few miles to dig out vehicles.

Eventually we began to see the signs of the rear of any army. Scattered all over the place were various ordnance dumps, service corps dumps, a variety of small units and a large hospital with a vast number of tents prepared with beds for casualties. We had to be very careful that our vehicles were properly spaced for enemy aircraft were in the vicinity. As we approached the front we began to hear the sound of gunfire in the distance.

I decided to stop at what appeared to be some small units – such as a petrol dump for example – in order to ask for directions to 13 Corps Headquarters. However, when I arrived there I found, to my astonishment, that it was a false dump made from cardboard as were the vehicles around it. It was part of a camouflage exercise and from the distance or from the sky it really appeared as though it was an active unit. I discovered afterwards that the position of these phoney units, complete with dummy soldiers, were altered daily so that aerial photographers would have the impression that here was an active unit. We continued to keep a very wary eye open for enemy aircraft and on a couple of occasions spotted some but they were not directly overhead so we just ignored them. Fortunately they ignored us too.

We arrived at a camp marked 'Rear 8th Army Headquarters' where the military police gave me further directions. I had to travel one mile west and by a burnt-out Bren carrier I should turn left on to C Track. Two miles further on we should see a 13 Corps sign. This was the first time that I had come across these tracks which were made by bits of wood knocked into the sand. At various intervals a simple painted sign would be found and from each sign another could be seen about fifty yards further on. We were warned to stay on the track which had been cleared of any mines but ten or twenty yards either side of the track could be dangerous

We then came to a sign which told us this was the 13 Corps Rear

Army Form G 1045
(Pads of 100.)

R.A.O.C. WORKSHOP INDENT
(To be rendered in triplicate. E.R. Part 1, 1932, para. 403,
or E.R. Part 3, 1933, para. 43 for T.A. will be complied with.)

Unit's No. ....
Unit **53 Field Rgt RA**

R.A.O.C. Serial No. ....

Station and Date **Deel 3/11/42** Commenced* .... Completed* ....

Job No.	Designation of Vehicle or Stores quoting Regd. No. when available.	No.	Nature of Service and Authority.	Summary of Cost {Repairs etc.	£	s.	d.
1	F.D.B. Quad A5419617		Prop shafts and Dynamos				
2	Field Quad A597216		Clutch and Prop shafts				
3	Fordson Scout P11674		Transmission				
4	Fordson Scout M6135						
5	Fordson 8 cwt M11855						
6	Morris 8 cwt 4421143						
7	Quad O.P 34768		Bogey wheel bearing				
8	Norton M/c 4590521						
9	Norton M/c 4544436						

Direct { Labour ....
{ Materials ....
Contracts ....
Travelling Exes. ....
Carriage of Stores ....
On-Cost† ....
Total Cost ....

* For R.A.O.C. use only.

NOTE.—A separate form will be used for stores in each Vocabulary Section.

(Signed) ....
O.C. ....
Approved
S.O.M.E. ....

O.C. ....
To note completion of service (land cost).
(Signed) ....
S.O.M.E. ....

3681/PMES/50.000 x 100/3-63

All in a days work. Nine trucks not fit to cover 1,000 miles of desert and passed to 10 Corps REME Workshop.

118

Echelon and when I enquired I was directed to travel a mile and a half down another track called the Sun Track. At a certain point I should see a sign proclaiming Moon Track and, with luck, one mile down this track would be the 53rd Regiment. We went along merrily although the noise of the shelling was getting louder and we could hear a great deal of activity. At this time we saw no enemy shelling nor any attacks by planes.

As we were travelling along the Moon track we saw the P Battery water cart coming in the opposite direction. I flagged down the driver who told me that the regiment was stationed about 500 yards further along. So I happily drove the final 500 yards and was delighted to see the 53rd Field Regiment at last.

The major of R Battery couldn't thank me enough for the gun; he had been worried because they were expecting to go into action at any time and he was short of the one gun. The Lieutenant Quartermaster Matthews actually said, 'Well done!' so I was very pleased.

The non LAD vehicles disappeared to rejoin their units and I was now in my correct position with the B echelon of the regimental headquarters. It was mid-afternoon by this time and, almost immediately after we arrived, the guns moved off to take up their positions. The Adjutant, Captain Drapkin, gave me a map reference which was actually just a spot in the desert, and I set up shop there. The LAD was now open for business.

The line eventually became known as the El Alamein line, but at the time nobody gave it a second thought never thinking for one moment that this name would have any more significance than the names of a thousand other places along the coast. The line stretched from the coast just past El Alamein station and across the desert to the Qattara Depression – an area impossible to be navigated by transport. It was a tiny battlefield, only about thirty miles long, but it was basically the bottleneck that had prevented the Afrika Korps from breaking through into the Nile Delta only twenty-five miles behind us. In this tiny battle field there were only two army corps: 13 and 10 Corps. A mixture of British, Indian, New Zealand, South African and various other small colonial units made up the 8th Army, that had just been taken over by General Montgomery. There was one other corps in reserve, 30 Corps, and in the battle of Alamein all the three corps played a very important part.

After I had seen that the LAD was in position and made sure that everything possible was being done to the vehicles that needed attention, I received a signal that Charlie Troop of Queen Battery had a problem with one of the guns. I spoke to Sergeant Neil, the tiffy*, on the radio, to get a good idea what the trouble was and I told

---

*Army nickname for a mechanic.

him that I would be over as soon as possible. I took the 8-cwt, with Eddie Taylor driving and, with a lot of difficulty, I found my way to battery headquarters. The prime difficulty was the minefields for although there were tracks to follow everybody was dug in and dispersed for safety. As we neared the battery nobody welcomed any transport at all for sometimes the mere arrival of a vehicle was sufficient to bring enemy shelling down upon one's head. Therefore as we neared the front we had to get out and walk.

At the battery headquarters I discovered that the front line consisted of the following: two of our minefields, then a no-man's land and then two German minefields called January and February. Some of our infantry were dug in on the no-man's land as were some anti-tank guns. Pip Battery (our senior battery, as this was the first time we were in action) was dug in at a position between our two minefields. To get to Pip Battery you had to carefully negotiate passages in the minefields which were marked by white tape and just wide enough for a vehicle. Queen and Robert Batteries were placed just behind these minefields.

The regiment would be firing at targets approximately 1 – 4 miles distant. The regimental headquarters were somewhere in the middle of Queen and Robert Batteries but about 300 – 400 yards to the rear.

The whole regiment was well dug in and the best possible use was being made of camouflage and sandbags. The camouflage nets were always left draped on to the vehicles even when on the move. Whenever vehicles stopped for more than a few minutes, the nets were automatically opened up with one or two stakes put around in an attempt to get the vehicle to blend into the landscape.

At the battery headquarters the office truck was sandbagged and half submerged in the sand. I was welcomed by Captain Johnson, the second-in-command. There was a great air of excitement in the truck with various staff sitting at maps and at the communication desk which was loaded with telephones and wirelesses. Suddenly, within a minute or two of my arrival, the first firing orders came over the radio and were immediately passed to an officer stationed at the desks with the maps in front of him. He was connected by a telephone line to Charlie and Don Troops. The regimental signallers had put in these lines the moment they had arrived for communication was of vital importance and telephones were much preferred to radio contact.

Within one minute of the orders coming through the firing began. I had heard many guns firing up to that point and I was to hear the firing of many more 25-pounder guns in the following two and a half years, but I never failed to be surprised by their loud noise. This time it appeared to be louder than ever because we were doing the firing. After three years of being in the army I was finally in action and helping the regiment to shoot back at the enemy. I had a sense of achievement and thought that although I did not know what was going to happen from then on, at least I had done something and could presume that we were damaging the enemy.

I walked the hundred yards to Charlie Troop and stood around the four guns watching how the recoil was behaving. I discussed them with Sergeant Neil and we made some minor adjustments to the recuperator systems, until they were firing beautifully. The gun that he was worried about had a fault that I had anticipated and I had brought the necessary spare part of the sight with me. It only took us about ten minutes to fix it on and we managed to do it between the firing so we did not have to report the gun out of action, which made Charlie Troop very happy.

During the time we were repairing this gun some enemy shells began to arrive and, for the first time, I heard a noise that was to become both very familiar as well as very frightening to me. There was the whee sound of a shell coming towards us and then the crump sound of its landing. I must have heard this noise thousands of times over the next couple of years and I was always alarmed by it. One tried to anticipate in which direction the shell was going and, in a way, we became quite good at this. There were many occasions when we heard the whee noise and would dive for cover after two or three seconds knowing that the shell would be landing quite near. At other times we could tell that the shell was going overhead and that we would be quite safe. Personally speaking, of all the unpleasant noises that I heard while I was in the army, this shell landing or coming towards us took a lot of beating.

I had now seen the first of our guns in action and my job was complete for the moment. It was getting late in the afternoon and, as there were no lights allowed whatsoever, I knew that I had better return to the LAD otherwise I would have difficulty in finding my way back. As we left the battery and were walking towards our truck, three enemy planes appeared. Taylor and myself made a quick dive for some shelter. Some bombs fell a short distance away and all hell broke loose. Everybody possessing an ack-ack weapon of any kind must have decided to open up and it was bedlam. This was my first taste of a battlefield with the heat, the sand, the noise of the bombers and the ack-ack trying to knock out the planes. There was the noise of shells, rifle fire and machine gun fire and I decided that it was not a very pleasant place to be – but at least I had had my initiation.

Once the enemy planes had left, we mounted the truck and first reported back at the regimental headquarters. As there was nothing particular to take action upon, we arrived back at the LAD just as it was about to get dark.

We began to develop a pattern that was to be repeated dozens of times over the next two and a half years and devised a routine of doing things. Whenever we moved at all, our priority was to get the

121

guns into their new positions. Secondly, we had to keep all the tactical transport in action which often meant that we were recovering vehicles and bringing them up from the last position after the regiment had gone into action elsewhere. If a vehicle required a major replacement, such as an engine or an axle, I would still have it towed to the next position in the hope that if we remained there long enough I might be able to get the necessary parts. The last thing I wanted to do was to send anything back to the workshop company because we could lose it permanently there.

Our third function was to liaise with the different batteries regarding the way the guns were functioning. I had to know from the fitters if they needed any spare parts or if there was any task that they were not capable of doing which we could handle at the LAD. I also had to do the same with the transport fitters because I was the link between the regiment and the REME. In fact a great deal of my time was spent in finding out what spares were required and chasing all over to any workshop company or stores depot where I could beg, borrow or steal our requirements.

We were always short of spare parts of every kind. Scattered all round the battlefields were vehicles that had been blown up and partially destroyed. Different people had cannibalised various parts from these vehicles on their way through, so one of the main jobs we had to do was to descend like locusts on any vehicle that was not repairable. We were after such useful components as petrol pumps, carburettors, spare wheels and tyres, in fact, any part that might be of use to us in the future. Vehicles that were severely damaged but still repairable would be towed back to the LAD and if necessary towed further to the brigade workshop.

We never knew how long we were going to be in any one place. Sometimes we moved within a few hours of arriving but at other times we might have two or three weeks in the same position. Obviously, during these longer periods, we utilised the time to put as much in order as possible. Our priority always remained with getting the guns in action and keeping them in action. Any time that a gun was out of action it had to be immediately reported as it was vital for the commander to know not how many guns he had to call upon, but how many guns could actually fire. Of the twenty-four guns in the regiment there were inevitably times when some of them were out of action. We got over this to a certain extent by using the LAD spare gun which we towed around with us to replace a damaged gun while it was repaired.

The blue was extremely hot and there was sand everywhere. We would be covered with sand the moment we walked a couple of yards. We constantly wore plastic goggles, issued for gas attacks, to keep the sand out of our eyes. After a short time in the open, our whole faces would be encrusted with sand and once the goggles were removed, we looked like clowns.

After two or three days we became settled into our routine. Soldiers are very easy people to adapt to any circumstances and we settled down very quickly. We rose at dawn to make full use of daylight and continued to carry out whatever repairs that we had not been able to finish the night before to tackle newly arrived tasks. There was a continual stream of people coming to us from the various parts of the regiment requiring technical assistance or a vital spare part. Sometimes we got a report in during the night of a recovery that was needed somewhere and a request to see if it was possible to salvage the vehicle. If a gun was in trouble, almost invariably I had to visit the gun site because normally the tiffies were perfectly capable of handling minor repairs themselves so if they sent an SOS then it meant it was something serious that needed my expertise. I would try to ascertain by radio what the problem was but we had to be very guarded how we spoke.

We obviously tried to help others not in our regiment who might be crying out for help. I had to be very careful for however desperate others may have been for parts my responsibility was to my own regiment. Therefore it was a question of judgement whether I should retain the part for myself or allow another unit to have it. Most other units, in turn, also tried to help me and I spent a lot of time travelling the desert trying to get any spare parts that we needed so desperately. I rapidly became acquainted with various NCOs, people in the different ordnance companies, REME workshops, Service Corps and so on. Usually by some coaxing and conniving and, even on occasions by doing a swap, we could do some sort of a deal. I always had to try to return to the LAD by dusk when I would brew up a quick meal and settle down for the night.

On one occasion I received an emergency request from one of the water carts which had to get to El Alamein Station to collect some piped water. It had broken down and needed a new petrol pump. I was able to oblige and afterwards we discovered a NAAFI canteen at the station where we went to have the usual cup of char with a wad. Whilst I was talking to the NAAFI lance-corporal in charge of the canteen, it transpired that I happened to have on the 8-cwt a carburettor for a 3-ton Ford. He was desperate for this component for his stores truck. I was able to do a deal with him and, in return for this carburettor, he sold me a box of twelve half-pound slabs of Cadbury chocolate. This was absolutely fantastic! I came away in triumph and was delighted to put this confectionery into my food box for some future occasion. Four or five weeks later, when we were hundreds of miles away from El Alamein, we found ourselves completely separated from our unit and our supplies. We had to eat our emergency rations and this box of chocolate was a godsend. I shared it around the detachment and for one day used the chocolate as our main source of food.

There was a variety of methods of sleeping. I had a waterproof bed roll into which my blankets were folded. All I had to do was to unstrap the leather strap, roll it out and it was ready. The outside cover had to be waterproof for even in the desert there was a lot of dew on the ground in the mornings drenching everything. There were many discussions about the best place to sleep. We had put sandbags on the floors of all of our vehicles to give us some protection should the vehicle go over a mine. Consequently a lot of men favoured sleeping under a vehicle where a certain protection from shelling or bombing could be obtained. Others decided that the vehicle itself was a target and the best plan was to sleep well away from any transport. We had been issued with bivouacs – simple tents, which were virtually two ground sheets buttoned together with a stick at each end and a few guy ropes. They were very effective and comfortable so some bothered to set them up whilst others merely lay stretched out on the sand and slept. Others slept in slit trenches which were sandbagged round for safety, for whenever we arrived in a new position we quickly dug trenches although sometimes we were too lazy to do so and, after the first shelling arrived, there would be a frantic amount of digging by everybody.

I normally slept under the tailboard of my 8-cwt Humber. This vehicle became a mobile home to me in every sense of the word. My food, my water and my bedroll were here plus everything else that I personally possessed. I was like a snail and, wherever I happened to be when it got dark, I at least had my truck. Should the shelling intensify, then I would place some sandbags around the tailboard and as the shelling worsened, the sandbags seemed to get higher and higher.

I carried a 45 Colt which was permanently strapped to my side. It was the first thing I could reach from my bedroll and I would never have dreamt of going anywhere without it. I also had my faithful rifle – issued at Leyton back in the Territorial days – behind the driver's seat where there was a special clip to hold it so that it was always handy. Hanging on the rifle were two Mills bombs for use in an emergency and finally the unit had a Tommy gun, also kept in the cab of the 8-cwt. All my men knew where it was and whoever was on sentry duty would carry it. In the morning, the last sentry would replace it back in the cab so that it would always be available.

The desert, oddly enough, was a very clean war. We were not pestered by flies and insects and, as there were no civilians in the area, there were no homes destroyed. Here there were just two armies fighting each other so, as far as any war can be called clean, the desert war certainly was. I think that it is fair to say that as long as there are going to be wars, the best way to do it is to find a desert, station the opposing armies there and let them fight it out. I think that the David and Goliath system is better still, where just one man is taken from each army. If the two opponents could just play table tennis and decide on the basis of that, then perhaps we would be getting a bit more civilised. Until then, deserts are very good places for wars.

Having said that flies and insects were no problem I must add that we had a very large tin of DDT powder which we sprinkled around our bedrolls to protect us against creepy-crawlies such as scorpions, which lived in the desert.

Our Leyland breakdown lorry continued to become stuck in the sand and useless in the desert other than for using the winch, for lifting engines and for a suspended tow. Finally, the Leyland broke its back for the chassis could not stand the strain and dented in the middle. Looking at the vehicle sideways, it had a V shape so we handed it in to one of the workshops and received a new Dodge breakdown lorry which was much better.

As time went on, we inevitably began to get casualties. Royal Artillery units very rarely have a lot of injured at one time, unlike an infantry unit – it's a question of attrition. On some days we would hear of perhaps three, four or five casualties. Some we knew very well and some were merely names. By now I could put a name to most of the faces in the regiment but it didn't seem to bother us all that much because in the army this process goes on all the time. I got to know some people very well and even became good friends with them. Then, suddenly, this person would disappear, perhaps being posted to another unit or further away. Sometimes I was posted and left my friends behind. Therefore when people were killed it appeared to be exactly the same, one day they were around and then we heard that they had gone and that was the end of the story. On the times when I was more involved in the incident, as happened on three or four occasions, then I remembered the event to a far greater extent and took a different attitude to it. Mostly when we heard the name of somebody who was no longer with the unit, it would register for a moment and then we probably forgot all about it and got on with what we had to do.

9
Before the Battle

I continued to write home to my mother every week although I must admit that after a while my writing got bigger because I simply did not know what to say. By now all our mail had to be censored and I found myself in the odd situation of having to do some of this censoring for my section. Some very peculiar things began to appear in my men's letters but obviously I tried to read the letters as though I did not know the writer, trying not to pry into personal affairs although this was almost an impossibility. In many ways I began to know my men far better, but under no circumstances could I let on that I had seen their mail or remembered any of it at all.

Obviously my correspondence home was also censored but fortunately I never knew by whom. As my letters were fairly impersonal it did not bother me unduly although occasionally, when I had a bit of time, I would write to my mother in Yiddish. My Yiddish writing was very rusty so it was a long laborious exercise but I knew from her answers that my mother was delighted. Usually she would have to get somebody to read my English letters to her so she really enjoyed having the pleasure of reading my news in Yiddish herself. I always thought that the person who censored my Yiddish letters must have found it very confusing when they tried to figure out even what language I was using although, if I remember correctly, we had to write the name of the language on the envelope. However, there were Palestinian soldiers serving in the desert who could have deciphered these letters.

After Montgomery arrived, it became fashionable in the 8th Army to be as unregimental as possible in the matter of clothes. Nobody was bothered about correct dress so most of the time we could wear what we liked and just be comfortable. We had to make sure that our heads were covered and take precautions against sunburn, although some men gradually tanned their bodies to the point where they were no longer affected by the sun, only wearing a hat, a pair of shorts, socks and boots. I personally never removed my shirt in the sunshine, having vivid memories of camping days at Hoddesdon and the Isle of Wight when, in a much less intense heat,

I had suffered with painful sunburn. My knees, arms and face gradually became brown – the tan taking years to disappear – but the rest of my body remained completely white.

Our Colonel, however, insisted on constantly looking totally regimental when he wore service dress. His particular idiosyncrasy was that he always wore a stiff shirt collar which was separate from his shirts and fastened by special studs. His batman went to a great deal of trouble concerning the washing of these collars. He made sure that he carried starch with him all over the world to enable him to keep the Colonel's collars in the best of condition.

We tried various ways of cooking our meals and some of the men became quite expert at turning simple tins of bully beef and so on into rather fancy dishes. We also had some odd foods given to us by the Quartermaster; odd in the sense that we were unused to such delicacies. We had one tin of South African guavas which were a sort of very tasty pear in a rather sickly juice. We had never seen such fruit in our lives before. The only thing was that instead of having a normal small tin we were issued with an enormous one containing 28 lb of these things! We put this giant tin on the tailboard of the GMC Stores lorry next to the gramophone and it became a routine that as anyone walked by the GMC he would dip in, take a guava, eat it and, at the same time, wind the gramophone and play one of the records.

We continued to learn some very hard lessons concerning movement in the desert, quickly discovering that travel over the desert is far more destructive on vehicles than is normal on the road. The desert may look smooth but it was a vicious trap for vehicles, sometimes being flat, soft sand and sometimes undulating. Our vehicles had not been designed to withstand such conditions so after a while we became desperate for replacement front and rear springs. After all a vehicle is only a box on a chassis and this chassis is suspended on the front and rear axles by steel springs which prevent it from constantly banging on to the axles. These springs were useless for desert purposes and we were forever changing axles and the springs attached to them. Fortunately, the springs, being made from steel, were rarely destroyed when a vehicle became a casualty and, even if it was burned out, the springs were salvageable. Thus we constantly scoured the battlefields to collect springs of all dimensions from any vehicle we found. We became experts at rebuilding complete springs from a variety of odd leaves.

A spring is really a flat piece of steel, around three inches wide and half an inch thick and two or three feet long. The complete assembly consisted of about six or eight of these springs bolted together. We therefore used to take these odd leaves and merely join them into the best possible combination we could produce. Sometimes a vehicle would leave the LAD with a definite tilt on one side because the replacement spring we had fitted on one side was a much tougher one than the original on the other side.

This spring problem became much more serious on our Ford quads because each quad was overloaded, as in addition to towing a gun and two limbers loaded with ammunition it also had to carry an enormous variety of personal and operational equipment needed by the gun crew including both normal and emergency food and water rations.

There were two prop shafts on these Fords because a quad was a four wheel drive vehicle with a short prop shaft to the front and a longer one to the rear axle. As the quads travelled along, hitting various bumps and oscillating up and down, weakened or broken leaves in the springs caused the chassis to suddenly come into violent contact with the prop shaft. This would then twist as though it were butter and eventually rip in half. When that happened, the vehicle came to a sudden halt and there was nothing to be done about it. This became a vastly serious problem as it was happening in every regiment so any available spare prop shafts were used up very quickly indeed. We had a massive problem in finding a solution and we only just managed to contain this problem. During the whole period in the desert we just about scraped through and every quad arrived at its final destination. This was because most of the quads that we had were Fords and fortunately all Ford prop shafts, irrespective of what truck they were on, were similar. They were hollow steel tubes, about three and a quarter inches in diameter with a knuckle joint at each end which fitted to the differential and the gearbox. These shafts varied in length depending upon to which type of vehicle they were attached. When we roamed the battlefield for casualties we would automatically remove the prop shafts from any derelict Fords. We would then cut the steel tubes to the length required for our quads and re-weld the knuckle joints on to each end of the prop shaft, thus reproducing a prop shaft that we required in the necessary length. It was not always the same diameter shaft but, as a compromise, it sufficed.

By this method we built up a stock of these prop shafts and were able to keep the guns mobile. Of all the problems that I encountered in the desert, this was the greatest. I used to have harrowing nightmares in which I saw the whole 8th Army stranded in the middle of the Libyan Desert as not one of our vehicles contained a prop shaft! I was reminded of when Napoleon said, 'For the want of a nail a horseshoe was lost, for the want of a horseshoe a gun was lost and for the want of a gun a battle was lost!'

My biggest nightmare was the one that would be the most terrifying to any armament artificer anywhere in the world. It happened in reality for the first time just before the start of the battle of Alamein when I was called out in the middle of the night to

Robert Battery. A gun had fired a shell which, instead of going
about two miles ahead towards the enemy, had landed about two or
three hundred yards in front of the gun. It was a miracle that none
of our infantry had been killed or wounded by this.

With an incident of this nature the drill was that the gun would
have to stop firing and the armament artificer summoned. As I was
the warrant officer concerned I immediately made my way to
Robert Battery. The night was pitch black so, although I had been
there several times in daylight, it was with great difficulty that I
managed to find the gun. Having some idea of what the problem
was I had taken with me some equipment and tools that I thought
might be necessary. The nature of this problem indicated that it
could be only one of two things. Either there was something wrong
with the charge or there was an obstruction in the bore so that the
force of the charge was used up in pushing the shell through the
restricted bore of the gun. If the rifling was affected and the correct
charge powder had been inserted then the next shell that was fired
would not proceed through the bore and there was a very big
danger that the whole gun would explode. Unfortunately there was
no way of checking if the gunpowder was faulty or had not been
properly put into the shell. If, on the other hand, there was an
obstruction then the gun had to be taken out of action with all the
problems that procedure involved. If the bore was damaged it
would have to go way back to a command workshop to have a new
barrel fitted.

My problem was that if at command workshops it was discovered
that the gun did not have an obstruction and I had pulled it out of
action unnecessarily, then not only would I look awfully foolish but
I would probably be hauled up in front of a court martial for taking
a perfectly good gun out of a very difficult battle situation.
However, if the gun did have an obstruction and I allowed it to be
fired then there was a very good chance of an explosion. Not only
could the gun crew be killed or wounded but so could I, because if I
pronounced the gun to be safe it was expected of me to stand there
while the next shell was fired to prove my confidence in my own
diagnosis.

At Stoke-on-Trent, in a lovely big workshop and in broad
daylight with a variety of tools on hand, we had been taught how to
check for any obstruction. We took an apparatus, put it into the
bore, spread gutta-percha round it and then unscrewed the
apparatus so that the gutta-percha pressed on the inside of the bore
to give us an impression. Then we would take out the apparatus and
the hardened gutta-percha and very carefully examine the lands
(part of the rifling) and impression made. We could thus diagnose
whether the obstruction was caused by any land failure. This
operation took about two or three hours under perfect conditions.

It was obviously impossible to use this method in the middle of the night, on the front line for we had neither the apparatus nor the gutta-percha on site. One old-timer had once said to me that if ever I were to get into this sort of position, there was a thing called a gauge plug bore which I could use. This is a piece of steel just slightly larger in diameter than the shell about to fired. He said that he had found that if he could push the gauge plug bore through the barrel of the gun it was most likely that no obstruction existed.

So, on this particular night at Robert Battery in the front line at Alamein, in the middle of the pitch black night and with an anxious audience of officers and crew, I covered the gun with the tarpaulin and switched on my torch. When I looked along the bore it seemed perfectly clear to me so I took my gauge plug bore, shoved it in the breech and depressed the gun to its fullest angle. My driver, Ted, stood at the other end and caught the gauge plug bore as it emerged through the gun.

I dared not display any lack of confidence so, once more, I kept my fingers and toes crossed. I turned to the battery commander and pronounced that the gun was perfectly safe to fire for the cause had been faulty gunpowder. Straight away the crew went into action and I stood about a foot away from the left wheel of the gun. When the firing order was given the noise nearly knocked me over but thankfully this time the gun had fired perfectly.

'Thank you, Q..' they said. 'Excellent bit of work.'

As I always say, 'My *mazel* (luck) held!'

During my army service I had to deal with this situation on five other occasions and only once did I have the luxury of working in broad daylight. I felt like a gynaecologist might feel, seemingly always having to deliver his babies in the middle of the night!

Gradually the talk increased about a major battle being about to take place. The old timers were very sceptical about these rumours as they had already been up and down the desert on previous sorties. However, this time the gossip was that Montgomery reckoned we were going to knock the Afrika Korps right out of North Africa; this sounded eminently believable to us newcomers. Talk of this new battle increased daily until finally we were officially informed that we were about to move into the battle positions.

This time Pip Battery moved in front of the first forward minefield which meant that there was nothing between them and the enemy minefield. Queen and Robert Batteries were both between the two minefields. This positioning took a lot of preparation and night after night men would go forward to prepare the new positions for all three batteries. Some infantry remained in front of Pip Battery but very few. When the positions were ready, the guns moved in at night and by the following dawn the whole regiment was very well dug in and camouflaged.

We were told that this battle was to be the largest artillery battle in which the British army had ever taken part. According to

Montgomery's own words later, there were actually 832 25-pounder guns in the line in the thirty-mile stretch from the sea to the depression. We were told that on the opening night of the battle, each gun would be called upon to fire approximately 1,000 rounds of 25-pounder ammunition so it was vital that the ammunition was ferried forward and stacked close to each gun position. This enormous task took many hours to prepare and was mostly done at night while the enemy was still fairly active. Fortunately there were no attacks upon us for it was considered a relatively quiet time and a quiet part of the line. We were therefore able to have everything ready in time for the opening battle.

This terrific barrage of countless guns and rounds of ammunition made the mind boggle at the amount of lethal steel that was going to rain down upon the enemy. The idea was that it would be so effective that our army would simply skate through.

A few days beforehand we were told that the battle was to start on the evening of 23rd October, but we refused to believe this date because the biggest secret of all in military life was the date and time that a battle was planned to commence. However, we were told that this time things were different and we had to have the exact information in order to cope with the vast amount of preparation needed to be done.

In the meantime various incidents occurred to keep us on our toes. On one occasion we had a sample of the terrible desert Kamseen wind which blew up very suddenly. For two days and two nights we were confined to the inside of our vehicles and the war simply stopped for it was impossible to drive. It was just like a thick, sandy snowstorm.

Rosh Hashanah came and went as did Yom Kippur but I was hardly aware of them although I did know the dates and tried to give five minutes thought on each of the days to the festival and to the circumstances in which I found myself. It was all so different from the Rosh Hashanahs and Yom Kippurs of a few years previously when I had been home as a civilian.

We also had one or two incidents of some night-time enemy parachutists dropping behind our lines. We all had to roam around trying to discover them. It was a very eerie sensation searching among the vehicles and we had to be very careful that nobody became so trigger-happy that they shot one of our own men. The worst time was when one parachutist was no more than two hundred yards from me when he was killed by a soldier in one of the batteries. I spent part of this night sitting with my back against the 8-cwt, my revolver in my hand, trying to keep awake in case a parachutist stepped into view and attempted to knock us out. We heard some further firing, some hand grenades being thrown and some damage being done before these parachutists were captured. They must have been very brave men to attempt such a dangerous mission but, as far as I know, they were all either taken prisoner, killed or wounded. Fortunately they only tried this stunt on a couple of occasions.

As the preparations for the battle became more and more advanced I noticed that the dumps of petrol, water, food and all the other ancillary commodities required by armies were growing larger and larger. The one thing that I was not happy to see was by a forward hospital where some men were busy digging graves in preparation for the inevitable casualties. I must admit that the idea of digging a grave before the man was even killed was not a very salubrious one. I remember Johnny Dale, the sergeant at RHQ who used to make crosses with men's names on them, always joked to me and said, 'Don't worry, Len, when I make it for you I'll make sure that you don't get a cross, but I'll do one of your double triangle things!'

'Thank you very much,' I replied, 'but try and do your own before you do mine.' He used to think it was very funny and at the time I suppose I did too. Now, when I look back at it, I fail to see any humour in it whatsoever.

A few hours before the battle we were all given an order of the day signed by General Montgomery. Sure enough this order said that he was sure that we would all do the best we could and that this time we were going to knock out the enemy and throw him right out of Africa. He also said that we were never going to be forced back again as had previously happened whenever the army had gone forward. Each man was given a copy of a personal message from the army commander; some immediately threw it away and others kept it as a memento. Generally speaking even the most cynical men were beginning to be affected by all the propaganda and the pep talks that we received. The Colonel made his rounds of the whole regiment being very friendly as he tried to do his best to impress upon everyone that this really was it. All levels of officers did likewise and the excitement began to build as the time got nearer.

I was busy chasing all over the place attempting to do various last minute preparations. In a certain way it reminded me of the time when I had been involved in amateur dramatics at the Boys' Club. Right up to the minute that the curtain went up there was always something that needed urgent attention and we never felt quite ready. Yet the curtain would rise and somehow the show would start.

There were two reasons that most of the men tried to get some rest during the day. Firstly to lull the enemy into thinking that it was still a very quiet period and that nothing much was about to happen and, secondly, because we all needed to be in as good physical shape as possible to endure the busy night ahead. By late afternoon of 23rd October everything was as ready as possible although we did not know the exact hour at which the battle was planned to commence. The most dangerous part, as far as we were concerned was the period just before we were going to start our barrage. If the Germans had known the time battle was to commence then just before that hour would have been the ideal moment for them to pre-empt our attack.

I decided to station myself at regimental headquarters with the A echelon to be very near to whichever battery might require my help. In the late afternoon the infantry were withdrawn from no man's land leaving nothing except empty desert in front of Pip Battery. We had no idea where the main attack was going to be and no idea of how Montgomery intended to fight this battle but, truthfully, nobody at our level was very concerned. We were only interested in the tiny piece of territory directly in front of us. There is an old Jewish saying about a small world in a large world and this struck me very forcibly when our small world was a tiny stretch of territory directly before our eyes.

There was a strange excitement in the air that we had never experienced before. Rank, which normally plays such a large part in the army, seemed to disappear. Everyone was talking to everyone else in a familiar way. Fate had put together this particular group of people at this particular time of their lives and at this certain point in history. Whatever happened from then onwards, we would always be united by the simple fact that we had all been together at the battle of El Alamein.

10
El Alamein

By nine o'clock on the night of 23rd October, the gun crews stood ready in position, awaiting the order to open fire. At a minute or two before 9.40 p.m. the first shells were loaded into the guns, the breechblocks were slammed shut and the various commands were given to the gun layer. At exactly 9.40 the order to fire was given and the barrage began.

It was complete bedlam. As far as one could be aware the earth exploded on either side of us. The flashes lit up the whole area as though it was a stage which had suddenly been illuminated. The shells were fired in groups by a very complicated arrangement in order to give each gun and its gunners a ten-minute rest each hour through the night whenever possible. During this break the gunners had to sponge out the guns with water because the metal had become so hot that the grey, camouflage paint on the barrels was so totally burnt off that the original steel colour showed through.

Throughout the night the gun crews worked like slaves. The noise was deafening despite the use of earplugs, which were generally ineffective, so most communication was by a variety of signs.

The first call for my assistance was received from one of the batteries very shortly after the barrage had begun and I made my way out to the first gun that was in trouble. I spent the night going from troop to troop, keeping the guns operative for most of the time. The most important thing from my point of view was that by morning all the guns should still be in action. During the night we had fired something like a thousand shells in each gun and I don't think that there were more than two guns out of commission at any one period. Fortunately on that night, the most important night of our regiment's history, the guns performed the job that they were asked to do. It all seemed to be chaos – organised chaos, coordinated chaos but nonetheless still chaos. Despite being exhausted and with our nerves at razor-edge, all our spirits remained high as did the excitement about being involved in action. Our attack appeared to be quite one-sided with very little fire returning from the enemy who appeared to have decided to go under cover to try to survive our barrage. Personally I did not see how anything could survive intact but, although history tells us that the Germans were very badly shaken, our barrage was not in itself sufficient to destroy them and allow us to break through the line without further fighting.

By morning I was completely shattered and delighted to return to the LAD to snatch some sleep. The entire battle of El Alamein lasted about ten days but I have no recollection whatsoever of knowing anything about its progress while it was going on. My sole concern remained, as always, the job that I was doing at any particular time. I suppose that every soldier in any battle knows little about the over-all picture, apart from the various rumours concerning units and casualties in our own very small area. Frankly, we paid very little attention to such news for we were all concentrating upon our own survival and I, in particular, with keeping the LAD together and functioning in the way we had been instructed. As long as the regiment's guns were firing, nothing else mattered to me.

For most of the ten days, we were attached to the 44th Infantry Division which was part of 13 Corps. We were loaned to the division and were transferred on two or three occasions to wherever extra artillery fire was required. Each time we moved was difficult both for me and for the unit as a whole. Most of the moves were done at night so there were the inevitable number of accidents and casualties mostly due to vehicles being the victims of mines.

During the battle there were fairly long periods of almost normality. There was not a continuation of the initial barrage by any means, for after the initial barrage everything else seemed an anti-climax. After firing a vast quantity of ammunition on the first night, the firing of relatively small numbers of shells over the next few days did not seem very dramatic. Even when we supported various local battles both the amounts of shells and the duration were much less.

I continued to spend the majority of my time dashing from one troop to another and supplying the tiffies with the various parts they required to put the guns back into action. One gun appeared to be unserviceable because its recuperator had been damaged, but we managed to replace this part by using one from a knocked-out 25-pounder that we found on the battlefield. This replacement recuperator worked satisfactorily so we put the gun back into action and the recuperator remained with the gun right up to the time that I left the regiment. This was strictly against the REME rules but all the gunners and the battery commander were happy that the gun continued to work perfectly.

On one occasion, when the three battalions of the Queen's Regiment were going to make a local attack, Pip Battery which stood in front of our own minefields with only no man's land between us and the German minefields, needed assistance. One of Pip's guns had sustained a cracked sight arm which meant that it could only fire on open targets without the benefit of the complete sight. Thus the gun could only be used against targets like a tank approaching it so, for our purposes, it was unserviceable. The sight bracket had fractured through, requiring a new bracket which could only be fixed in a base workshop. I examined this gun and decided that there was a rather unorthodox method that I could utilise. The one thing that was plentiful in the desert was barbed wire which was held by three or four feet of mild steel posts of angle iron. I took one of these posts and decided that it was feasible to weld it to that part of the bracket which still remained attached to the gun. This would do as a temporary repair and, by re-aligning the sight, the gun could go back into action in the normal way. The problem was that there was no way that we could get the gun out of its pit, back through the minefields to the LAD and finally return it to action.

After some thought, I decided that Jack Wragg could help us to make this repair actually on site in the gun pit. Jack was a very phlegmatic individual whose role in the LAD was that of a welder. We only had one bottle each of oxygen and acetylene, both of which were guarded more than any other commodity as we knew that there was very little chance of replacing them. When I explained the situation to Jack he was willing to have a go so we put the welding equipment on to the 8-cwt truck and, together with a couple of soldiers from troop headquarters, we carried the equipment across some four or five hundred yards through the minefield. It was about 3 a.m. by the time we reached the gun position and it was pitch dark. We prepared the gun by covering it with a tarpaulin and the members of the gun troop stood all around the tarpaulin to ensure that the edges were firmly fixed in the sand. Not a glimmer of light could be seen emerging from it as the last thing that we wanted was for enemy artillery to try any counter battery attacks upon us. As we worked under the cover we could still hear the usual firing of various guns and a small amount of enemy shells arriving back on to our positions.

I had already tied the angle iron to the remaining part of the gun bracket and Jack welded both sides of the angle iron until it appeared to be very firmly secured to the gun. We then repeated this performance with the gun sight and welded the broken part back on to the angle iron. This took about half an hour. We had no way of knowing whether the first shot would crack the welding so we made it quite clear to the battery commander what the position was. He accepted this and thanked us for our efforts. We removed the tarpaulin, carried back our oxygen and acetylene bottles and told the troop commander that he could now fire a shell. After realignment of the sight they then fired and all seemed to work perfectly.

As Jack and I thankfully drove back to the LAD I said, 'Jack, if you never do anything else in this war, but putting this gun back into action you have more than done anything that could be expected as your contribution to winning.'

As we had stood on the gun site just as dawn was breaking and the visibility began lengthening, we had watched troops of the Queen's Regiment walking past us in battle formation towards the no man's land. We wished them good luck as they passed and they seemed quite cheerful as they disappeared into the darkness ahead. I discovered afterwards that they were forming up into a position about 400 yards in front of our guns prior to the attack that they were about to make. It later transpired that these three battalions had encountered a lot of opposition and suffered tremendous casualties. Twenty-four hours afterwards they came past our guns again and we were told that barely one battalion could be made from the three battalions of men that had originally gone into the attack. I found that relatively unimportant sideshow a very moving sight; that small battle of the Queen's was, for me, the most memorable scene of the whole of the desert warfare. I was really thankful that I had not been in one of those units that had suffered such losses.

We continued to move around to our positions, doing as we were told and trying to snatch sleep whenever possible. There were times during the ten days when I believed that the whole battle had been a failure for we had not moved one inch forward nor had we broken through the enemy lines. Then, at the end of this period, as I was coming from the LAD towards the regiment, I suddenly saw a quad with a trailer and one of our guns coming towards me. I stopped my vehicle and flagged down the driver who was from Robert Battery. For a moment I thought that we were actually retreating. I asked him what was going on and he told me that the regiment had been told to get out of the line and to make their way independently to a map reference some eight miles behind the line. As I carried on forward along the track more and more of our vehicles came hurtling by me until I arrived at one vehicle which was stationary. Here I saw the Adjutant, Captain Drapkin, who informed me that the regiment had been ordered out. I had to see to it that we got to a position some miles behind the line as quickly as possible.

I went on to the three battery headquarters where, as always, there were a few vehicles that were giving trouble. It took three or four hours before I managed to get the last of them out of their positions and on their way back to the point where the regiment was now assembling. It was midnight on 3rd November by the time that I arrived at where the regiment was now laagering and at the regimental office, I was told that the army had broken through the enemy lines. The 7th Armoured Division was the division that was going to chase the retreating enemy and try to destroy him as much as possible. I was also informed that our 53rd Field Regiment was now attached to the 7th Armoured Division for this purpose and that we were now part of the 7th Armoured. The LAD was temporarily going to be detached and we were now all under the command of a REME major who was going to organise the recovery services over the desert area along which the 7th Armoured would travel.

This REME major explained how it was all going to work. The whole armoured division would, at first light, start moving from the position they currently held. This was, as far as I could see, a huge area containing hundreds and hundreds of vehicles of all shapes and sizes, from all types of regiments. Everything was jammed so closely together that if enemy aircraft had come over the could have devastated the entire division; fortunately none were about that night.

The major instructed me that after the whole division had departed I was to report to him when he would give me further instructions about how my detachment would follow on. I tried to get a couple of hours' sleep and when first light came I could hear various vehicles beginning to vacate the area. Our job was to help anybody to get moving, irrespective of their original unit.

Any vehicle incapable of travelling one thousand miles across the desert had to be left behind. After discussion with Colonel Greenhalgh, we decided that there were thirteen such vehicles in our regiment that came into this category. These thirteen vehicles were left with my LAD in addition to another vehicle needed to return the drivers to the regiment. At 10 a.m. on 4th November, after attention to some other vehicles, I took the fourteen trucks to the nearest service corps which was fifteen miles away. All I was given there was a small signed, piece of paper stating that thirteen trucks had been received from 53rd Field Regiment.

By lunch-time practically everything that was going to move was on its way. My LAD's job was to follow a route fairly near to the coast with the army travelling along the desert parallel to the coast road. Along with other LADs, we had to do our share of recovery and repairs. As we were now attached to an armoured division, we encountered a wide variety of vehicles, some of which we had never previously experienced. The only armour that we had in the 53rd was Bren gun carriers and once we had had a small Honey Stuart tank used for reconnaissance work. We were kept very busy simultaneously trying to do our work and travelling.

We went through part of the line that the army had broken through leaving behind us, on the old Alamein line, a large part of the German army that were still fighting a retreating action. As we quickly passed through the line so a new situation arose for us as the Germans were now behind us. We thus had to keep a wary eye out for all sorts of German rear echelon activities which were trying to support the remaining part of the German army still fighting in the line, not yet able to retreat.

It was a most unusual sight that we saw as we travelled along through the old battlefield. There were many, many bodies scattered all over the place. I never really got used to the sight of dead bodies. I don't think that anybody did. We had seen quite a few of our own casualties before the break-through but now we were looking at the part of the line that had actually taken the brunt of our barrages.

There were also many knocked-out vehicles, damaged tanks and burnt-out trucks amongst the rubbish and paraphernalia of a battlefield. We had to be very careful to avoid mines but periodically we would hear one explode as a soldier either trod on a mine or a truck was blown up. We gradually made our way through until we left the old German line behind us and reached open desert. And all the time we performed our usual tasks of giving assistance to anybody that required our services.

We were next told that for our race across the desert we were going to be part of what was called the 7th Armoured Division Replenishment Column. Apparently the 7th Armoured Division was now chasing forward at a terrific rate so it was more important to keep up with them and to give them support than it was to repair the odd abandoned vehicles. Although we were attached to this REME major, whom I never saw again after leaving the place at which we had originally laagered, we were, to all intents and purposes, on our own. I was in charge of my LAD and there was nobody I had to report to, nobody to give me instructions and nobody to provide us with supplies. After we had travelled quite a long way across the open desert, I had to permit the use of our emergency rations. Until we could catch up with the regiment we would have to manage with what we carried by way of food, water and petrol. We followed the 7th Armoured Column travelling hour after hour across virgin desert, hardly seeing any other person or vehicle. When we came across any abandoned German sites we investigated whenever possible and took anything that we thought might be of some use to us in the future.

We allowed ourselves about twenty minutes before it actually got dark, to prepare our stop. We would have a quick brew up with the old flimsy can system and very quickly heat some mulligatawny and bully beef. We would then put out our sentries and settle down until daylight. The biggest danger was from the odd planes that came over still trying to prevent replenishment from getting to the forward units of our division.

During the day we saw prisoners being marched to the war camps. Some of them were Germans but the majority were Italians;

thousands of them. Whole units of Italians had completely surrendered and when we saw them marching into captivity it was strange to see just one British soldier in charge of them, leading the way. Once, when I was in a vehicle with the second-in-command – a regular major – we saw a group in the distance consisting of a tank, some vehicles and about forty of the enemy. The major promptly said, 'Let's go!' I had no choice but to accompany him and the two of us drove very warily to within a hundred yards or so of this group. We then got out and walked towards them. We had our revolvers in our hands as we marched across the desert looking, I expect, like a couple of idiots, being so vulnerable. Then we saw a white flag on the tank and the party turned out to be Italians looking for somebody to whom they could surrender. When I examined the tank I found that it was completely in order: full of ammo with not one shell having been fired and the racks of the shells of the gun were completely filled and unused. The Italians seemed very pleased, talkative and quite happy being captured but the various Germans that we saw always seemed dispirited.

We had to be very watchful about loot. Naturally we felt entitled to take anything useful that we found on an enemy. The German vehicles did not seem so hot to me but their fully-equipped tool boxes were magnificent in comparison with those in our vehicles which merely seemed to contain a hammer and a chisel. We considered any tools, spare parts and welding equipment to be fair game and we also disarmed anybody we saw – although many had thrown their arms away before surrendering. One German officer officially handed me his beautiful Luger as a token of surrender. This was a wonderful piece which had been specially made for him and had his family crest engraved on the butt and I put it into my own kit as a souvenir of the war. The best item was on a knocked-out German vehicle which was surrounded by a number of bodies. There I found a three-barrel sporting gun in perfect condition. It was in a wonderfully constructed box and was absolutely the finest craftsmanship you could possibly imagine. It had all the parts for cleaning with a place for every component in the box. On both the case and on the gun was the S.S. insignia with the name of the captain who owned it, obviously of minor nobility. This I also kept, considering it to be a souvenir.

When we were two hundred miles from El Alamein and about thirty miles from the coast road to Tunisia, most of the replenishment column had dispersed to find their various units and I was left on my own with the LAD. The only orders that I had was to rejoin the 53rd Field so I decided to head for the coast road because most of the army was travelling along it. I discussed this with the NCOs and my major instruction to my unit was that nobody was to leave the LAD for any reason whatsoever without my permission. I was determined of one thing which was that when I reached the regiment I was going to have a complete LAD to report to the Colonel.

A surprisingly large part of the army were actually separated from their units and the system of supplies to these sections and sub-units had broken down. We were all left to our own resources so everybody was trying to barter with other groups, exchanging commodities like tinned bully for tinned fruit. We had sufficient water because of the extra allowance allocated for radiator repairs, and we were able to syphon petrol from various abandoned vehicles that we came across. Food was our biggest problem but we managed to somewhat twist the arms of those who needed us to repair their broken-down vehicles and thus were able to add to our rations. I also had the famous chocolate that I had acquired at the El Alamein NAAFI prior to the battle.

By some mistake in administration, I suspect, one of the batteries had been given a small Daimler armoured car. This was a fantastically made vehicle with a steering column system that could be pulled right round to enable the driver to move backwards just as fast as driving forwards. This was ideal for units which might suddenly have to get the hell out of a situation by reversing down a road. Unfortunately this Daimler had hit a mine which destroyed a couple of front tyres. Although we had managed to patch it up again and again, the inner tubes finally became irreparable. I had to give the order to write it off and leave it in the desert simply because we did not have any spare inner tubes. It was really a tragedy to abandon such a very expensive vehicle and I, on my own decision, had to authorise it to be left in the desert; presumably it remains there to this very day.

We spent three or four days slowly working our way past Mersa Matruh, up the road to Sidi Barrani towards Bardia. We were travelling along the famous coast road that the 8th Army had traversed so many times. It was so chock-a-block with vehicles that any out of order ones had to be pulled off the road and on to the sand. If it seemed as if a two or three hour repair were necessary, I would leave a fitter with the appropriate spares and a motorbike and instruct him to catch up with us later in the day. We continued to acquire stores whenever possible and I had to be fairly strict with our food, dividing it fairly amongst our different vehicles.

We also had the danger of enemy aircraft which would occasionally bomb our vehicles. Any damaged vehicles were pushed off the road so that we could continue our journey. We also continued to be vigilant about mines which were disguised as innocent items that a soldier may be tempted to pick up or kick, such as tin cans; these were very dangerous. If there was one thing that made our soldiers respect the danger from mines, it was the periodic sightings of individual bodies and vehicles which had been a victim of these gadgets. We never got used to the smell of the dead. There is a peculiar, terrible smell that a body acquires soon after being killed in the desert. In many cases the dead were not buried for quite a period of time, for this was mainly the task of the special units that followed up on to the battlefield.

11
To Tobruk and Back

The advance seemed to stretch for hundreds of miles and I was in the midst of thousands of vehicles heading forwards. My only orders were to link up with the regiment and help as many people as possible in the process. I presumed that the regiment was with the advance units of the 7th Armoured Division, but I had no real idea whatsoever as to where the regiment was. Again I was left totally in charge of my section and all facets of my training and experience were now being utilised. I was pleased that I felt no difficulty in making responsible decisions for my small group of reliable soldiers. Thus from the end of October to 10th November I was the 'Field Marshal' in charge of my own little army. Obviously I would eventually have to account to the regiment for my movements but until then I was on my own. It felt amazingly lonely to be a small group in the midst of a vast army which never had any contact with us unless they required our specific assistance.

After Bardia the next town of any consequence was Tobruk. Travelling along the coast road, we usually bypassed small towns and, to avoid congestion, we often travelled on the sand alongside the road. There were certain bottlenecks such as Halfaya Pass where we simply had to wait our turn to progress.

We were kept extremely busy, snatching sleep whenever possible; if I had had a unit ten times the size, there would still have been plenty for us to do. As we had to keep moving there were no permanent or semi-permanent depots of any kind being set up. There was also the hazard of the pockets of Germans putting up a rearguard defence along the route but it was our job to advance, not to mop up.

After Tobruk I tried to ascertain the whereabouts of the regiment but as I did not know to which brigade of the 7th Armoured Division the regiment was attached, no one could give me any information. I had to be extremely careful because as we travelled across the desert it was possible for us to overtake the whole 7th Armoured Division and we could find ourselves the leading unit of

143

the 8th Army. Eventually we found someone who did indeed think that the 53rd Regiment was left behind and that I had actually gone past them. According to this soldier, the 53rd Field had been pulled out of the line at Tobruk and another unit had taken their place. This rather surprised me but I decided that my job was to be with the regiment, not in advance of them, however interesting it might appear.

I thus cut back across the desert and, whilst the rest of the army was going forward, I was actually travelling backwards. I laagered the LAD on the side of the road about ten miles outside the town and set off to search for my unit. Tobruk had been the scene of much prolonged fighting so its whole perimeter was surrounded by all the paraphernalia of old battles. When I came to within striking distance of the large arch which was the entrance to Tobruk, I encountered a Royal Corps of Signals van which sent a message for me to one of the brigade headquarters. I was delighted to discover that the 53rd Field was laagered about five miles the other side of the town.

I collected the LAD and triumphantly returned to the regiment. At last I began to recognise various familiar faces and as I got out of the 8-cwt and walked across the sand, I saw the Colonel and the RSM standing by the regimental headquarters truck. They were both glad to see me and to learn that my LAD were without casualties. I made my report and the Colonel said, 'Well done, we actually had a good report of the LAD from the REME major. We have been pulled out of the line and are waiting for the whole regiment to collect at this area!'

For me the most important aspect of this meeting was that in view of the good work that the LAD had performed in the Western Desert, the Colonel promoted me on the spot to WO1; an armament sergeant major! The RSM gave me one of his WO1 badges and then produced a bottle for us to have a drink on it. I promised the other headquarter members of the sergeants' mess that on the first evening possible we would have a mess party to celebrate my promotion. Then I returned to my LAD where I was heartily congratulated by the members of my unit.

The regiment was to be pulled out and returned to Beni Yussef camp near Cairo for re-fitting and rest. Once we had repaired the one or two vehicles that needed our attention, we began to travel through the desert, back along the route via Bardia, Sidi Barrani and Mersa Matruh. We had previously heard rumours of an Anglo-American invasion of North Africa and now that we were out of the battle area, we heard that on 8th November they had actually landed in Algeria and were advancing towards Tunisia. Apparently this was called 'Operation Torch' and was proceeding quite successfully. This meant that the Germans and Italians (Rommel's Afrika Korps) were now going to be caught between the British 8th

Army coming from Egypt and the Anglo-American Army coming from Algeria. It was thus probably that this was the beginning of the end in North Africa. We presumed that after we had recuperated we would return to assist in the final chase-up.

I was astonished to realise that in this terrific advance, many men, guns and trucks had been separated from their regiments and were only now finding their way back.

A few months previously, just prior to going into the blue, an Egyptian Groppi ice cream seller had been allowed in to the camp. In Egypt, Groppi ice cream was equivalent to Lyons in Britain and several of us were delighted to buy tubs of ice cream to eat while we were waiting for one of our trucks to receive a minor adjustment. As we had already tidied the camp-site, instead of throwing the tub's lid on the ground, I put it in the top pocket of my overalls which I normally only wore when performing some recuperator work on the guns. It was necessary to be very clean because of the hydraulic system.

As we approached Cairo, I saw that one of our gun quads had stopped apparently suffering from some petrol trouble. After a look at the engine, I quickly realised that the petrol pump's cork washer had cracked meaning that the petrol pump was sucking in some air and not functioning efficiently. As we were now within a couple of hours from Cairo, I decided that a temporary repair would suffice and to make a gasket from a piece of cardboard. Fortunately I happened to be wearing my overalls and when I put my hand into my pocket I found the old Groppi lid. Lo and behold, it fitted the petrol pump of the Ford quad perfectly. All I had to do was to cut out a hole in the centre and put the lid back on to the pump for the engine to work perfectly. I instructed the driver to visit the LAD at the first convenient moment to get this temporary washer replaced with a proper cork one. This was another example of our 'making do' techniques which occupied so much of our time. The end of this story is that the driver was negligent and did not report to the LAD. To my astonishment, after six months and several thousand miles of travelling, one of my fitters discovered this temporary repair during a routine examination of the quad. The driver said that he had left the ice cream cover in place because it worked much better than the previous cork gasket.

After various stoppages and halts we finally arrived at Beni Yussef where for the first time for some period, I was able to relax without worrying about sudden summonses to attend to one emergency or another. Beni Yussef was a huge permanent tented camp specifically designed for units returning from the desert. Here all the different parts of our unit were to be serviced and made ready for action as soon as possible. The men were to be issued with 48-hour passes into Cairo which would be spaced out over the period of the following week or so. However, the LAD were busier in this resting state than in the battle areas because every vehicle, every gun and every piece of equipment in the regiment had to be checked. All temporary repairs had to be made good and we also had to deal with new replacement vehicles which had arrived.

As the senior REME in the regiment I had the authority to bypass the normal channels and go directly to any of the depots to obtain whatever parts I could. I was mainly concerned with two huge depots in the Cairo area, one was the REME workshops at Tel el Kabir and the other was the ordnance depot for technical spares at Abbasiah.

The main casualty of our LAD had been the Leyland breakdown lorry. Fortunately it lasted until we reached Beni Yussef when I handed it in to the base workshops for overhaul. We were then given a new American Dodge breakdown lorry with which we were very pleased. Unlike the Leyland, the Dodge had a completely enclosed cab – the Americans at least were civilised enough to realise that drivers also needed protection from the elements. It was very fortunate that we did exchange vehicles because at a later date we encountered severe weather conditions that would have been unbearable in an open cab.

I systematically made contact with the workshops and the MT spares supply units. We had used up a vast amount of our spares – they were our life blood – so day after day I chased around Abbasiah visiting different depots spread over several square miles. I successfully acquired a large collection of spares, including many that were not on our establishment but items that I managed to wheedle out of the storeman because experience had taught me that they were very necessary. Fortunately many of the storemen at Abbasiah were Jewish soldiers from Palestine so my Yiddish once again came in handy, much to the astonishment of whichever driver was accompanying me.

I had another stroke of luck at one of the TK workshops in that almost the first person I bumped into was my old ASM Paddy Doyle, the Regular Army ASM who had been permanently attached to the Territorial Unit in Leyton. He was a very strict but very fair man with whom I had always got on very well both at Buntingford and Colchester. He had now been promoted to major and was in charge of a group of workshops. He was as delighted to see me as I was to see him and gave me every assistance I needed. I was able to arrange any repair of our vehicles that required base workshop attention and Old Matt, Captain Quartermaster Matthews, was astonished at the ease with which I did so.

Paddy Doyle told me that another of our Leyton comrades was the sergeant in charge of one of the paintshops. Bill Hales had been a painter at Ford Works before the war and had lived part of his early life in the East End. He had many Jewish friends and even spoke a few words of Yiddish. I remember that when Nat and I –

back in the early days of the war – used to play solo, Bill used to join in. We discovered that on occasions he would use Yiddish expressions for the cards such as saying *shipa* for spades and once we roared out laughing when as I was going to play a card he suddenly said, '*Nisht!*' The other players were baffled but I had understood him perfectly.

Bill and I had a reunion drink in the sergeants' mess where we both enjoyed talking about old times. When he asked me if I would like to have all the regiment's vehicles repainted, I looked at him in astonishment because it was extremely difficult to acquire even a small can of paint. Our vehicles had really taken a bashing and looked very ragged so I eagerly accepted his fantastic offer. I arranged for him to come out with a lorry fully equipped to spray our vehicles and dashed back to arrange with the Adjutant that over the course of a week, section by section and troop by troop, all our vehicles, guns and limbers would be resprayed and newly camouflaged. All the signs were also repainted and all the top brass were overjoyed for there is no doubt that when we left Beni Yussef our regiment looked absolutely spick, span and brand new.

Next I contacted my cousin Johnny Helman who had gone out as a soldier in the Buffs, The Royal East Kents, in the winter of 1940. During his time in the desert, he had had a serious accident whilst in action in Tobruk and been hospitalised in the Cairo area. The army authorities had set up an organisation to manufacture as many of the items they required as possible and one of the most important of these was uniforms. Johnny had been a tailor in civilian life and he was now a sergeant in charge of a section of civilians making army uniforms in a new factory in Cairo.

When I contacted him to tell him that I had a 48-hour leave in Cairo, he arranged to be able to join me. I went to Cairo with some friends, including Tommy Sinclair, and Johnny arranged for the five of us to stay in a small civilian hotel – a welcome change from army conditions. Johnny and I spoke for hours on end and I was delighted to see that he had fully recovered from his injuries. He knew Cairo well enough and guided us to the various parts of interest. I had my fortune read at the pyramids by an Arab wearing a long gown. He asked me my name, drew some hieroglyphic-looking signs with a long stick in the sand and said various mumbo-jumbo incantations. For a small sum of piastres he predicted that I was going to be perfectly well and safe and would return home very soon. He was right on the whole but his idea of very soon is another story! However, I'm sure he told every soldier the same forecast that they yearned to hear.

Cairo was a fascinating, busy, stinking city absolutely chock-a-block full of people, containing slums and some high rise buildings alongside them. Johnny took us to some simple but good restaurants so we had a most welcome break from army food.

There was a big open air cinema at Heliopolis, a suburb of Cairo, where *Gone With The Wind* was being shown in two parts screened on alternate nights. As we were in town for two nights we decided to catch both parts of the film. On the first evening we visited the cinema we discovered that the second half of the film was showing and although we found it a very interesting story we had to guess what had occurred in the beginning. We intended to watch the first part the following night – it not really bothering us seeing the film the wrong way round – but when we arrived we discovered that the cinema was full to capacity with no room for us. It wasn't until at least a decade later that I caught up with the first part of *Gone With The Wind* when it was re-released in London. I've always thought that it must be something of a record to see a two-part film with an interval of ten years between each part – especially having viewed the parts in the wrong order!

All in all, we enjoyed our short break in Cairo. We had some photographs taken before we returned to the 53rd Field where we took up duties once more.

It was about that time that I purchased a small portable radio from one of the chaps in Tel el Kabir. It had been removed from a broken-up civilian vehicle but was in perfectly good working order. When I clipped the radio to a car battery it played beautifully and we could listen to music or whatever else was being broadcast in its range. It sounds a very small thing today but I and most of the LAD derived more pleasure from this radio than any other of our possessions. It was our sole source of recreation and I carried it through many countries for a long time. It needed repairing over and over again by various army workshops but it was one of the mementoes that I finally brought home with me, and it was still going strong. I had the names of the places I had visited and the battles this radio had survived painted on to it and, at one stage, had a wooden box made to encase it.

A short while before the war a publicity stunt had been arranged to encourage enlistment to our regiment. Since it originated from Bolton the entire Bolton Wanderers Football team had been enlisted into the 53rd Field. Harry Gosling, the Captain, (who was later killed in action) was made an officer and various other members of his squad gradually joined different sections throughout the batteries. My friend Tommy Sinclair had been a young player and he had also played for the Scotland national team, Boys' Division, signing at the age of sixteen for the Wanderers, at that time one of the great first division teams in the British Football League. Their star player was a centre forward by the name of Westwood who had also played for England and he became the Colonel's personal driver where he remained all the time I was with the regiment.

Since our regiment was so football-orientated we had interbattery knock-out competitions during our time at Beni Yussef. Our LAD managed to get a team together in which I played – not because I was any good but to make up the numbers. Naturally we got eliminated after our first game but nevertheless we thoroughly enjoyed ourselves.

People were also very football-minded in Cairo which housed a team called 'King Farouk's Football Team'. This was a professional team that so dominated the Middle East that nobody could ever remember the last time they had been beaten. Somehow it became known that the famous Bolton Wanderers were actually in the area so a match was arranged at the stadium in Cairo between King Farouk's 11 and the 53rd Field. Naturally the whole regiment went to watch and there were several thousand civilians also present.

Previously a team from the complete British Army had been soundly defeated by King Farouk's squad and now it was not the British Army nor even a corps or division challenging this mighty team; just one regiment fielding a challenge to the Egyptians.

Harry Gosling was captain and I think that most of the other players were also first team-mates from the Bolton 1939 team One was from their reserve team so although it was a pretty formidable line up none of them had played seriously for quite a while, having just returned from the desert. Our chaps splendidly rose to the occasion and thrilled us by actually winning this match by one goal to nil. The English-speaking paper in Cairo ran a headline stating something like, 'Out of the desert came the Bolton Wanderers to defeat the famous King Farouk's 11' and our regiment became famous in the 8th Army. From that moment we were always termed as the chaps that defeated King Farouk's 11.

We eventually received news that the regiment was to move on 23rd December when we would be making a ten day trek to join PAI (Persia and Iraq) Force north of Baghdad. As we would be travelling on Christmas day it was decided that we would celebrate the festival on 22nd December and pretend that it was the 25th of the month. Accordingly the Quartermaster issued rations and the cooks did everybody proud so we had a wonderful day. I, together with all the members of the sergeants' mess, followed the usual custom and took the men their morning gunfire into their tents and the rest of the day was spent in various revelries. A camel and his owner were allowed into the camp and we all took turns in trying to have a camel ride whilst in the evening each mess had its own party. There was also a concert arranged in a huge tent and, when volunteers were requested I, in my enthusiasm, mounted the stage and produced my *Little Nell* act. I added a few topical jokes and, as most of the men had happily had a few drinks, I was greatly cheered for my efforts. Some days later, when talking to the Colonel, he even referred to the fact that I had been enough of a sport to take part in the men's activities and said that this was very good for morale.

149

However, this being the army, our movement date was changed at the last minute to 28th December. The Quartermaster managed to get hold of a new allowance of rations and the cooks again produced wonders so we celebrated Christmas 1942 twice and had the pleasure of enjoying an extra day off duty.

Finally, after a few usual last minute hitches, we departed from Beni Yussef, my vehicle being the last of the regiment to move. At all costs we had to avoid leaving a vehicle behind at the Middle East Forces workshops because once we went into PAI Force we would never be able to reclaim it. So, by hook or by crook, we had to get everything to the destination given to us each morning.

The journey was relatively uneventful with a number of stoppages which we coped with by the usual system of relaying messages, men and parts to the distressed vehicles. Sometimes the Don R (dispatch rider) had to chase up to one of the stores lorries to obtain a part, for, although both our stores lorries were mobile, they continued to operate. We had many tricks up our sleeves to keep a vehicle going such as the method we used to clear petrol blocks. We used to fill a small two gallon tin with petrol and attach a tap and a rubber hose. This contraption would be tied in some convenient spot allowing the petrol to drip directly into the carburettor.

At night the regiment would laager at about 6 p.m. and we would reach them some time later at about 8.30. However, on a couple of occasions we were so busy that we had to work throughout the night and sleep in shifts during the journey the following day.

Our camps were set up in a square patch of the desert and on each corner was positioned a 3-ton lorry with its headlights fully on to illuminate the whole area. Thus the sentries around the perimeter could guard against thieves. These thieves were a terrible problem and were actually known to crawl in under the lights in order to steal rifles from the side of sleeping soldiers. We were all very careful and this never happened to us.

12
Palestine and Iraq

Some time during the second day of our journey from Egypt we crossed into Northern Sinai and the Gaza Strip, entering Palestine. That night we camped in a desert stretch north of Hebron.

For me, going into Palestine was a very emotional experience. There were no border guards or boundaries and no way of knowing exactly when I reached Palestine. The terrain was unaltered and the Arab villages we saw appeared no different to those we had seen previously.

All my life I had learned about Palestine, Jerusalem and the Holy places. This, everybody had always told me, was from where the Jews had originated; my history and the roots of my life were in this foreign-looking country. I had often wondered about Palestine, although the Zionist idea was really quite as alien to me as it was to most of the youngsters from my sort of background. My generation had been brought up with the idea that as soon as was possibly practical we had to become good Englishmen whilst still remaining very much attached to the Jewish religion.

The convoy rode on into Palestine through much semi-arid country. We passed various farmhouses and villages but for the first several miles I saw no sign of any Jewish influence or Jewish settlement. Towards the late afternoon I stopped on a road outside a farmhouse because one of our quads had broken down. One of the LAD vehicles was already on the scene and there was some work going on under the bonnet of the vehicle.

There were three small boys watching this group of soldiers, most of whom were just standing around whilst a couple from my unit repaired the minor electrical fault on the quad. A couple of the soldiers tried to make conversation with the boys in the usual friendly manner of British soldiers. When I approached I realised that the small boys, who could not have been more than four or five years old, were chattering in Hebrew and the soldiers were trying to make themselves understood by sign language. I checked that the repairs were progressing well, for it was already late and we still had to catch up with the convoy, and then spoke to the boys in Yiddish.

Two of them were unable to understand me but the third spoke perfect Yiddish and got very excited, as did the other two. I was asked a thousand questions in one minute such as, 'How are you a soldier? Are you a Jew? How could an English soldier speak Yiddish and be Jewish?' – He simply could not understand and was quite thrilled by me. While I talked to him the other boys rushed into the farmhouse and returned with their parents who were very pleased to meet me. We conversed for several minutes and they told me that they were part of a small group in this farmhouse which was actually part of a Kibbutz consisting of about eighty Jewish settlers and which had only been operating for about a year. All of them had originally come from other parts of Palestine so they were in a very difficult position being the first real group of Jews in that corner of Eretz, on the main road into the Gaza Strip and Egypt. They were charming people full of questions which I had to translate to the other soldiers, who were somewhat surprised to discover a group of Europeans farming in this area. I don't think the soldiers had ever heard of the word 'Kibbutz' for it was something that few people knew about at this time.

We all became very friendly and the kibbutzniks pressed me and the twenty other soldiers to remain with them for the night. 'Stay,' they said, 'and we will have a very nice evening. We will introduce you to the other members of the Kibbutz, have a sing-song and a party.'

They were really genuine in their invitation but, unfortunately, I had to explain that it simply was not possible for us to stay as I had a responsibility to the regiment as a whole. Once the soldiers realised that we were invited to stay the night they did everything they could to persuade me to agree, saying that we could easily catch up with the convoy in the morning. However, I was the one in charge and, most reluctantly, I had to decline.

In the meantime the mother had returned to the farmhouse and, after a few minutes, she came out with a couple of other women carrying trays loaded with a huge mound of honey cake and plenty of lemon tea for everybody. The soldiers were overwhelmed by this hospitality and many of them remarked that it was something that could never have happened in an Arab community. On the contrary, whenever there were Arabs nearby we had to be very cautious since so much had been stolen from the convoys.

We all enjoyed this interesting interlude from our normal duties and I took the name and address of the Kibbutz, promising that if ever I was passing by again or had any local leave then I would certainly return for a longer visit. Unfortunately another visit was not to be, so all I managed was to send them one or two postcards wishing them luck in the coming months.

As a final gesture they presented us with a whole box of Jaffa oranges to be shared out amongst our group. I promptly did this and everybody was overwhelmed. I was in a euphoric state from the very fact of entering Palestine, with its historical associations, and then having this wonderful reception from the first Jews that I met. Having completed our repairs, we left the site in an exuberant mood being waved goodbye, farewell and shalom by what had grown to be a fairly large group of people from the Kibbutz.

On the third day we crossed the River Jordan and the Judean hills. I remembered that this was where Moses had struck the rocks with his staff and produced drinking water. We entered into Transjordan where we camped outside the small town of Mafraq. Once we crossed the Jordan, I was amazed how quickly the green of the coastal strip faded away into scrubland, then arid country and finally desert.

For the next few days we travelled across the Syrian desert through the old route from Mesopotamia to the Promised Land where very many thoughts occurred to me at different times about the history of my people. In fact the beginning of what we know as civilisation all took place along this same route.

We followed the pipeline because it was parallel to the road. The pipeline went via Rutba and a couple of pumping stations where four or five people lived in solitary splendour, keeping an eye on the pipeline. Then the desert road abruptly ceased for no apparent reason. The process of building the rest of this road had halted for the moment; a moment which became several years – as the road to Baghdad was not completed until long after the war.

The landscape now changed from pure desert to very rocky ground with huge boulders scattered all over the place as though some gigantic eruption had taken place. These boulders resembled very large marbles that had been rolled across the ground and abandoned, so the convoy had to negotiate its way carefully around these obstacles. There was a certain amount of scrub life and one would imagine that when it eventually rained shoots would rapidly emerge from the ground and some sort of vegetation would grow here and there.

For literally hundreds of miles there was little sign of any inhabitants although occasionally we would spot a Bedouin family group. These consisted of one or two men standing still, a woman completely covered in black, a few goats and perhaps some children playing around a couple of black tents. They always seemed so isolated with nothing specific, as far as we could discern, to keep them in that particular spot, miles from anything else. Yet they seemed to be content with their solitary lives.

There was never any sign of life when we camped – within our stockade lit by headlights blazing from each corner – yet by the time we departed the next morning (mine was always the last vehicle to leave) a small group of Bedouins would have appeared. The moment we left they would pounce, removing every scrap of wood, paper or refuse. The camp would be picked clean since presumably everything they found was of some value to these people.

Our routine never varied, so day after day more vehicles would be awaiting our arrival to receive repairs that evening. The whole LAD with all our resources were fully stretched and despite being kept busier and busier we managed to complete them all.

On the seventh day we were unable to leave the camp until 5 p.m., having spent the entire day working on a number of vehicles, so the last LAD vehicle did not arrive at the next camp until 3.30 the following morning. By the time I arrived there most of that day's repairs had already been carried out but we still had to make sure that everything was right for the move the following morning. Fortunately, this camp was close to Habbaniya aerodrome so I was able to get some assistance from the RAF squadron stationed there. Their fitters were very helpful, supplying us with some very badly needed spare parts and I later discovered that this one squadron of the RAF controlled an area of several thousand square miles with virtually no help from the military at all.

On the ninth night we laagered outside Baghdad which, compared to Cairo, was a very Far Eastern city in appearance. Not one person in the streets seemed to be free from some sort of eye disease and all the men wore caps similar to our army forage caps, quite different from any headgear we had ever seen on other Arabs. The main recollections that I have about Baghdad are the smell and, at night, the sound of millions and millions of frogs, which abounded in the surrounding marshes. As for the stench it was the worst I had ever encountered and made even the 6th District of South Africa's Cape Town smell like paradise by comparison – and that's really saying something. In fact, some miles outside of the city we simply ceased to use our maps or compasses and merely pointed our vehicle in the direction of this diabolical smell!

After Baghdad the last stretch of our journey was straightforward. Our destination was about a hundred miles north of Baghdad, almost on the Persian border and about thirty miles away from Eskikifri, a small town completely surrounded by a mud wall with various gates, which were closed at night. It was like something out of the ark and would probably remain as such forever, the life of its residents having already seen no change for thousands of years. I learned afterwards that malaria was so rife in this area that every person in this town suffered with a bout of this disease every single year. It was horrific.

On arrival at this camp my first duty was to report to the commanding officer and to inform him that the regiment had arrived safely with every vehicle except one that had left Beni Yussef now in our new camp on the Iraq/Persian border. Our record had been spoilt when, at the last moment twenty miles out of Baghdad, some idiot of a driver had left his 15-cwt truck on a steep slope whilst he answered a call of nature. He had become so accustomed to driving in flat areas and deserts that he had forgotten to put on his handbrake! Fortunately, his two passengers had also dismounted so there was no one on board when the truck promptly rolled backwards over a cliff. The truck was so badly smashed up that it had to be taken back to the base workshops in Baghdad and I had to report that it was doubtful we would ever again see this vehicle.

We were now in one of the most remote and inaccessible areas of the world. The natives were mostly Kurds who were forever at war with the government in Baghdad. They refused to recognise this government so any visiting Baghdad officials had to be protected by a company of Iraqi troops.

Soon after we arrived in the camp, the commanding officer called the senior people together and, although I held a very junior rank, I, being in command of the REME, was included. The CO explained the situation and laid down guide lines as to how we were to act. As this was the first time since leaving England that we were in a static position nowhere near a battle zone, his main concern was that we should maintain our standards whilst being prepared to play our part in whatever we might be called upon to do at some later date. The problem would be that as we were a regiment in a desolate, unimportant area we would be starved of new equipment and could gradually deteriorate into some sort of holding force.

The CO informed us that we were awaiting the arrival from India of the various units that were to be assembled as the 8th Indian Mountain Division and that our regiment was now part of the 131 Brigade.

The Indian divisions had always been organised along similar lines since the Indian mutiny. No Indians were allowed to be Royal Artillery, so each brigade (of which there were normally three in the division) consisted of two battalions of Indian infantry, one battalion of British infantry, a British Royal Artillery Field Regiment and all the various ancillary units of support. As the Field Regiment of the 131 Brigade, we had to become accustomed to the idea that we were now part of a formation with a chain of command through the regiment, through brigade and through to division. As we had to integrate within the brigade and the division all of us had to familiarise ourselves with all the brigade's different units and personnel.

As far as I was concerned, I had to acquaint myself with the brigade ordnance section for MT spares and gun spares amongst other organisations. I had to learn the differences between British commissioned officers who were Indian, and Indian commissioned officers who were in different ranks, as were Indian NCOs and Indian warrant officers. There were all sorts of new ranks I had to learn; *Nike* – corporal, *Havaldar* – sergeant, *Jemadar* and *Subadar* –

equivalent to British army ranks of lieutenant and captain. I found all of this extremely interesting as I began to know and become friendly with quite a few different types of Indians.

I often spent many evenings at the various units where we discussed all sorts of politics, moralities and ideas from the Indian culture. I had previously known little about the Indian way of life and found it all quite fascinating. We had Punjabis, Sikhs, Pathans, Gurkhas and several other races in the division, with Hindu and Muslim being the main religions. However, the Hindus were split into a number of different sects and I enjoyed listening to all their stories as I tried to understand the different mental processes that lay behind their customs.

One Hindu friend of mine said that he believed it to be impossible that any European, however long he spent in India, could ever fully understand the Indian mentality or the enormous pressures of the caste system and religion that motivated all the different races in their different ways. The best we could hope to do, he said, was merely to try to avoid offending any of the religious groups and to maintain the harmony which was necessary in dealing with the various Indians that we met in the division. For example, Gurkhas were classified as British other ranks and were therefore entitled to similar rations to them and to enter into their NAAFIs unlike Indian other ranks. How the tortuous process came about that Gurkha soldiers were classified and considered as British other ranks was one of the mysteries of army life.

As we were now in a division, a REME captain appeared on the scene. Captain Coffin was a typical middle class, pleasant young man who had left England about a year ago to be attached to the Indian army and was the REME officer of the 8th Indian Division, responsible for their various Light Aid Detachments. For a while he was the chain of command through which I had to go for all my requirements, but sadly he drowned under mysterious circumstances later on during the war.

As we had to maintain the morale of the men during this lengthy lull, it was decided that the camp should be laid out in the same way that the main streets in Bolton were laid out. An intensive amount of activity was put into preparing this virgin stretch of desert to this end. Firstly, stones were used to form the camp's perimeter and further stones, normally small boulders, were placed a foot apart in rows to constitute the streets. Before very long the whole centre of Bolton was reproduced and signs were erected depicting the names of Bolton's main streets. This was then taken even further, with the site where the regimental headquarters was parked being called by the name of the area which housed Bolton's Town Hall and the MO site being termed by the name of the area where Bolton's hospital stood. Even the battery quartermaster was called by the name of a large local store in Bolton! After a while the small boulders forming the road were all painted white and the whole project began to get out of hand. The RSM justified it as a way of keeping the men busy and it certainly was an example of the odd sort of thing that occurs in units in isolated places.

We continued to be vigilant against the perennial trouble of Arab thieving. The value of the items that they stole was so great to them that they risked being shot. We had to have alert perimeter guards day and night and once more used vehicle headlights to illuminate our camp. There was also the danger that our food would attract the attention of the vicious and dangerous wild dogs that roamed the area. The possibility of rabies was also a threat so it was decided to appoint an official dog killer. Our armourer, Pete Adams, was chosen as he was considered an excellent and safe marksman so he spent much of his day patrolling the perimeter, firing at any dog he spotted.

Since the days were hotter than anywhere else we had been, we consequently got into the habit of starting work very early, having a siesta from noon to 4 p.m. and then working till later in the evening. We slept in small bivvies but to keep cool during our siestas we dug about six feet down into the ground where we found it to be far more comfortable in the heat of the day.

We kept our water in canvas bags which we got from the natives and these were hung on the vehicles so that they were actually constantly in the sun during the day. The outside of these bags was coated with a mixture of baked sand and water and, amazingly, the hotter the sun shone on to the bags, the cooler the water inside became. Eventually these bags could be seen attached to every vehicle in the regiment and the men would periodically take drinks from them.

Another item that we procured from the natives was the sheepskin jacket. These were very crudely made and could be bought very cheaply. The sheep's fur was on the inside so these jackets were extremely warm at night when it got really cold indeed. Such jackets were unknown in Europe at this time but some years after the war they began to be imported into England where they now remain very popular. Whenever I see one it reminds me of the days I spent in Iraq.

Our most bountiful commodity was crude oil. We had a number of large marquees which we used for various activities such as messing and for storage. We devised a system of heating these marquees with the use of this oil. We dug a one-foot square channel which ran right the way through the length of the marquee. At one end we had a tank of crude oil with a tap attached to it which allowed the oil to drip down to a plate of sheet steel on the ground. We also had a can of water which dripped on to the steel sheet at the same time as the oil. We lined the channel with tin from our flimsy cans and then covered it with sand. Some rag waste, impregnated with oil, was placed at the entrance to the channel so that when the mixture of oil and water dripped down, fire was shot along the channel. Surprisingly, this was a very efficient central heating system and I rigged up several of them up in many of the marquees. We used to spend most of our evenings in these cosy mess marquees despite the system being somewhat of a fire hazard. There were a couple of occasions when marquees were unfortunately burned down and all the stores therein destroyed, but nobody seemed to worry unduly because the advantage of having a warm place to go to at night far outweighed what little we lost.

Keeping the men occupied remained our priority and to this end the camp was scoured for people who were able to teach such things as foreign languages. A series of instructive events was organised and my contribution to this was running a driver/mechanics course at the LAD.

During this three-week course we taught the basics of driving and a rudimentary knowledge of vehicle maintenance. I was only able to cope with about fifteen men at any one time and I insisted that they should all be volunteers. Each of the batteries sent five men along for the course which was a great success for the majority of the soldiers were very keen to learn motoring skills. We ran this school during the whole period that we were in the area, in addition to carry out out our normal work but, as we could use our trainees to assist us on certain jobs such as decokes, it enabled us to get a lot more work done.

I also gave several talks about vehicles explaining how they worked and the functions of basic components such as gearboxes, clutches and differentials. I also took part in testing the men and passing them as drivers at the end of the course, although I was not too strict for I considered that as long as the basics of driving were understood further skills could be picked up with practice. As far as I know all of my students became perfectly successful driver/mechanics and so we achieved the ultimate objective to increase the number of men competent in this field.

My other task was to give various talks on the 25-pounders and guns in general to each of the troops. I developed some set lectures concerning the history of artillery, the development of the guns and the maintenance of the guns. I became like a music-hall turn! I only kept in that which seemed to interest the men and discarded topics which seemed to bore them, so that in the end my talks became quite popular, although I never kidded myself that they were particularly enjoyable. I always said that it was easier to sit and listen to me talking about guns – around which their whole lives revolved – than it was for them to do drill or some of the other less amenable army exercises.

Once the various officers' messes became established I took up residence in the regimental headquarters sergeants' mess. Along with the RSM, I was the most senior in the mess which meant that I was at the top of the tree of our twenty members. All that this really meant was that I slept in a bivvy by myself and had a few more home comforts around me. We attended a large number of parties at the various messes – up to two or three times a week when we were not on manoeuvres – and naturally my rendering of *Little Nell* was performed so many times that everybody must surely have also known it by heart. However everybody seemed to enjoy these revelries and, after a few drinks, nobody minded singing the same songs over and over again.

I was also invited to parties at the Indian workshops and ordnance sections. These were very different to the British ones. A big fire would be lit in the middle of the desert and about 300 men, mainly Indians, would sit around it. The Muslim and Hindu cooks would bring in a live sheep, kill it and roast it. After the sheep had been eaten with chapati and rice we would sit around the fire partaking in such activities as singing and dancing. I would sit in the front row with the other British people and I spent several thoroughly enjoyable evenings at these parties.

We had a system of loaning books, so I was never without something to read. When it so happened that I had to take a 3-ton lorry along with two drivers to collect some stores in Beirut, I spoke to the seven or eight other readers in the division and we each put a few pounds into a kitty, collecting about £30 altogether. As I could only afford to be away from the unit for four days, we virtually drove the 700 to 800 miles non-stop, taking turns at driving and only pausing for meals. Somehow I managed to find the time to visit the American bookshop, which contained a terrific variety of books and seemed to be carrying on as though there was no war. I spent a wonderful couple of hours selecting a number of books and when I explained to the manager what I was doing, he very kindly gave a discount plus adding one or two in free. Thus I returned triumphantly to the regiment with a considerable number of volumes. These were joyfully circulated amongst the various contributors and over the next few months we all had the pleasure of reading some new books that had been injected into the division.

As a by-product of my trip to the Beirut bookshop, even more people in the division considered me to be eccentric for I had now actually spent money on books!

I went to Baghdad a few times, staying some hours each time, chiefly visiting the base workshop and stores. I also went into a synagogue on one occasion for wherever there were Jewish communities I tried to find the time to go the synagogue and pay my respects. There was a fair-sized Jewish community in Baghdad although I had no way of recognising any Jew other than in the temple. It was a very Sephardic synagogue and very Oriental in appearance but nevertheless I was made to feel both at home and very welcome. The Bimah, the Ark, the *tallisim* and all the religious artefacts were more or less what I had been used to, as were the prayers and method of praying. It was extremely interesting and I thoroughly enjoyed my visit there.

A craze for gazelle-shooting became popular amongst both the soldiers and the officers. The area we were in was fairly undulating territory, part desert and part scrubland. Amongst the wild animals were the gazelles which were magnificent creatures with enormous horns up to seven feet long. Gazelles usually travel in small herds and I only once accepted an invitation to join in the hunt.

The tarpaulin was removed from a 15-cwt truck and six men stood on the back of the truck, attaching themselves to the framework with the webbing that normally held the tarpaulin. They were armed with the standard Enfield .303 rifle. The driver together with a mate – who acted as look-out – would head across the desert and when a herd of gazelle was spotted the driver would head towards it as fast as he could. Those standing had to hang on like grim death until near enough to take a shot. Of all the crazy ways of hunting, this one was certainly the maddest. Everybody got very excited especially the driver who headed towards the herd like a raving lunatic. Several people on the back of the truck would start shooting without the slightest possibility of hitting anything and well before they were in range. On the one occasion that I went no gazelles were actually killed and I was very pleased about that. The truck bounced up and down like a yo-yo for the ground was very uneven and full of potholes so it was a wonder that no one was hurt. This form of hunting continued until eventually one of the vehicles overturned and the Colonel put a stop to it. It was fortunate that he did because somebody would certainly have got killed. Personally I was very sorry for the gazelle and it seemed a great shame when I did see one that had been killed. However, I must admit that I had no compunction about joining in the meal that was prepared!

Gradually we became a division going on manoeuvres around the oil town of Kirkuk, around Mosul, into the north and east of Iran and as far down as Basra in the South by the Persian Gulf. I spent most of my time collecting broken-down vehicles all over the region and trying to keep everything moving in working order. As I was my own boss it was simple to enter the various towns that we encountered. These towns were out of bounds to the various units that were on manoeuvres but as the REME warrant officer I was expected to enter the towns to try to acquire any spares that we needed. I always made use of this facility and looked around the towns whenever possible. I usually found that most of them contained a small MT section which, if it wasn't of the British or

Indian army, belonged to either the Iraqi or Trans-Jordan Frontier Force. This Force was something of a comic army since they wore such peculiar hats! Nevertheless they were helpful, for although they would not give us any spares they were usually open to barter.

These towns were very interesting and varied. Kirkuk had oil rigs all over the place and was very orientally medieval having hardly ever seen any Europeans. There were virtually no roads, only alleys between the houses that led to a market place. On each side of the alley would be open-fronted shuttered shops displaying their wares such as boots, jewellery and bakery goods. Up until the oil came, Kirkuk had remained unchanged for hundreds of years; now they used oil in every possible way for heating, lighting and cooking. There were very few women ever to be seen on the streets. If you were walking down a narrow alley and there was a woman fifty yards away, the moment she spotted you she would immediately turn round and disappear. These women were covered from top to toe in black and completely veiled.

Parts for vehicles were very scarce – particularly tyres, so we had to keep a very careful eye on our spares to prevent them from being taken by the soldiers for barter.

Kirkuk's houses were mud-baked and the funny part that struck me was that the inhabitants had flattened out our flimsy cans and used these sheets of tin, covered with a layer of mud, to patch up their outer walls. It was odd to look along a street of patched mud huts and to see areas of tin glinting through in the sunshine.

The people in Kirkuk, Mosul or well into Persia (Iran) seemed much the same. There were no borders of any kind and I don't think the people bothered whether they were in Persia or Iraq. It seemed to be the same story when we went down south as far as Basra which was a much bigger city containing a few roads but really just a larger edition of Kirkuk or Mosul.

I was told by the CO that the new 17-pounder anti-tank gun had arrived in the division but that nobody at all knew anything about it. As I was the expert on guns, division had asked him to send me to the anti-tank regiment to give them the lowdown on this new gun. I discovered, to my surprise, that in the whole of PAI Force, the number of armament artificers could be counted on one hand and that I was a much rarer bird than I had realised.

This was not very helpful for me because I didn't feel like pointing out to the CO that, in the same way that nobody else knew anything about the 17-pounder, neither did I! Whilst I was in England I had heard that it was being produced and I knew that the previous anti-tank gun in use was a 6-pounder which was better than the one before which had been a 2-pounder. People had gradually realised that something larger was needed to knock out a tank and this 17-pounder was supposed to be the answer.

Anyway I promptly went to the anti-tank regiment where I was made very welcome. I asked to spend two or three hours alone with the gun to examine it. As I did not mention that I had never encountered one before they all thought that I was an expert on it but, once again, I said 'Thank God' very heartily when I found that the handbook accompanied the gun. By studying this handbook alongside the gun I was very quickly able to put together sufficient knowledge to enable me to tell the gunners what they needed to know about it. In actual fact it was a very simple weapon as it was intended to fire open sights on to tanks and was thus much simpler indeed compared to any other piece of artillery which had to fire blind several miles distance. I spent three days with the regiment and when I returned to the 53rd Field the Adjutant told me that my help had been very much appreciated. So once again I got myself out of trouble by a bit of careful bluff and manipulation.

By then I had well and truly discovered that in the army it did not seem to matter what you actually knew – it was what people thought you knew that was most important. It may well be that in the years since then I have discovered that the same applies in civilian life.

When a Turkish general came to inspect the whole division it was a tremendous event. We were told that we had to really put our best foot forward and parade as though we were the Brigade of Guards. The reason for this was that this particular Turkish general had inspected a German division one week earlier as Turkey was neutral at that time. Both the Germans and the Allies were trying to entice them into the war and to convince Turkey that each was going to win. Up until our North African victory the Turks had been sure that the Germans were going to succeed but now that the Americans were on our side the Turks were undecided as to who was going to be the victor. We were told that the German division had very much impressed the general so we really had to pull out all the stops.

There was a gaggle of red tape Army GHQ officers with our colonel, our general and the Turkish general. They visited each of our batteries in turn. As the party reached each battery the battery major would shout '109th *Field Battery Royal Artillery, attention!*' (This was Pip Battery). Then the whole unit would come to attention to be examined.

The same happened at Queen, 210th Battery and Robert, the 438 Battery. When it was the Signal Detachment's turn, their captain – to keep up the whole magnificence of the occasion – shouted out, '*Royal Corps of Signals attached to the 53rd Field Regiment, attention!*' and the 45 men of this section were examined, inspected and congratulated.

The LAD which merely consisted at that time of some sixteen men was the tiniest section in the regiment. However, we had the longest name. When it was our turn I shouted, in my best parade voice, '*Royal Electrical and Mechanical Engineers, Light Aid Detachment, attached to the 53rd Field Regiment Royal Artillery – attention!*' My brave little band promptly sprang to attention and were duly inspected. This provided the only light relief of the day as, luckily, this Turkish general had a sense of humour. He gravely saluted me and examined my men but he was grinning all over his face. Since he was grinning General Russell and our colonel grinned so everybody was happy. I hate to think what would have been the outcome had I selected a more sour general but it seemed appropriate at the time and I got away with it!

Lance Montgomery, the regimental doctor, became a very good friend of mine although he was quite an unusual character. Before the war he had been a member of the Oxford Group Movement which was a religious group considered to be a very right wing organisation. Yet after I had had many conversations with Lance I found him to be a genuine person who really was sincerely religious. If all the Oxford Group people were like him then there was nothing wrong with that movement. He was fascinated by my views on religion and history but I was really astounded that such an intelligent man as him could be so dogmatic and simplistic in his attitudes to religion and Christianity. As his sect based their ideas on personal prayer between themselves and God, he used to spend daily periods of time in silent prayer, presumably talking to whatever deity he thought was his particular friend. He was unusual in that he tried to get everybody not to join the Oxford movement but simply to pray. Many a time we heard stories concerning men going to him with, for example, venereal disease and, before being given any treatment, being persuaded to kneel to God for forgiveness and to pray to be healed. They went along with it because in the end he was a caring person and a helpful doctor.

The malaria precautions continued to be very strict and we took the yellow pill daily. In fact the men had to line up with the NCOs watching them put the pill in their mouths because in many cases the men would simply pretend to take it. We also used the anti-mosquito ointment which we liberally smeared over our exposed parts. One hour before sunset we had to roll down our sleeves and put on our long slacks in order to cut down the risk of malaria. The army were very strict about this procedure and Montgomery had introduced the bowler hat system for any colonel whose regiment exceeded the quota of either malaria or venereal disease. As far as malaria was concerned it was pot luck to a certain extent because nobody could avoid getting bitten by mosquitoes at different times, so a certain amount of the disease was impossible to avoid. Apparently there was one period in the First World War when the British and the Turkish armies, who were fighting each other, had something like 90 per cent from each army suffering from malaria causing the whole war to come to a standstill for a period of

My first income-tax demand caught up with me in the Iraqi desert.

months. Fortunately we never reached such a bad state and were able to keep our incidence of malaria down to a relatively low figure.

Our regimental padre was a Protestant from Ulster and he was another unusual character. He tried to be one of the boys and, in the whole time I knew him, we never discussed religion, God or anything of that nature, but he was a very helpful person. There were several times when one of my LAD came to me with personal problems that I quite frankly had no clue how to deal with so at least I could pass these men across to the padre who appeared to be of some assistance to them. When some very difficult times came along he was of especial use when there were casualties and took charge of the burial arrangements, saying the necessary prayers.

We stayed in PAI Force for four months. I was extremely busy the whole time and was probably one of the few sane people left in the regiment at the end of the period. There is no doubt that the lack of a proper occupation in these remote areas definitely created the condition that the French call cafard. However much we tried to keep the men occupied after a while the rot began to set in. Indiscipline began to come out of the ranks and to counteract it the junior NCOs began getting tougher. This in turn created more problems and some bad feelings between the men and the officers. Gradually there began to be a deterioration in the very high morale that we had experienced following our desert victory and we began to hope that our stay in this camp would end very shortly. We were afraid that we would be forgotten and that the regiment would sink into oblivion as a holding unit.

We were joined by the 52nd Field Regiment, a Manchester Territorial unit, the sister regiment of our 53rd. Coincidentally, when I went over to their LAD to introduce myself to the warrant officer in charge, he turned out to be Charlie Bacon, an old friend of mine from Leyton. I was able to tell him quite a bit about the situation in our division and we had some good social times together visiting each other's messes.

We were all very relieved when at the end of May 1943 orders finally came for the division to move. We were delighted to hear that we were going to Latakia in Northern Lebanon on the Mediterranean Coast. We were especially happy because there is no doubt that that part of the Middle East was considered to be one of its most pleasant areas.

13
Latakia

We rejoined the Middle East Forces on 29th May 1943. The North African war had just finished – a complete victory for the Allies – so the 8th Army would now have to have a new role to play. We were all very happy to be going to such a pleasant part of the Mediterranean Coast with no possibility of having to return to the dreaded Western Desert.

I had been afraid that I would be transferred from Iraq to another part of the world without having the chance to see Palestine. I was especially pleased for as Latakia was very near to Eretz, the majority of our store depots would be in the Haifa area. I was determined that this time I would see a lot more of the country and meet many more of the Palestinian Jewish settlers.

The journey back across the Syrian desert was very similar to our crossing four months previously. The route only varied halfway across the desert when we headed north through Syria via Damascus. We travelled across the mountain range through Baalbek, Homs and Hama and finally arrived on a site overlooking the blue Mediterranean, just north of the small town of Latakia.

While we were in Iraq we had often wondered why our division – really an infantry division – was sometimes referred to as a Mountain division and as to why we had received mountain training. After the war I learned that Stalin had kept asking Churchill to prepare an army to fight in the South Russian Caucasian Mountains, near Northern Iran. The Wehrmacht were advancing in Russia and obviously planning an attempt to reach the oil supplies of the Persian Gulf, via Iran. It was therefore extremely important to block the route of any German advance in this area and for this purpose the 8th Indian Division was prepared. Fortunately the Russians managed to hold the German army at bay so that, apart from supply lines, no British or Indian divisions were actually sent to partake in any fighting in Russia.

I was so frantically busy that if I had not had Jack Wragg as my batman I would never have had any idea of the whereabouts of my kit or as to where I would sleep at night. Jack organised everything extremely well and made my existence much easier. As I was not a cigarette smoker I was able to reward him with my monthly ration as well as a small amount of money. He was delighted because he was a heavy smoker so my contribution helped him out enormously. Jack was always even tempered, with the dry humour of the typical Brummy and I greatly valued his friendship.

One day, when I was roaming round a small town hoping to exchange a particular spare with a section of the Iraqi army, I left the 15-cwt truck parked with its driver in a narrow alley. Thirty yards away from our vehicle I suddenly heard shouting and saw three natives trying to steal items from our truck. The driver was standing outside, smoking a cigarette and unable to reach his rifle, strapped in its usual position inside the cabin. I immediately ran back, yelled and brandished my revolver in the air. As soon as the men saw me approaching them with a weapon in my hand, they hurried away without taking anything.

As a result of this incident I purchased two daggers. The habit of carrying short daggers was beginning to spread amongst many of the troops, so I gave one to the driver and kept the other for myself. From then on I wore this leather-sheathed dagger in my right sock; fortunately I personally never had any occasion to use it although I did hear of several incidents where soldiers had successfully defended themselves with these daggers against Arabian and later Italian muggers.

At Latakia my camp bed was positioned in the middle of a cucumber patch. I was thus able to lie down in the afternoon, stretch out my hand and rummage through the soft earth to extract a small cucumber. These were delicious when peeled and sprinkled with salt. The whole camp used to enjoy these snacks although I gradually had to stretch further and further away from my bed to reach them! The cucumbers just about lasted out our stay.

We were able to listen to various stations on my mobile radio and, with our remaining one gramophone record which we had managed to salvage after our desert journey, we were well supplied with a variety of music.

As we were the nearest REME detachment on the main coast to Turkey we were sometimes called upon to assist any military or air force vehicle that needed attention in our vicinity. I soon realised that there was a steady stream of 3-ton lorries driving through Turkey and loaded with a variety of equipment. The Royal Army Service Corps drivers always changed into civilian clothes after leaving Latakia. When I fell into conversation with one of these drivers he explained that they were supplying military equipment to Russia via Turkey. As Turkey was neutral, soldiers had to wear civilian clothes on their way through Turkey and could only return to uniform upon entering Russia to deliver the goods. There were many things like this which went on during the war and that were not generally known about. It was only by giving a little technical assistance to these people that we became more aware of what was going on.

As I was not responsible to any senior, I was able to roam the surrounding area in my jeep. I always had the excuse that I was searching for spares so I was able to visit towns such as Aleppo, Hama, Homs, Tripoli, Beirut and Damascus. I also went to some of the many small villages that were scattered over the whole area. There were some very remote places in the mountains where in many cases we had to park several hundred yards from the village, walking the rest of the way. Only a donkey was able to carry anything along these very narrow mountain tracks. I was always an object of curiosity in these villages, probably being the first British soldier that had ever bothered to explore them.

Unfortunately, just as I was enjoying myself, I developed a high temperature which confined me to bed for a couple of weeks. Lance Montgomery diagnosed malaria but did his best to avoid sending me to hospital because once taken away from the regiment one never knew when or if one would be allowed to return. Since our camp was very comfortable he was able to treat me himself. He decided to set a date for my temperature to drop as should it continue to remain high for too long he would have no option but to have me hospitalised. Jack Wragg looked after me. My temperature continued to rage and I sweated profusely, only desiring to be left alone. Fortunately my fever broke on the very day that Lance designated to be the deadline for my remaining under his care, and I then made a speedy recovery.

The RSM, Jimmy Burrows, the only other warrant officer class 1 in the regiment besides myself, was posted away. He was a regular soldier who was getting a field commission. His replacement was the former battery sergeant major of Pip Battery, an old Bolton Territorial and a very good friend of mine. It was a great pleasure to have him as RSM for Jimmy had never allowed it to be forgotten that he was a regular soldier forever acting as though he was 'on parade' twenty-four hours a day. Tommy Yates was quite a different character being a jovial, burly man and, whilst still very regimental in outlook, he kept his discipline by the use of a much friendlier manner.

In the vernacular of Bolton dialect, the RSM was known as t'RSM which was often shortened to Tara. By the same system I, as the ASM was termed as t'ASM pronounced Tayessem, which was very difficult to abbreviate. The broad accented men from Bolton (or Bowelton as they used to call it) did manage to contract it to something like Tay.

Once, when Tommy had to go to collect some papers from Haifa and I needed some stores from the main Haifa depot, I decided to accompany him on the 200 mile journey along the coast. We took a 3-tonner driven by a young soldier from Bolton who had a twin brother serving as a gunner with Pip Battery. The route to Haifa was along a magnificent stretch of road which had had tunnels dug in the cliff to allow vehicles to take a more direct route.

There was a transit camp just outside the city of Haifa so we decided to stay there for the night before attending to our various chores first thing the next morning. In accordance with his instructions Tommy phoned through to the regimental office as soon as we arrived, in order to inform them of his position and to see if there were any other messages for him to deliver whilst in the area.

After some difficulty he made contact with Latakia and as he was talking to the Adjutant I noticed that he went very white, obviously having heard some news that had shaken him rigid. After finishing on the telephone he told me that our driver's twin brother had been swimming with the regiment that afternoon. He was a poor swimmer and in the mêlée that went on in the water he had got into difficulties and accidentally drowned. The Adjutant had told Tommy that we had to break this dreadful news to our driver. We decided that it was best to wait until we had completed our work the following day and to give him the tragic news on the road back to the regiment.

We then dumped our kit into the first available tent, went to the mess and had a meal, the driver eating in the men's mess. We were both deeply upset and were dreading the moment when we would have to tell this young soldier about his twin's death.

I had the surprise of my life the following morning as I stepped out of the tent to go to the ablutions, for simultaneously emerging from the tent next door was none other than Billy Raven, my old friend from the Boys' Club. We were both absolutely astonished. He was in a Reconnaissance Corps Unit and about to return to it after a seven day leave. I delayed our departure by an hour, all I could manage under the circumstances. Billy and I sat in the tent to enjoy a long reminiscent talk about our youth and the whereabouts of several of our friends, now scattered all over the world. Between us we knew about the fortunes of many of the old club members and we both enjoyed this brief reunion. All too soon we shook hands, wished each other good luck and looked forward to meeting each other again back in Fordham Street – once the war was over. This actually happened as Billy is one of the club members that I have met many times over the years. He became one of the leading lights on the Old Victorians Committee which raised money for charity by running various functions.

We drove to divisional headquarters, where Tommy dealt with his paper work, and then carried on to the enormous Ordnance Depot at Haifa which consisted of a number of corrugated metal huts brimming with stores of every type and description. Most of the personnel here were Palestinians many of whom were Yiddish-speaking Jews with limited English. Once again I amazed my companion with my skills in Yiddish which was a definite help in acquiring certain stores which were in very short supply. I was also given several names and addresses and many invitations by Kibbutzniks who urged us to spend any leave time that we had at their homes.

All this was marred, however, by the knowledge hanging over us that very soon we were going to have a very sad task to perform. Sometime during the afternoon we stopped to eat the unexpired portion of our day's rations in the traditional army manner. We decided that now was the time and we broke the news to the driver. He was completely overcome. It was really pitiful to see him and to listen to him as he muttered that he had promised his mother that he would look after his twin brother.

Accordingly, I took the wheel for the remainder of the journey and we were very relieved when, later at night, we reached Latakia where we could hand over our driver to his close friends who could comfort him in a more suitable manner.

Generally, the regiment's morale had recovered and a leave rota was instituted entitling each soldier to seven days' leave at a leave camp on the beach in Beirut. At the end of May the regiment moved to a site just five miles north of Beirut and here, we were informed, we would receive our mountain training.

I became very friendly with Danny, the son of the owner of the land on which we were now camping. Danny was my age and studying at the American University of Beirut. His home was a large farmhouse twenty miles into the mountains north of Beirut. He was a Christian Arab and we often discussed the very complicated religious and political situation in the Lebanon and Syria. Actually, it wasn't really a discussion, more lectures by him to me. I learned a great deal about the fight for the control of Lebanon between the British and the French. Pre-war Lebanon, he told me, was French-controlled as was the rest of Syria. However, the British were taking advantage of the fact that France was now occupied by the Germans and was thus in a very difficult position with regard to her colonies. These French colonies were backing break-away groups who desired to set up an independent Lebanon state. Lebanon had been nominally given its freedom by the small unit of fighting French forces that still remained in the country and by the British that were actually in occupation. This new, independent state was intended to be a Christian-dominated country as the Christian Arabs were the richest and most powerful section of the population.

Danny was obviously from a wealthy family and very well educated. The main produce of his family's farm was silk and I was often invited there where Danny showed me how the silk was produced. Dotted around the farm were what looked like beehives on long poles. Here the silkworms lived and produced their thread.

Danny's house was very oriental and of an open design. It was sparsely furnished with many rugs on the floor upon which everybody usually sat.

When he took me into one or two of the villages in his area, mostly Muslim Arabs, I noticed that the conditions there were extremely primitive and that the one nearest to the farmhouse, along a virtually inaccessible track, was just a collection of mud huts. In the centre of this village were two communal ovens where I watched chapatis being baked. I called them chapatis because that's what our Indian troops called these flat pancake-looking breads; I have no idea what the Arab name is. This dough was rolled out on to a flat plate and stuck on the ceiling of a simple oven. A woman then set a few twigs alight on the base of the oven and a grill, half way down, caught the chapatis once they had dried sufficiently to fall from the roof. It was a very simple yet very effective system of baking bread.

Danny showed me another very interesting facet of village life. In the corner of one of the mud huts stood a wooden stake and chained to it was a naked boy. Danny told me that this creature was a lunatic. I was sickened by the fact that this child was treated as though he was a mad dog. They would have killed a mad dog but an insane boy was left tethered to a stake in the ground. The boy looked at us like an animal would stare and I found it all to be a very shocking sight. It reinforced in my mind how near the primitive is to the ultra-modern. This unfortunate lad was chained inside a mud hut, yet just a mile away lived the university educated, intelligent family to which my friend belonged. Presumably Danny's father was Lord of the Manor and when I met him he was very courteous like an old-fashioned patriarch. It was all very difficult to stomach.

My turn for leave came on 7th June and I went with Tommy Sinclair to the Beirut camp which was a very simple place, just a series of tents on the beach with canteen facilities. I spent a very relaxing few days reading and eating in NAAFI and YMCA canteens. It was a great pleasure just to be relieved of the continual calls for assistance and we had a wonderful 'holiday'.

I took Tommy to the Beirut Sephardic synagogue where we received a very friendly reception. We had tea with the Beadle in the secretary's office in the back of the synagogue. The most interesting part of this office was that all around the walls were portraits of the synagogue's past presidents and in every case they depicted a man wearing a fez. This headgear was very popular in the Turkish regime but after the First World War – as a symbol of independence from Turkey – everybody had stopped wearing the fez.

On our return to the 53rd our mountain training took a very serious turn. After being used to the flat deserts we found it very tough to cope with the narrow roads and the problems of transporting large numbers of vehicles through the mountains. If only one transporter broke down the whole army could be jammed, so our recovery difficulties were massive.

The regiment was issued with twenty-four jeeps. These were, without doubt, the greatest weapon of the whole war as far as ordinary soldiers were concerned, being the most practical form of transport over mountainous and muddy terrains. We also had mules and muleteers attached to each unit and I was amazed how sure footed this animal was. Even when they were highly laden the mules seemed able to travel over terrain that a cat could not have managed.

We discussed the possibility of stripping the 25-pounders into various parts to enable us to fly separate components over a mountain range – using an Auster light aircraft – where the gun could be reassembled on the new site. A great deal of time was spent by several of the tiffies and myself in experimenting in this way but with only partial success. There was a limit to how much stripping-down was practical and in the end, probably because there were not enough aircraft available, this idea was abandoned.

In the middle of July, after the powers that be considered that we had had sufficient mountain training, we were once again on the move. Our next site was just over the eastern border of Palestine in Syria and I was delighted with its position. I was only a half hour's drive from the Kibbutz Tel Hai where I could thus spend all of my free time.

There was a monument at Tel Hai to a man called Joseph Trumpeldor. Apparently he was a Russian Jew, an ex-officer who had lost one arm fighting in the Russian war. He had come to Palestine as a pioneer and was one of the founder members who had organised the defence of this Kibbutz on the hill. It was continually being attacked by Arabs who could easily cross the border from Syria. Trumpeldor had died defending his home from one of these attacks.

In the valley beneath the Kibbutz was an Arab village and I could never understand why the Arabs chose to live in this mosquito-infected area and had completely ignored the very much cooler and healthier hilltop.

I made many friends at Tel Hai and had numerous discussions about Zionism, the Jewish question and Jewish history in general. I learned a great deal of what these pioneers were trying to achieve and greatly admired them. In many ways they were turning the traditional ideas about Jews topsy-turvy. They were basically farmers who believed in doing all the domestic and farmwork themselves on a strict rota basis. It was the most democratic form of life possible with virtually nobody having any possessions. All their work was done for the benefit of the Kibbutz and for the good

GRAND GYMKHANA & FÊTE

DES POLICIERS LIBANAIS
DE L'ARMÉE BRITANNIQUE
ET
DES FORCES FRANÇAISES COMBATTANTES

PRESIDEN D'HONNEUR
Dr. EYOUB TABET   (Chef de l'Etat)

VICE-PRESIDENTS

Lt. Gen. W. B. HOLMES. CB., DSO.
Maj. Gen. Sir Edward SPEARS.
KBE., OB., MC.
Mons. JAWAD BOULOS.
 (Ministre des Affaires Etrangeres).
Col. J.A. BARRACLOUGH, DSO.,
OBE., MC.

Mons. JEAN HELLEU.
(Ministre plénipotentiaire au Levant)
Gen. Chadebec de LAVALADE.
 (Comdt. en Chef au LEVANT).
Mons. HENRI PHARAON.

Col. M. MARGALIN. O.L.H.

Les Prix seront distribués par Donna Maria SURSOK
à 19 heures

COMMISSAIRES

Lt.-Col. H. GARGOUR.   Major. S. OGDEN-SMITH.   Capitaine J. MARECHAL.

J U G E S

Commodore B. C. BROOKE. R. N.
Mons. ELIE CHIDIAC.
Colonel ANGENOT.

Sqn. Ldr. COOPER, R.A.F.
Lt.-Col. R. N. GUEST. M. C.
Mons. TRABOULSI.

Tous profits aux Croix-Rouges et aux caisses de Bienfaisance
des trois forces policières

Prix du programme   P. ...

Fête celebrating the birth of the Lebanon independent republic.

173

of all the Jewish settlers in Palestine with a view to some future Jewish State.

Next I was sent to Jaffa on a two-day course. This was a very hush-hush establishment where I was prepared to train the regiment for combined operations. Here I was given information concerning the waterproofing of vehicles and guns from landing craft in the event of an invasion. Our basic equipment was sheets of waterproof material and plenty of adhesive tape.

On my return to the regiment I prepared four sheets of notes with simple instructions on how best to waterproof our vehicles. Paper 1 stated the tasks that had to be done prior to embarkation and mostly concerned the waterproofing of carburettors and exhaust pipes. (The guns had to be treated in a different manner.) Sheet 2 contained instructions on what to do during the disembarkation; literally how to come off the landing craft into the water, if necessary, and how to drive on to the beach. The third sheet concerned what had to be done immediately after landing such as ripping off the waterproof sheets that had been previously positioned, and the fourth sheet contained the final instructions on removing all traces of the waterproofing as soon as possible after landing.

Each driver was carefully instructed on how to carry out these simple orders with the senior person on each vehicle or gun having possession of these four separate, so that they could be given to the driver at the correct time for him to carry out the set procedures. We rigged up some ramps so that the drivers had the opportunity of practising driving down, as though entering into the sea, and disembarking. We tried to simulate the conditions under which we were likely to be in any real landing.

In the event of the regiment making a beach landing, I was to be in the CO's craft. This would land prior to any of the guns but after the observation officers with the first infantry had set up observation points. My job on the beach would be to see that any vehicles or guns that might have got into any mechanical difficulties were removed from the area as quickly as possible.

By the time we had completed this training we were uncertain as to whether we were supposed to be an infantry division, a mountain division or part of the Navy! In order to get some idea of our destination, we began to look at the maps for places containing both beaches and mountains; Italy and Greece were the places most mentioned.

14
To Italy

The 8th Army under Montgomery and the United States 7th under Patton, had landed at different parts of Sicily in early July and proceeded to advance rapidly across the island. Mussolini was overthrown towards the end of July and Marshal Badoglio now headed the new civilian Italian government.

On a more personal note, I received a cable at this time, informing me that I was now an uncle for the second time. My sister in law, Freda, had given birth to a son called Neil who had the Hebrew name of Nathan, after my late father. I was overjoyed at this news.

Meanwhile things were moving very fast. The Allies landed in Italy on 8th September and, at first, it appeared as if Italy was finished as far as the war was concerned. The Germans, however, had different ideas, and immediately sent six divisions from the north to the south of Italy with instructions to throw the invaders back into the sea.

The 8th Indian Division was moved to Tripoli at the end of August and began to board ships in the harbour. This was our second attempt to embark as some weeks earlier Pip Battery had already boarded the ships but this campaign, a mystery to us at the time, was cancelled before the rest of the regiment could be put aboard.

Some years later I read in Winston Churchill's memoirs that the original idea had been that our division should invade the island of Rhodes. Fortunately, as it turned out, this plan was superseded at the last minute when it was decided that we should go through what was jokingly termed as 'the soft underbelly of Europe'; namely Sicily and Italy. At that time it was unknown to the British that two armoured German divisions were recuperating and resting on Rhodes, so if we had landed there we would have been in for a very sticky time.

In mid-September 1943, I set sail on a United States Liberty ship. These vessels were constructed by the hundreds and literally meant the salvaging of the supply system from America to Europe. Without these Liberty ships it would have been impossible to move the vast forces and supplies that were needed.

The ship I was on carried a diverse selection of about two hundred of the division's vehicles and their drivers. I never could understand why the 'genius' staff officer had concocted such a daft mixture; it made no sense whatsoever but presumably the gentleman had some warped theory of his own.

There was one officer on board the ship. He was a British captain and a regular Indian Army Officer. The quicker I pass over his story the better because he was the epitome of all the stories that one had ever heard about junior officers in the British Indian Army. Fortunately he remained in his cabin – for the entire trip. He was certainly there on the only occasion that I talked with him, when I first boarded the ship. This was when he gave me the good news that as I was the senior warrant officer, (in point of fact, I was the only warrant officer) I was therefore appointed the ship's RSM which meant that I was responsible for all the arrangements whilst we were on board including discipline and catering.

Fortunately there were some cooks available for I needed to arrange a number of different messes at different parts of the deck. The British soldiers only needed one mess but the Indians required several sub-messes to cope with the different diets of Muslims, Sikhs, Hindus and Gurkhas. Fortunately a very helpful Indian Havaldar from Brigade headquarters was on hand to advise me about the different food requirements so I managed not to offend any religious customs.

After the first day I had more or less organised both the feeding and the sleeping arrangements. The latter were really simple, as I merely allocated a section of the deck for each group, and individuals just slept on any space available.

The big problem concerned the toilets. There were no facilities provided on Liberty ships for toilets or ablutions for the large number of soldiers that we had. The carpenters had rigged up two rows of very simple, temporary toilets on the stern of the deck. These rows faced each other and gave very little privacy. The flushing system involved the liberal use of a hose and a contraption which pumped water in and flushed the waste matter back into the sea. This explained why the lavatories were at the rear of the ship; our rubbish could be left behind us.

Unfortunately the afore-mentioned 'genius' staff officer had forgotten to place an Indian sweeper on board. These were low caste Indians who were deemed to be too inferior to be soldiers. They were civilians who worked for the army and who wore uniforms with no insignia. Each unit used their sweepers to perform all the menial tasks.

One line of toilets was allocated for British use and the other for Indian use. Naturally, whichever unlucky British soldier was assigned toilet fatigue would spend that day moaning his head off as he followed his orders to wash the deck with the hosepipe and sprinkle the antiseptic liquid all over the place so as to keep the toilets clean and relatively free of infection.

My problem began twenty-four hours after setting sail when I was approached by the three havaldars who were the Senior Indian NCOs on board. They very sheepishly informed me that they were unable to detail anybody for latrine duty. To put it mildly my first reaction was one of astonishment and my second was to say, 'Well, if you can't, then clean it yourselves!' My third reaction was to ask, 'Who the hell do you expect to clean it?' I pointed out that in a few hours' time the ship would be uninhabitable due to the stench, not to mention the threat from bubonic plague!

They agreed with me entirely and then came the suggestion that perhaps I could tell the British soldier to extend his area and do the Indian row at the same time as cleaning the British toilets. I suppose, on reflection, this seemed very logical to them and it taught me a great deal about the Indian Army.

I was probably one of the few warrant officers in the British Army who could keep calm under these circumstances so I very quietly pointed out that no, I did not think this was a good idea and I managed to refrain from mentioning that I was anxious to avoid a mutiny by the British soldiers!

We decided to walk across to the stern and to quietly try to sort out this little problem. By now the smell was no longer a joke and the British soldiers were beginning to mutter certain remarks, albeit under their breath, that were hardly complimentary towards the Indians.

I examined the situation very carefully. Then I managed to fix another hose to the pump and to increase the pressure so that we had two much more powerful jets of water. By standing at the end of the row, I was able to convince the havaldars that whoever operated the hosepipes was not really physically *in* the toilets. After all, if one stood at the end of the line one could be deemed to be facing either way. After I had demonstrated this concept for about ten minutes – during which time I must confess that I got rid of most of the rubbish myself – they were more or less convinced. If the Sergeant Major Sahib was standing, yet not standing in the latrines and just happened to be pointing the jets of water in that direction, then, yes, they supposed it could be done by the Indians.

They eventually detailed some sepoys to carry on with the job and I promptly departed. The whole episode reinforced my experience in demonstrating how tactful one had to be when dealing with people of different religions and philosophies.

For the next few days, the convoy steamed slowly ahead. We carried our life-jackets at all times and kept a wary eye open for both aircraft and submarines. Fortunately we were troubled by neither, apart from spotting one lonely plane. On the fifth day I suddenly fell ill and my temperature shot up. I was afraid that I was in for another bout of malaria but as we had no doctor on board, I still took my anti-malaria pills and I lay, wrapped in a blanket, under the shelter of a lorry on deck for twenty-four hours. My temperature then disappeared and I soon felt much better. Later, when I spoke to Lance Montgomery, he said that it had probably not been malaria at all but sandfly fever.

On the ninth day the convoy arrived at Malta where it stayed overnight in the relative safety of Valetta Harbour, within the boom. Our arrival coincided with the surrender of a large part of the Italian fleet which was already anchored in the harbour. This was a most incredible sight for as we entered the harbour we passed within 200 yards of the mighty *Vittorio Veneto* battleship which was decked in flags as though having won a gigantic victory. As we looked upwards from our tiny vessel, we could see how beautifully in order everything was on board and noticed how spick and span were the rows of sailors who saluted us. The Italian Naval Band played a variety of tunes from light operas to folk music; yet it was obvious to us all that this one ship alone had the power to have completely destroyed our entire convoy without the slightest difficulty.

When we awoke the next day we found that we were on our way again and this time everybody realised that our next stop would be mainland Italy. We reached Taranto Harbour in southern Italy on 25th September 1943. From the sea, everything looked very normal with Taranto appearing to be a large and important harbour and city. After some hours we entered the port where there were the usual navy ships scuttling around, keeping a wary eye open for enemy submarines.

We had to join a long queue of ships which were awaiting their turn to be unloaded but fortunately there were some infantry landing craft in operation. After a further long wait the landing craft came alongside us and all the soldiers were able to be ferried to the port. Once again I realised that the sea was not my favourite place and we were all very thankful to be back on dry land.

The military police had total control of the port and had erected signs all over the place so that everybody knew what they had to do. I marched my couple of hundred drivers to two very large buildings that had been earmarked as waiting places. One building was for Indian other ranks and the other was for the British. All the vehicles were then gradually unloaded and the drivers summoned to take over their vehicles and sent to rejoin their units at various staging waiting posts around the city.

The port seemed very deserted with many of the buildings having been bombed or shelled. A few Italians had been retained to help the Military Police but most of the lifting facilities had been put out of action. However, one crane was still functional and there was a

178

long queue of ships waiting for the REs to unload them.

After I had handed over my drivers to the military police, I was now free of my responsibility for the men. My next task was to reach our regiment's assembly point so I spoke to an MP sergeant major. He told me that all the troops, except drivers, had to rejoin their units, each of which had been allocated a position in an area of about five to ten miles north of Taranto. The 53rd Field's collecting point was near a village called Castellanetta. He warned me that, apart from fruit and grapes, there was a great shortage of food in the region as the civil administration had completely broken down. The farmers had all sorts of food but many of the villages and towns were experiencing great hardship. The sergeant major also warned me that many women were setting up in business which was creating several problems.

Taranto was in a very poor area of the country and had deteriorated even further owing to the war. Every commodity was in short supply and the medical services were quite inadequate. Venereal disease was rife. There was no money available for the Italian lira had been banned (the Fascist lira) and as yet the authorities had not issued the military money that was due to be introduced. All that was left was barter.

Apparently the prostitutes were available for the recognised fee of one tin of bully beef or any other type of meat. Consequently, apart from the VD problem I would also have to deal with the problem of rations being stolen in order to pay for the services of these women. Normally, I had never had to have anything to do with this sort of discipline because the anti-VD precautions in places like Cairo or Baghdad were taken by the unit medical officers and permanently stationed warrant officers in that area. But we had no back-up services in Taranto for we were the first troops to arrive there, so I had to take charge.

The military police sergeant major, recommended three procedures which were: 1) Get tough with any stragglers. I had to make sure that anyone seen where he had no right to be was arrested and returned to his holding unit; 2) Get very tough on any food pilfering since as it was very difficult to land stores the only available rations were those that we had brought with us; 3) To set up a prophylactic station the moment I got to the 53rd holding area.

I managed to get a lift with a motorbike dispatch rider who was taking some letters to the 131 Brigade via our assembly point. He drove through the city where we saw plenty of people who appeared indifferent to our presence as we passed through. It was quite a pleasing sort of town although it had obviously sustained some bombing and shelling damage. There were very few motor vehicles about although we did see some horse and donkey-drawn carts.

The weather was beautiful and the countryside was punctuated with various farmhouses but the villages seemed very dilapidated. The people were very poorly dressed but most of the villagers called friendly greetings to us. There were Mussolini slogans, such as 'Victory for Italy' scrawled on every wall available and in some cases an attempt had been made to cross out certain words. I did not understand Italian at this time so it all meant very little to me.

When I arrived at the regiment, there were about a hundred men already in place including ten from regimental headquarters. I reported to the Adjutant at the RHQ which was situated in a vineyard. The whole area seemed full of vineyards and orchards. There were enormous bunches of black and white grapes and the trees contained ripe pears, plums and apples in abundance.

The Adjutant told me that there was nothing much to be done until the whole regiment had arrived when we would have to get ready as quickly as possible to begin the move north. He also told me that just before embarking Bert France had been taken ill, probably with malaria, and they had had to leave him behind at a base hospital. I was now short of a corporal and as Bert was one of our key people I was very sorry to hear this news, especially as the chance of him being returned to us was remote.

Since the RSM had not arrived it was my duty to set up the prophylactic station. The men, being unoccupied, had already begun to drift off to the local village, irrespective or orders to the contrary. There seemed to be plenty of cheap vino available which was hardly surprising considering the vast quantity of grapes in the region. Many men had also appeared to make contact with the local women.

Just as I began to make the arrangements, the RSM arrived and took over the task with my assistance. We quickly invented various tasks to occupy the men such as tidying up the vineyards and digging slit trenches, even though we knew that there was not the faintest chance of the enemy being anywhere near. We also set up a tent with washing facilities and made the prophylactic packs available. There were no questions asked when any man took one of these packets from the box that we left just inside the door of the tent. These packs contained preventative measures, ointments and cleansing materials which would hopefully prevent them from getting venereal disease. We literally had to force these kits on to all the men although a lot of them protested that they didn't need them; but the RSM was not in the mood for nonsense.

We put a guard on the food that had arrived for by trying to prevent food being stolen for barter purposes, insisting that the men have prophylactic packets, providing cleansing facilities and giving very lurid warnings about venereal diseases, we hoped to have some sort of control over the local prostitutes who were not at all slow in coming round to the camps.

As we could not expect any support units for some considerable time, the LAD and REME units would have to abandon any vehicle or gun that we could not repair. Fortunately, at this time, I could see no sign of the enemy so it was a question of our own speed of reorganising and getting everything in order for the time when the division had to take -part in the fighting.

A number of parachutes had been left in the vicinity by the units who had landed during the earlier invasion. Terry Lewis had cut several lengths of this green camouflage silk and he gave me one of these pieces. He told me that the village tailor would make me a pair of pyjamas from this silk in exchange for a very small amount of barter. As I was busy, Terry arranged this service for me and I kept them as a souvenir. The funny part was that I had never previously owned or slept in pyjamas and I am quite sure that neither had 99 per cent of the other men in the camp. One evening, just before dusk, it was very amusing to see several soldiers walking around wearing luxurious green silk pyjamas! I never actually attempted to wear my set and eventually they were lost later on in the war.

The Adjutant explained the situation to the RSM and myself. Apparently the paratroopers and the other landing troops had met little opposition when they landed in the Taranto area and they were now racing towards Foggia. This was the key to the whole strategy for there were several airstrips in the Foggia area and thus it was crucial that we took both the town and the airstrips before the Germans. They were reacting in a much faster manner than had been expected and several divisions were grouping and racing down Italy to attempt to destroy our invasion forces before we could build up sufficient strength. We would have no chance without the airfields at Foggia.

Our role was to chase up to join the British units racing north and to get as far as possible before the enemy destroyed us.

The US 5th Army had landed at Salerno on the other coast of Italy and were very heavily engaged in fighting. It seemed that the Germans were more concerned with that side of Italy which controlled Naples and Rome and Field Marshal Kesselring had already declared his determination to throw the 5th Army back into the sea. As we were talking a runner arrived with the news that the 8th Army had successfully taken Foggia on 27th September. This meant that the RAF would immediately start flying in and we had to get the regiment on the road as quickly as possible.

I began to set up an LAD but I had no equipment and no vehicles, just an allocated piece of land. I decided that the best thing I could do would be to return to the port and to direct any vehicle of the 53rd to our assembly area. Captain Matthews, the Quartermaster, had obtained a civilian truck from somewhere and I realised that the few trucks that we had seen being driven around had been commandeered by the military. He was using this particular truck to ferry stores from a brigade service corps unit that had disembarked. I got lifts to and from the port on this truck which made life much simpler for me.

Once, when I was standing by the dockside talking to a driver of one of our quads, I heard a loud explosion. The liberty ship which was third in the queue for disembarkation suddenly began to settle in the water and at first there was quite a bit of panic. Nobody knew the cause of this explosion and could only assume that an enemy submarine had got inside the harbour boom. Everybody was running round in circles, the naval ships were darting around like lunatics and hundreds of Indian soldiers began to line the liberty ship's decks. Some began to jump into the water and swim to the dockside. There was no danger to them – even non-swimmers would have been perfectly safe – but nobody knew if there were to be any further explosions.

It was soon realised that the ship had hit a mine on the floor of the dock basin. We were all thankful that it had not exploded earlier since at least fifteen ships had previously passed over the same spot. After a short time the ship lay still on the sea floor with the top deck still above water. Thus, as it transpired, anyone on board who had just wandered up to the top deck would have been perfectly safe.

I learned afterwards that Charlie Bacon and the LAD of the 52nd Field Regiment had unluckily been on this ship. All their vehicles and stores were now submerged on the lower decks and it would be several months before any of it could be salvaged. Thus Charlie and his entire LAD found themselves on the dockside without as much as a bicycle or a pair of roller skates, a spanner or a pair of pliers. This was extremely serious for the regiment, bearing in mind that the brigade workshops had not yet arrived. After a few days he was given a 3-ton lorry and he managed to scrounge a few hand tools from various vehicles. I gave him some spares and equipment which were surplus to my requirements but I had to be very careful not to leave my own unit short. It took him several months to become adequately re-equipped and function as a REME detachment. This did not seem to worry him unduly since Charlie was a very happy-go-lucky fellow; after all, if he had no equipment he could hardly be expected to do very much, could he!

15
The First Battles

In early October, as soon as the whole division had finished disembarking, we began our race northwards to reinforce the units that had made the first contact with the enemy. The plan was to form a line on our side of the mountains, about fifty miles north of Foggia between Campobasso and Termoli on the Adriatic Coast. I use the term 'our side' because this mountain range forms the spine of Italy and was the dividing line between the west and the east. The 5th Army was more or less on the western side whilst the 8th Army were fighting on the Adriatic side. These two armies were thus separated, for most of the time by mountains.

We heard that the 5th Army had taken the port of Naples on 2nd October which cheered us up no end because now we had both proper port facilities at Naples to accompany the airfield facilities at Foggia. We now felt able to hold whatever the enemy threw against us.

The following few weeks were a complete shambles. We soon realised that Jerry intended to fight for every inch of the country. His intention was to prevent the build-up of our forces and totally to destroy our 8th and 5th Armies. One has to remember that the German army still considered themselves to be the greatest fighting machine in the world. Even after their defeat in North Africa they never allowed themselves to contemplate the possibility that our small number of troops could be much of a threat to them; especially when many of our forces contained Indians whom they considered racially inferior.

It did not take us long to appreciate why we were called the 8th Indian Mountain Division, for all the problems that we had experienced in our training began to come thick and fast. The roads were in an appalling condition and very vulnerable to destruction by enemy engineers which made movement very difficult for us. Fortunately the weather remained beautiful and was certainly all that we had expected. To us, Italy was the land of sunshine.

We continued our advance as the enemy fought their retreat but we moved at a snail's pace, no more than three or four miles a day. Whenever we stopped there were vehicles to repair plus accidents and casualties that needed attention. As soon as everything had been straightened out and we had all transferred to the next position, the next order to advance would be given. Most of my time continued to be spent dashing hither and thither, trying to keep in contact with the various batteries and regimental headquarters. Time after time I would arrive at where we were supposed to assemble only to discover that the next move had already been made. Or, having left the LAD in the early morning so that I could hunt for spares, I would return very late at night to a new, unfamiliar position although I always tried to reconnoitre any new position before giving the LAD the map reference.

Once again I was truly thankful for Jack Wragg's services for however late I arrived, he always ensured that my kit was present and that my camp equipment had been so arranged that I could at least get some sleep. Irrespective of the hour, Jack always had a meal prepared for me and without him my life would have been far more difficult.

As yet I had no back-up as the brigade workshops were unable to operate in these conditions. A brigade workshop could neither function on the move nor could it operate and move every couple of days; it just wasn't practical. So, either they were a long way behind me which meant I was virtually out of touch with them or they were approaching us but were not yet operational.

We became very expert at determining the best site for the LAD to set up shop. The one essential was some hard-standing so that we could perform such repairs as axle changing or those that involved removing the engine with the use of the breakdown lorry.

In front of every farmhouse, no matter how meagre it might be, there would be a paved area once used for threshing corn. Thus I soon realised that the best place for my site would be in the vicinity of a farmhouse where, if we were lucky, we could also use the building when the weather became inclement. Most of the farmhouses in the forward area had been deserted due to the danger, although once the army had moved on some of the family would return. These farmhouses were usually nothing more than a large barn with a large open space on the ground floor and a ladder to the upper part which was usually divided into two or three bedrooms. In the living area there would be a large open fireplace which was also used for cooking. An iron hook would be hung in it holding a large iron cauldron. Here the woman of the house would cook her family's meals. The fuel for the fire would be twigs collected from the surrounding areas. There would be some simple items of wooden furniture such as chairs, tables and chests of drawers and around the upper walls a variety of food could be seen hanging either for storage or ripening purposes. Foodstuffs were also hung to make them less accessible to vermin such as rats and mice. All sorts of farm implements could be seen scattered all over the floor and, to me, these scenes were reminiscent of some eighteenth century paintings of rural Britain that I had once seen.

There were no proper toilet facilities apart from a bucket at the back of the farmhouse. Some small attempts were made to achieve some sort of privacy by placing planks around it but this was barely adequate. The bucket's contents were used as manure; nothing was wasted in these economic circumstances. Water was either provided by a well or, if it was a more prosperous farm, there might be a pump. I never saw any taps providing water in any of the farms in this area. There were plenty of streams and rivers where the women would do the washing, thumping it on to nearby stones. We soon learnt that they would be delighted to do our washing as well, for a small payment and, to my astonishment, it was always returned to us scrupulously clean; perhaps it was in contrast to our own efforts. We paid for this service with either food or scarce goods such as needles and at least the problem of clean laundry was easily solved!

As soon as I found a suitable base I would send a message back to the detachment and Frank Storey would then organise the move. However, to quick a move could result in finding ourselves in front of the guns. This was most unpleasant for we would then not only be vulnerable to normal shelling but also on the receiving end of small arms and mortar fire. The main advantage of being ahead of the guns was that we could take our pick of any deserted farmhouses where we could promptly get settled. If I deliberately waited until later some civilians may have already returned to their properties, especially when the fighting appeared to be somewhat intermittent. Then I would have the problem of persuading them to vacate the farmhouse but I usually compromised by working out a system whereby I would place my men on the ground floor and allow any civilians who desired to do so to use the less safe upstairs rooms. I preferred to persuade these farming families to move as far away as possible from the battle area because of the physical danger to them but in many cases they had nowhere else to go and, as all their possessions were on their farm, they were naturally reluctant to leave.

At first we and the Italians were very wary of each other. None of us spoke any Italian but once we had begun to learn some of the language we realised that they were wonderful, good-hearted, family-orientated and very friendly people. The majority of them were not the slightest bit interested in politics or Mussolini and his Fascist movement. They were simple people who were trying to continue their existence in very difficult circumstances. I felt a great deal of compassion for these Italians for we saw hardly any villages that had not been destroyed, there was no civil administration and there was a terrific shortage of food. All the villages and small towns were crowded with refugees. Food was scarce and all sorts of terrible incidents occurred. In my small way I did whatever I could to make their lives easier. For instance, as no medical facilities were available, when I donated an aspirin to a youngster with a temperature, they did not know how to thank me enough.

Gradually I picked up some colloquial Italian – I am terrible at learning languages – and I was eventually able to carry on quite an intelligent conversation. As we were such a small detachment we had a great deal of contact with the civilians in whose farmhouses we stayed and this certainly helped me to learn the language. Unlike the Western Desert, we were involved in a civilian-occupied war zone and, whether we liked it or not, became involved with their problems.

At one farm there was a very sick, old grandfather who, despite giving him whatever medicine we had available, died. I used the 15-cwt truck to carry his body and the mourners to the church several miles away where he was buried. Although technically we were dealing with an enemy family, my soldiers behaved with tremendous decorum during the whole period of the man's illness, funeral and wake. One has to respect the innate goodness of our soldiers who behaved in such a civilised manner when it came down to individual circumstances. Despite being away from their homes and in a situation where they were liable to get killed themselves, they still had compassion for the tragedies of others.

The biggest danger we faced was from the shelling, particularly in the mountains where there were few roads. Vital points, such as crossroads, had been pinpointed for attack as the enemy knew exactly where these congested places were situated having already fully mapped the area a day or two before they left. Our military police would put up signs warning drivers of the most dangerous places but, as there was often no alternative route, we had no choice but to continue along the dangerous routes. We did try to make new tracks to bypass danger areas and were successful in some cases, but generally we were forced to scurry along them as fast as was possible. However, travelling at speed created more problems than it cured because it meant that more vehicles were accidentally damaged and it was my LAD's job to recover and repair them if possible. I tried to institute a rota so that everybody took a turn on the recovery team and thus spread the danger more fairly and I soon realised that the very large Dodge breakdown lorry attracted enemy shelling. This lorry seemed to especially excite the German observers so we tried to use smaller vehicles for recovery but when we had to have a suspended tow it became very difficult.

Our first river crossing was over the Biferno. The enemy had destroyed all the bridges so the Royal Engineers had to construct a Bailey bridge across the river. A Bailey bridge requires approach roads on both sides of the river and these were usually paths made up with small bricks or rubble as foundation material. During dry weather some rivers became merely a trickle enabling jeeps and other of the smaller four-wheeled vehicles to cross without too much difficulty. The jeeps were lifesavers enabling me to cross rivers where the water was so high that it covered my boots as I was driving. There were only a few occasions when the jeep would fail us and then we had to use the breakdown lorry's winch to manoeuvre it to the shore. However, when it rained all larger vehicles had to use a Bailey bridge with all the risks of the enemy shelling.

We had been very puzzled when we had first learned about the Indian company of mules. Many men made jokes such as 'this is the Indian method of portable food' but these animals really came into their own in this part of Italy. They were fantastic animals who certainly lived up to their reputation for stubbornness. They were able to carry stores, piled up to a height equal to that of the mule itself. They appeared to achieve the impossible by merely balancing these loads, let alone successfully crossing rivers and mountain paths thus laden. In the pitch black of the night mules were the primary method of transporting shells from our lorries to gun sites; the alternative was manpack which, on the few occasions it happened, was the biggest nightmare of my life. It was almost impossible for a man to keep his balance on these mountainous tracks but the mules had little trouble and were the only method which never let us down. It was always very sad to see a mule that had been killed by the enemy; they had to be left where they had died for no one seemed to have the specific responsibility of burying them. Obviously they were eventually interred but it was always a long time later, well after we had left the area.

When we came to cross the Trigno River we had the additional problem that the weather was becoming wetter and, with the rain, came the mud. We struggled on for a few more miles but the conditions finally brought everything to a halt. By mid-November, General Alexander, Supreme Allied Commander in the Mediterranean Theatre, had no choice but to stop the advance. We were now bumping up against the forward defences of what we were told was the enemy winter line which, on our side of Italy, was along the River Sangro whilst the 5th Army was facing Monte Cassino which overlooked the Liri Valley and the road to Rome.

It is impossible to describe how much mud affected us. We used to think that we had problems in the desert with sand but, compared to mud, sand is wonderful! Now that we were literally up to our necks in mud it was an effort just to walk and each step sank us further into the ground. Often the mud would rise over the top of our wellington boots. From first thing in the morning to last thing at night we battled to keep the tracks open with the use of stones and pebbles.

Our only satisfaction was the knowledge that Jerry was encountering the same difficulties with supplies which resulted in some easing up of the shelling. This was a godsend because between the shelling and the mud, we preferred the latter!

Everybody had been getting very jittery for the shelling never appeared to stop. Sometimes it might be intermittent but the threat was always present. Perhaps for a few hours all would be quiet, then suddenly, we would hear the all too familiar whine and the thump as the shell landed. If it appeared to be coming in our direction we would promptly dive to the ground and try to get any cover we could.

There were one or two very brave people – either heroes, deaf or barmy, I'm not sure which – who seemed to be able to ignore the shelling and just carry on as normal. I certainly was not one of them as I disliked the shelling immensely and made sure that I kept busy whenever we were in an area that was being attacked.

We still had to deal with the pests of mines and booby traps. Even if a mine detector had surveyed the area there was still no guarantee of safety. Often a vehicle would suddenly explode along a path that had been continually in use for a week, when an enemy mine decided to come to life. German booby traps were particularly nasty tricks, often attached to the most simple of utensils, such as innocent-looking pails by the side of a farmhouse. Sometimes a booby trap would be detonated when a door was opened for the Germans used a great deal of ingenuity to maim us.

We had to impress upon our men never to take any chances whatsoever and to keep out of unauthorised areas. At first they found it a novelty to take odd items from deserted houses and sometimes a soldier could be seen comfortably seated on an armchair placed in the back of an open top lorry. However, after several people had been killed or wounded by these booby traps, this thieving ceased. We took a very hard line with any soldiers found looting, although most of it was very minor pilfering from deserted buildings. Mostly the soldiers picked up stupid things like furniture which they threw away after a few days, although sometimes a pig or some chickens would mysteriously disappear, no doubt making a good supper for those concerned.

We all had our pet fears and without a doubt mine was a fear of lying in my bivvy at night. I was always at my worst whenever the planes came overhead to drop their bombs and I would often find myself shaking. I would try to hold my arm to stop my tremors but I soon realised that the best cure was to get up, stand outside and simply watch the bombers. The real trick, as far as I was concerned, was to keep occupied whenever there was any danger for as long as I was busy I was in control and I felt fortunate that unlike most of the gunners who had to spend hours between bursts of activity, I always had plenty of work to do.

When three or four of the guns began to develop problems, my spare gun sights came to my rescue and I was able to fix them promptly. Naturally, I had never let on that I had previously acquired these spares before we left England; they were my own secret reserve. Soon afterwards, the Adjutant sent for me to tell me that the CO had been complimented by the Divisional Artillery's commanding officer. They had noticed an odd fact from our returns, for apparently our record of guns out of action at any one period was much better than the division's other two artillery regiments. Colonel Greenhalgh was delighted with this report; his compliments were passed on to me. It was wondered, the Adjutant told me, if I had any particular explanation for this success, but I kept a straight face. I was determined not to mention my unofficial sights and simply said that it reflected well on all the regimental tiffies, the LAD and the whole regiment's efficiency. In my view, I said, it was because we were a competent crew of soldiers. The Adjutant was overjoyed and remarked that that was what they had all presumed; so we left it at that.

As a result of this discussion it was decided to set up a special gun workshop with the prime responsibility for repairing the divisional guns. Personnel were taken from the three brigade workshops and the officer chosen to be in charge was a friend of mine, Captain Sambrook. He was a British officer in the Indian army who had progressed from a council house background, through grammar school to university, and he was an extremely good engineer. I could not have been happier that it was him with whom I would have to deal and his section helped me enormously to keep the guns in action. Tommy Thompson, a regular soldier, was his staff sergeant and, in the quiet periods. Tommy Sinclair and myself were always made welcome at their section whenever we joined them for a cup of tea and a chat.

By the third week in December, we were once again on the move and crossing the Sangro River was our next objective. At first it appeared to be no different to the other rivers we had crossed. The infantry attacked during a lull in the weather and everything proceeded as normal with the guns crossing via the Bailey Bridge. By late afternoon the guns were in place and I decided that I could now take the LAD across. My only problem was with a Stuart tank from Queen Battery that had severe fuel problems. Sergeant Storey and one of my other men were taking a long time to carry out this repair so I decided to leave a 15-cwt truck with Frank and instructed him to rejoin us the next day by which time the tank should be operational.

It took us about three hours to reach the end of the queue crossing the river and it was not until late evening that I managed to establish the LAD in a farmhouse just outside Orsogna. During the night the weather suddenly worsened and it poured with rain for hours. Everywhere became flooded and the River Sangro changed from being a gentle flowing stream of about fifteen feet wide to an absolute torrent with steep, unapproachable banks on both sides. The Bailey bridge was completely awash and impassable; not even a jeep could cope in this situation.

We were in quite a predicament having the infantry and most of the artillery on our side of the river but the entire backup of the army stranded on the other bank. Our only good fortune was that the RAF was now well established in Foggia and were able to give us air cover. However, it was an absolutely golden opportunity for the enemy but, as it transpired, they were more concerned with holding the 5th Army and protecting the road to Rome.

The Royal Engineers worked like Trojans and everybody tried to assist them. Ten days later a new triple length Bailey Bridge was ready and the build-up of supplies managed to cross the river. During this construction period, a trickle of supplies had been ferried down to the river by mules and loaded on to small boats. Once on our side, more mules had brought the goods up on to the road. The enemy continually shelled the Engineers as they worked but although a couple of shells did strike the bridge, they did not cause any serious damage that could not be quickly repaired.

The poor mules were also prime targets and I was absolutely sickened to see dozens of them lying dead on either side of the bridge. It was bad enough for us, but our mules could really have had no argument with any mules that happened to have been working for the Germans.

Frank Storey eventually arrived with the repaired tank, saying what a great time they had had. They had made friends with an Italian family, celebrating with the whole village each evening while we were daft enough to be cut off on our side of the river.

16
The Winter Line

The division took the town of Lanciano and on 24th December we started our preparations for Christmas. Although we knew that Christmas Day would be spent in the line, we hoped that if it proved to be an uneventful time the cooks would manage to provide us with some seasonal fare and we would be able to celebrate the festival in our usual military manner. However it wasn't to be, our luck was out. Lunchtime on 25th December saw the regiment on the road and still moving forward. I think this annoyed everybody more than any other thing the enemy was responsible for during the whole of this period.

This small advance petered out primarily because the 5th Army was completely stalled on the other side of the mountains. It was not really practical for us to move further up, because then we would risk being cut off and destroyed. There was now no alternative but to stop for the rest of the winter.

By 28th December 1943 we had reached Ortona on the Adriatic coast where we settled ourselves in to a large unoccupied farmhouse. After a couple of days, two or three Italians returned so I allowed them to use the upper floor and moved the whole LAD into the relative comfort of the lower floor. It was somewhat crowded but at least there was room for us all to sleep inside the building. The weather was now very cold and there had been several snow falls, so we made ourselves as snug as possible for what we hoped would be a period of relative calm. We were now facing the main Gustav line. At last we had the opportunity to perform all the maintenance tasks that we had been forced to neglect. We also had time to recover from our difficult travels, to clean ourselves properly and to get our kits in order. Although the temperatures were very low and snow had settled on the ground, there were some lovely sunny days when we were able to indulge in a variety of activities that cheered us all up.

Naturally, we were not left alone to mind our own business for very long. No sooner had we made ourselves comfortable than some bright spark of a staff officer decided that the line was a bit too ragged for his liking. As it was not strictly according to his teaching at Staff College he decided to straighten out the line and to move various units into neater positions. We were informed that we were occupying a space that had now been allocated to Pip Battery. We were forced to move to an area which turned out to be mostly occupied by Queen Battery who had already requisitioned all the habitable buildings. We had no alternative but to live in the open and sleep in our bivouacs. This did not suit us at all and we were most displeased at the prospect of a prolonged stay out in the open during the worst of the winter.

We were now situated on the top of a mountain slope. About 25 yards away, just on the other side of the ridge, were the eight gun positions and Queen Battery's headquarters, all of which were dug in, sandbagged and heavily camouflaged. This was necessary because there was a deep rift in the mountain and, with the aid of binoculars, Queen had a very clear view of the enemy artillery pointing towards them. They could also see the German soldiers going about their business although, obviously, the enemy gun positions were also very well camouflaged. The valley was basically inaccessible although as no infantry was normally stationed there, it was just possible for odd individuals to climb down and up the other side. The two hostile batteries faced each other, both keeping a wary eye open for any sudden, silent, night-time raids. Fortunately all remained very quiet with most of the activity still being contained on the other side of Italy. These mountains did not really provide suitable terrain for warfare.

A type of truce situation appeared in that both sides seemed to have decided to sit out the bad weather without too much of a show of military enthusiasm. As long as no one was actually seen to be doing anything, no action was taken. It was only when more than one vehicle was on the move that it would encounter any firing, and then it was only fired upon so that the small ration of daily shells could be utilised. There were one or two days when no shells at all were fired. When a troop duty officer changed, the one who was going off duty simply fired half a dozen shells to use up his quota.

We dug ourselves trenches, four feet deep by six feet long, on to which we placed our bivouacs. Normally two soldiers shared a bivouac but myself and the senior NCOs had one each to ourselves. We spent a considerable amount of time making these bivouacs comfortable. At one end we cut a makeshift ladder into the earth which we covered with some sort of tarpaulin, laid down in a series of steps, to prevent the earth from crumbling. The really clever bit was at the other end where we invented a variety of fireplaces and grates. We made chimneys out of our ever useful flimsy petrol cans as, with some ingenuity, it was very easy to transform these into funnel shapes. One end of the chimney would protrude from the ground a couple of feet away from the end of our bivvy while the other end was attached to the back of our makeshift fire. There were masses of twigs about, which we collected for fuel and, although there was always plenty of smoke, with a little fanning and a lot of luck, most of the smoke found its way up the improvised chimney.

We covered the ground inside the bivvy with sacks or any other material we could acquire and around the surface of the bivvy we placed a couple of rows of earth-filled sandbags. Our bivvies were safe enough sleep-places unless they were victims of a direct hit.

It was amazing how warm and comfortable we could be, even if there was a storm raging outside. Some men even pinned pictures of their wives, sweethearts and children on the wall of the trenches. If there was a snowstorm at night, pickets had the duty to shovel off the snow to prevent an accumulation of it causing the bivvy to collapse on top of the unfortunate occupants. By good fortune, backed up by terrible threats, none of our LAD pickets ever failed us but I did see some snow-logged battery gunners who took a very dim view of their avalanches.

Although we had lost our cosy farmhouse, we still needed some hard standing for our vehicle repair work. To that end I got permission to use the threshing area of a nearby farmhouse. This building was occupied by some Royal Engineers who were cleaning the area of mines and booby traps. Ten days later, just as we had begun to acclimatise ourselves to residing in our bivouacs, our luck once again changed. The Engineers decided to move on having considered that our surroundings were now cleared of mines. We were quickly off the mark and once again we were grateful to move indoors. This time we were determined to stay put until the spring weather arrived.

It remained cold but when it wasn't actually snowing or raining, we coped without too much difficulty, as long as we were warmly dressed and active. On the few days when the sun emerged there was a real beauty in the scenery that astonished us.

Just about this time Captain Simpson, one of our troop commanders, turned up at the LAD. He had been on a flying course and, to our amazement, arrived in a light Auster aircraft. He landed his plane on a tiny handkerchief of a field about 300 yards from our unit and informed us that he was now attached to the regiment for local and low flying observation purposes. He was accompanied by a 3-ton lorry, manned by a corporal and a private whose job it was to carry the special high octane fuel needed for the plane. The lorry also carried a roll of wire netting, about 20 feet wide and 50 yards long, for the idea was to set up this portable landing strip on a suitable site as near as possible to the regimental headquarters.

On several occasions when I was talking to Captain Simpson, he would suddenly announce that he was going to pop off and have a look around. Sure enough some fifteen minutes later he could be seen buzzing at almost tree-top level, over enemy territory. It was really strange to listen in on the operations radio at RHQ and to hear him give a running commentary as he described the complete situation of the enemy below. Surprisingly enough he was quite safe as the enemy knew full well that anyone who was daft enough to fire at a pilot would immediately bring the whole divisional artillery down on their heads. The same applied when the enemy observer flew over our lines. Nobody dreamt of firing at him; all we did was to immediately make for cover and pretend that we weren't there!

Captain Simpson had quite a sense of humour and seemed to think it particularly funny to shell enemy latrines. He told me that whenever he saw a few Germans using the makeshift latrines he would call for artillery fire on the position, saying that he could see some tanks assembling. As he was solo in the Auster nobody could argue with him and, as it was a principle that whatever the air observer requested he got immediately, the shelling would take place. He had a theory that even if he was not causing enemy casualties he was at least making them too nervous to use the toilets! The idea of Germans with tummy cramps seemed to amuse him.

What was of particular importance to me was that the Auster now came under the repair system of the regiment. So now my LAD was responsible for carrying out all sorts of minor repairs on aircraft and we became quite proud of our own private airforce. Naturally, most of the pilots overreached themselves some time or another when they flew too low and observed things that each army could not allow to become general knowledge. Their rate of casualties became extremely high and very few of them lasted for more than three months without getting shot down. Captain Simpson was fairly lucky, because when he was eventually fired at he managed to bring the plane back over our lines. He was also very fortunate in that his only injury was a broken leg. I saw him strapped up on a stretcher, happy as the day was long, as he was taken away to hospital by ambulance.

As there were very few pipe-smokers in the unit there was no shortage of tobacco; it was the pipes themselves that were unavailable. By now I had got into the habit of smoking my pipe almost permanently and owned two pipes, both with improvised stems. Breaking stems was one of my specialities, probably because I was always crawling under vehicles having first put my pipe in my pocket and, inevitably, snapped the stem on several occasions. One day I happened to come across an old copy of the *Tatler* magazine where I saw an advertisement for a firm called Loew's of Regent Street. This company was selling beautiful Briar pipes for one pound. I mentioned this to my friend Sergeant Joe Barker, of Robert battery, who was also a dedicated pipe-smoker, and we decided to order ourselves one of these pipes. Several months later, after I had completely forgotten about it, I was delighted to receive a beautiful briar. It arrived with a covering letter saying the price had now doubled but since I was a soldier on active duty I need not bother to forward the other pound and they wished me good luck and enjoyable smoking. However, when I spoke to Joe I was surprised to hear that he had not received his pipe. We thought about it and decided that it was probably still somewhere in the army Post Office 'pipeline' and would arrive shortly.

A few days later I heard that a stray shell had landed on Joe's gun position and he had been killed outright. It's an odd thing to reflect, but I remember being very annoyed with Jerry for killing him before Joe had had the pleasure of using his new pipe. After further reflection, I thought that at least it was fortunate that the one pipe that had arrived had been for me and not for Joe, as it would have been wasted on a man who sadly would not have lived to enjoy it.

We still had the same attitude to casualties that we had formed in North Africa. In every army one continually becomes friends with many people who might suddenly be posted away and would then disappear from our lives. I suppose we considered the casualties in the same way. They had been 'posted' and therefore we did not expect to see them again. The only exception to this was when casualties occurred in an incident in which we were personally involved. Then the effect lasted a bit longer but it still soon passed from one's memory and life carried on just as usual.

Montgomery left the 8th Army in December and returned home to take charge of the British Army that was now preparing for the Normandy invasion. He was followed by many of the veteran 8th Army divisions, which now contained a mixture of nationalities including Indian, Poles, French, Italians and New Zealanders. We considered ourselves very unlucky in not being sent back to Blighty but, as we were part and parcel of the 8th Indian Division, we had to remain.

It was obvious that before long there was going to be an advance on the Adriatic side of Italy and that the main bottleneck of Cassino on the other side would have to be taken. During our period in the line, several battles had taken place between January and March 1944, in a vain attempt to break through the Cassino bastion. Both these battles involving the United States 5th Army and the British 8th Army were unsuccessful. In an attempt to bypass Cassino and thereby force the enemy to retreat for fear of being cut off, a seaborne force landed at Anzio about sixty miles north of Cassino. But they too were unable to break out of the seven mile bridgehead they had captured and were very fortunate in that they avoided being overrun and annihilated by the skin of their teeth. The Allied casualties were very heavy and they had to stay dug in on the beach until the break-out which did not occur until 23rd May.

Soon after this breakout, I met Bert Morley, an old Leyton friend of mine. He was with the Brigade REME workshop and he described to me how part of the company he was with had had to act as infantry. They had manned the perimeter trenches to allow the other part of the unit to carry out essential repairs on the guns and trucks to keep the brigade fighting. He reminded me that he was thankful for the infantry training we had both received back at Wivenhoe Park at the beginning of the war.

We remained in our comfortable farmhouse until late February when the division was stretched over a 20-mile front near Orsogna. We stayed like this for a couple of weeks to allow a complete regrouping of all the new units to take place as by now most of the British divisions had left. This fortnight seemed very eerie and we felt very lonely indeed for instead of being surrounded by a whole variety of our troops, as was usual in the forward areas, we were able to travel quite freely without any sign of other units. There was no shortage of farmhouses for us to occupy because there were so few troops in the area. There were also no soldiers of any kind between us and the enemy so we had to be very watchful in case any Germans decided to come across to try to capture some prisoners.

We used several minor roads to keep contact with the rest of the 53rd Field so I had to warn everybody to be extra cautious. Our maps were not very accurate and there had already been several instances when men had taken the wrong byroad and found themselves behind the enemy's front line.

We were beginning to think that the whole of Italy was made up of mountains when, in early March, the division moved across one mountain range and into another mountainous area on the west side of the Appenines. We had terrible troubles as we travelled along the narrow tortuous roads that Jerry had already devastated. Fortunately the weather began to improve and, apart from hearing the occasional shell and spotting a few enemy planes, we saw little actual combat. As always, the enemy's worst legacy was that of mines and booby traps. There were no set patterns to these devices which made everybody nervous.

We were finally pulled out of the line at the end of March. This was a godsend as the division had been in action without a break since landing at Taranto the previous September. We moved into the Benevento area, which was a small town about sixty miles south-east of Cassino. This was a picturesque, rural area and absolutely ideal for rest and recuperation. It was also a perfect tactical position as from here we could be sent to either front in the shortest possible time.

I did my best to allow the LAD some relaxation but we were exceptionally busy. We had to carry out a wide range of repairs that had not been possible to do whilst the regiment was in action. I also organised an inspection of every gun and vehicle in the unit and made a successful trip to the ordnance depot that was expanding at Naples.

From here I obtained a whole truckful of spare parts to replenish our own rapidly depleting stores, including a 25-pounder gunsight which, at that time, was certainly worth its weight in gold. I took Harry Beaumont with me, as he was the lance-corporal in charge of the LAD stores. He was absolutely overjoyed to be able to choose spares that we desperately needed and it once again taught me that in a bureaucratic system like the services, the personal touch achieved far more than a thousand official forms ever managed.

We had a great party at the sergeants' mess which was occupying a large barn that we had discovered. This was the first time in a long while that all the regiment's warrant officers and sergeants had been able to gather together so we used this opportunity to exchange many tales about our adventures and to drink a toast to all our missing comrades.

At the end of this fortnight's rest we were told by the CO that our next action was to be at Cassino. However, before the regiment moved, about twenty representatives from all the regiment's batteries and sections were to be taken on a visit to the battlefield to familiarise ourselves with the area and the plan of battle. I went along as the senior REME person.

As we approached Cassino all the signs of battle became apparent and a general air of despondency seemed to hang over all the troops in the area. Many people were of the opinion that the German position was impregnable and that after three tries there was little hope for our chances in what came to be known as the 4th Battle of Cassino. The monastery on the mountain dominated the entire valley and had a clear view of the whole flat plain for a distance of about twenty miles. Not even a mouse could scamper there without being spotted and shelled. In front of the monastery was the town and in front of the town was the Rapido River.

The part of the plain where our unit was to set up our guns contained a road which ran at right angles to the river, straight down the plain and right up to the destroyed bridge that had once spanned the Rapido. Our infantry was dug in by the river bank and the enemy was installed on the opposite side of the river. At that time it was quite a narrow river with little water running through so it did not appear to be a terrible obstacle, although boats were still required to cross the Rapido. In many ways the narrowness was a disadvantage because the Germans had a bird's eye view of whatever went on. The advance would thus have to begin with a river crossing against a very determined and well dug in enemy.

The job of the 53rd was to position our guns on either side of this road as near as possible to the river so that their range of fire was as extensive as possible. Our guns had to be invisible to the enemy and accompanied by all the stocks of ammunition required for the opening barrage of the battle on 11th May at 23.00 hours. All our preparations had to be done at night and in silence so that the enemy would be unaware that a thousand guns had moved into the area. The main tactical point was that of complete surprise and the enemy was to be lulled into thinking that no further attempt was planned to attack Cassino frontally.

The 53rd was to be brought about ten miles behind the line, into a field that was hidden by a fold in the ground. This was one of the few places that could not be observed from the monastery. We were to deploy the regiment in various stages from the holding position into battle stations.

We returned to the 53rd and prepared to move into our holding area. We were very busy on some last minute repairs at the LAD and, as was quite common, I missed a night's sleep. Then there was a change of plan and we had to move into position the following night so by the time the whole unit was in place I had not slept a wink for over forty-eight hours. As soon as my jeep arrived, I lay down on the grass and, quite oblivious to everything around me, immediately fell fast asleep.

The whole regiment was parked in this field for several days as we tried to camouflage the transport and the guns, dead scared that a stray enemy plane would spot our build up. All vehicles were forbidden to move during daylight and, as there was only the one main road leading down to the river, a strict rota system was in force. The 53rd was allocated four lorries, one for each of the batteries and one for the RHQ party. These lorries had to be at the entrance to the road at a given time which was controlled with clockwork precision by the military police. If a lorry was just a minute late it simply missed its place in the queue. Once on its way, the lorry would travel down the road, without lights and as quietly as possible. When it neared its position it would cut off the main road and cross the fields to its allocated battle position where the squad would unload camouflage nets, digging tools and cookhouse stores. Traffic was only allowed to travel towards the river, from dusk to 3 a.m., for fear of accidents, so from 3 a.m. to daylight the transport travelled back to the holding units. The squads that had been left at the gun positions rigged up camouflage and began to prepare the gun pits. It was absolutely imperative that by daylight no enemy observers should have any indication that gun positions were being prepared under their very noses. During the hours of daylight no soldier was allowed to emerge from under the nets for any reason whatsoever.

The build-up continued on the second, third and fourth nights when all essential stores and equipment were ferried into position, including the vast amounts of ammunition that had to be manhandled to the gun positions and prepared for firing.

17
Cassino

During the build-up to the battle of Cassino most of the regiment in the holding area had nothing to do during daylight. The usual exception was the LAD who were busy with a flow of minor problems. I don't think a single half hour ever existed when something did not go wrong with some vehicle somewhere.

During one lull when I was chatting with Tommy Yates, the RSM, and observing the regiment scattered across the field, he suddenly said, "There's something peculiar going on. I can feel it in my bones. Let's go and find out'

I had no idea what he was talking about but I followed him. He walked in a very odd manner, trying to look as unobtrusive as possible, as we passed along the side of a hedge. After a few minutes we cut through a sheltered path where, to my astonishment, we stumbled upon a line of about twenty soldiers, who were looking very sheepish indeed at being discovered.

'What the hell's going on?' Tommy roared.

There was a flurry in the bushes and, lo and behold, a female head appeared. This unfortunate lass turned out to be a local village girl who had unexpectedly found a method of making a fortune in a single day although, by the time we arrived, she looked a physical wreck! Tommy made sure that she was escorted a considerable distance away from our unit and issued terrible threats to her in case she had any ideas of returning or sending any substitutes. His final remark to me was, 'If she's poxed up, half the regiment's in trouble!'

The guns and crews finally moved into position on the night of 10th May so we all had to spend the following day as quietly as possible and without moving from under the cover of the camouflage nets. The big question we were all asking was whether Jerry had any idea of the preparations that had taken place. If he did, then we could well be in for some very unpleasant surprises. Only time would tell and meanwhile we received the usual message from the army commander saying how confident he was of a successful outcome to the battle.

There were about six vehicles that had been damaged by shellfire as they had travelled back and forth along the road to Cassino. These vehicles together with all their stores had been pushed onto the fields off the main road at the various spots where they had been hit. As we were anxious to retrieve them we were finally given permission to attempt their recovery on the night of 10th May and had about two hours in which to do the best we could. All the other transport had finished with the road at 5 a.m. and, although day break had begun it was very misty due to the low lying ground near the river. Since the visibility was poor for the enemy we were fairly safe to work in the area until about 7 a.m. when the sun would finally break through.

We had to use the jeep for this recovery attempt since the Germans systematically shelled the road at regular intervals. We were not allowed to take the breakdown lorry simply because it was far too visible. It was easy to tow most of these vehicles with the jeep's towrope but there was one nerve-racking job which we left to last. There was a Royal Corps of Signals jeep, full of radio equipment, which the Signals were most anxious to retrieve. It was sited only ten yards from the river and its rear axle differential had been damaged so it had to be removed by the use of a suspended tow. Naturally our recovery jeep did not possess any kind of crane or jib, so we decided to jack up the back of the RCS jeep, remove its rear wheels to prevent it from bumping on to the ground and attach it with ropes to the back of our jeep. We slowly moved off and eventually managed to crawl back to the LAD with the signals jeep.

Two of the other shelled vehicles, were so badly damaged that they had to be written off but we managed to patch up the other four and return them to action. All in all we were very pleased and considered that we had done a good job.

All the time we were working on this recovery we were in the midst of a well dug-in infantry platoon and every so often a burst of machine gun fire took place right under our noses. We were not at all popular with the infantry who kept telling us, in very impolite terms, to get the hell out of there before the whole Jerry artillery spotted us. We assured them that we were as anxious to get out of their way as they were to get rid of us!

During the day of 11th May, our artillery regiments produced the normal amount of routine shelling to convince the Germans that this day was no different to any other day. At exactly 23.00 hours the order *'Fire'* was given and the 4th battle of Cassino began.

For the next several days, amidst all the chaos that was around us, the LAD worked day and night. Most of my time was spent with the gun positions helping the troop artificers keep the guns firing. After a very short period the barrels of the guns became so hot that all their paint had completely burnt off. As always, there were a couple of guns that gave us the most trouble but at no time did any gun stay out of action for very long. The only exception to this was a

Robert battery gun that seemed to have suffered a direct hit from an enemy shell. Five of the six gun crew were killed instantly and the one survivor, a bombardier was wounded. I knew him well because he had been on the regimental headquarters Quartermaster's staff and had only been transferred back to a gun position about ten days beforehand. He was thus really unlucky to have been wounded but fortunate not to be killed.

It was my grisly task to evacuate the gun and examine it in preparation for giving evidence at the subsequent Court of Inquiry. However, before I could even begin this examination I had to tow it down to the river in order to wash off the blood and bits of human remains attached to it. We used makeshift brooms to clean it. Before sending it back through the chain of command to the workshops, I gave it a thorough examination at the LAD and, to my surprise, I discovered that it had not been struck by an enemy shell. It appeared that one of our own shells had exploded probably due to the speed of loading the gun, the next shell had been brought forward too fast and it had recoiled when it fired, hitting the fuse of the shell that the loader was holding in his hand. This was certainly the worst accident that happened to the 53rd Field, proving that no amount of training or experience could guarantee 100 per cent safety when dealing with explosives.

My conclusions were confirmed when, some weeks later, the Court of Inquiry heard my evidence and also when, a few months later, the wounded bombardier returned to the regiment and stated what had actually happened also blaming the speed with which they were trying to feed the gun with ammunition.

The 8th Indian Division reached San Gimignano by 19th May and Rocca Secca two days later where we were all delighted at the unexpected return of our own Corporal Bert France who had always been such an enormous help to the LAD and a first-class fitter.

My main problems were keeping track of the regiment's various sections and maintaining the LAD in what was a very chaotic and mobile situation. Most of the time I received hardly any instructions from above and had to use my own judgement regarding the best way to function. I had to decide what was not feasible owing to lack of spares and time and to assess how necessary the object was that we were trying to repair for the particular situation in hand. As always, we tried to do our best to assist anybody in trouble, irrespective to which unit they belonged.

I continued to make many more friends among the Indian soldiers, admiring their courage and cheerfulness under the most difficult circumstances. They always appreciated whatever assistance we were able to give to any of them and their gratitude was always expressed by the offers of cigarettes and very hot, very sweet tea. We never saw two Gurkhas standing by the side of the road unless they were brewing up a cup of tea and whenever we stopped to speak to them, they would inevitably grin as they immediately offered a welcome, refreshing drink of this tea. Whilst repairing their vehicles I would often have interesting discussions about history and politics with *havaldars* and *jemadars*. I was familiar with the usual British imperial view of India and its different types of people but it was fascinating to hear the point of view of the Indian himself, whether he be Hindu or Muslim. Little did I realise that before many months were to pass, these theoretical differences were going to explode in the sub-continent, creating a civil war as well as the splitting up of the old India as we had known it under the Raj.

The regiment crossed the River Melfa at the end of May and advanced against heavy resistance through to Varallo reaching Guarcino by 4th June. We then pressed on to Casola through some very difficult mountain terrain. Our first breakout of the Cassino position began to turn into a chase; never a rout but certainly a chase. From then on the speed at which we could advance to Terni, Spoleto and Foligno was decided by the enemy who were defending all possible strategic positions with small groups of men so well dug-in that they were difficult to attack and destroy. They had blown up the narrow roads and all the possible bottlenecks so the Royal Engineers were incessantly working to try to keep some sort of road open for our advance. There were certain spots where every vehicle had to be winched up a gulley to get through to the next part of the road. From a recovery point of view, life was almost impossible.

On 4th June we heard that the United States Army had entered Rome. This was followed, on 6th June, by the really big news that the Allies had invaded Normandy. At last, I myself began to see that the war could indeed possibly end fairly soon.

We moved continuously and were often the first Allied soldiers to have arrived along some of the rarely used sidetracks that led to some very isolated hamlets, villages and individual farmhouses. The inhabitants of this region lived such a quiet life that many of the children had never descended the mountains to visit the plains. At first we were greeted somewhat warily by the local people but, as was usual, we were soon made very welcome by the vast majority. My Italian had improved to such an extent that I was able to establish many friendly contacts with the help of an English-Italian dictionary which I had bought and carried with me everywhere, as did many of the other soldiers.

One day we reached a very remote farmhouse, near Assisi, where we were the first of the Allied soldiers to arrive. We were welcomed by the farm's owner who spoke English with a very Yankee-Italian accent. In his enthusiasm, he had covered the farmhouse door with a large number of flags to greet us; that they all depicted the stars and stripes did not matter. He told us that he had spent several years in the USA, had saved his money and returned home to buy this farm. He had been praying and waiting for the moment that the Allies arrived and didn't care at all that we were not the Americans; the fact that we spoke English was good enough for him. He had saved some very special bottles of wine for this historic moment and invited us all to have a party. We thought that this was a terrific idea so we agreed to settle ourselves into the ground floor of his farm. As we first had to complete our usual tasks we arranged for the party to take place that evening and also included in the invitation the Captain Quartermaster and our friends on his staff who were just down the road.

By 9 p.m. that evening there were about twenty-five of us sitting around the ground floor on our usual various makeshift beds. I remember making ourselves comfortable and the full box of vino bottles. The farmer's wife had done us all proud producing, as if by magic, a splendid selection of cakes and fruit. The party began and, as far as I was concerned, as it started – so it finished. Although we had some real expert drinkers amongst us, men that we used to call 'hollow legs', I was not one of this breed. On the few very special occasions when I had drunk too much I had always experienced difficulty in walking and talking but at least I had always known exactly where I was and what I was doing.

At this party, however, although I distinctly remember having my first drink of this special wine, I can recall nothing else until I awoke the following morning, fully dressed on my bedroll. I was in a dreadful state. I had obviously been sick and I had a splitting headache, generally feeling absolutely awful with the king of all hangovers. Everybody around me kept saying what a marvellous party we had all enjoyed and telling me how I had danced about and kept them all in stitches with the stories I had told. Apparently I had been the life and soul of the party. The only excuse I can make was that this vino must have been pure alcohol as it certainly took me about three days to recover. The very noise of our guns – the Germans had decided to join in at this time – was enough for me to make a firm resolve never to again drink so much and certainly not to trust Italian home-brewed vino!

Meanwhile the whole army was meeting with very stiff resistance in the Assisi/Perugia area. On the outskirts of Assisi I struck personal gold. Amongst some damaged buildings there was one whose sign contained a painting of a tobacco pipe, proclaiming that it was a pipe factory. I felt compelled to explore this ruin. Although it was practically derelict and had been evacuated, it still contained some machinery and boxes. In what was apparently the storeroom I discovered a box containing a stemless pipe which had not even been varnished or painted. However, on one of the lathes I found several part finished stems and suddenly, as far as I was concerned, the war could mind its own business; I was involved with my pipe. I promptly gathered some files, emery paper and sandpaper, married the pipe with one of the stems and produced a beautiful brand new Briar pipe. It actually lasted for several years and I even had a couple of new stems made for it years afterwards when I was back again in civvy street.

Assisi became one of my favourite Italian cities and contained some of my fondest memories. Everybody had been looking for a reason to visit Rome which had been very strictly put out of bounds since the last thing the army wanted was any trouble there. As there were no REME or Ordnance depots in Rome I couldn't find any of my usual excuses to visit the city.

Fortunately, our new Adjutant, Captain Squires, had dropped his pocket watch and felt lost without it. He gave it to me to see if I could do anything with it and, after fiddling about with it – more by luck than by judgement – I somehow succeeded in getting it working again. He was so delighted at this that, when I mentioned I was about to celebrate my birthday on 30th June, he gave me a one-day pass to Rome. The authorities had only just begun to let a very small number of soldiers into the city so I was thrilled to spend my twenty-fourth birthday seeing the eternal city for the first time.

The first place I made for was the main synagogue where I spoke to several Italian Jews. They told me about some of their miraculous escapes from the Nazis and it was really the beginning of the horrific stories we were all about to hear. These Italian Sephardic Jews were the first that I had encountered that spoke no Yiddish whatsoever but fortunately my Italian had progressed sufficiently to carry on conversations with them, admittedly with some difficulty. I joined in one of the daily services amongst many who had lost various close members of their families. I tried to give them as much hope as possible, because, with luck, I thought their missing relatives would be eventually released from captivity or emerge from wherever they were hiding in the still unconquered parts of Italy.

I was very amused to note that several of the pedlars selling holy trinkets on the steps of the Vatican wore small badges with a Magen David in their buttonholes.

When I returned to the 53rd there was somewhat of a lull in the fighting as far as our brigade was concerned because there was a reorganisation going on. We then advanced north of Perugia, circling Lake Trasimeno and crossing the mountains to Siena. By the end of July we reached Poggibonsi where I received a message to report immediately to a map reference where I was to meet the CO.

I found Lieutenant-Colonel Greenhalgh in a clearing off the main road. He was standing by a group of vehicles and he explained that these were the advanced mobile tactical headquarters of the

8th Army. The General Officer Commanding the group, Lieutenant-General Oliver Leese, and his top staff officers were also present. I was told that one of the White scout armoured cars had developed a problem and that, as there were no REME workshops within a hundred miles, my CO had offered the General the services of his LAD. Thank you very much, Bob!

The scout car was full of maps and radio equipment with two banks of three men sitting in two rows, each with a radio set. On examination we soon realised that the front wheel assembly was broken. The scout car was a ten wheeled vehicle and all of these wheels were driven which enabled it virtually to travel wherever a truck could go. Unfortunately on this particular vehicle there was no way of neutralising or bypassing the broken assembly on the front wheels which meant that without the acquisition of new parts it would be unable to travel on the road.

One of the red-tabbed officers told me that my unit had four hours to repair the scout car after which time they would have to transfer all its equipment on to an ordinary 3-ton truck. As this procedure would take about an hour, I had three hours to give them a firm yes or no.

My LAD carried no spares suitable for a White scout car which, being manufactured in the USA, was really a freak vehicle to be in the British army at all. However, we rapidly stripped down the front wheel assembly to discover, as we had suspected, that the main Timkin roller bearing had collapsed. Whilst we were working the car continued to be busily used by its occupants with a great deal of activity going on involving the radios, messages, discussions, pouring over a whole variety of maps and a lot of coming and going. It occurred to me that it resembled a film studio and had nothing at all to do with the real war to which we were accustomed.

The problem facing me was simple – it was the solution that was difficult. The half shaft holding the wheel was about 6 cms in diameter and the inner rim of the assembly housing would accept a bearing of 10 cms diameter. All I needed was a new roller bearing, 1" thick, with a diameter of 10 cms and a central hole of 6 cms across. I personally doubted whether such a component existed in the whole of Italy let alone having any idea where it could be acquired within the next hour or two. However miracles do sometimes happen so I sent Flynn on the motorbike back to a small town we had passed through about 15 miles away. When we had been there we had continued our usual practice of stopping at a couple of deserted engineering factories and garages to look for any useful tools or spares. I remembered that in one of the repair garages there had been a storeroom containing a number of spares that had appeared to be of no use to us; we could only carry a certain amount. I seemed to recall that this storeroom had contained a number of different kinds of bearings which I had just

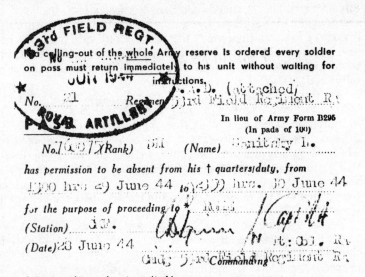

One day pass to Rome on my 24th birthday.

ignored. I gave Flynn the exact specifications of required bearing and told him to return as quickly as possible. On no account should he stay to argue with any Italians who might turn up for, although we normally never took anything from any occupied place, this was an emergency and to start issuing a note that one day the British Military Authorities would reimburse the part's owner was far too complicated.

Flynn returned after about an hour in a great flurry, making sure that he was seen to be the hero of the piece by all and sundry. By this time everybody on the army headquarters staff was very interested to see whether we were going to succeed in returning the White Scout car to action. Flynn dumped on to the ground a pile of assorted bearings out of his small haversack. Naturally I pounced on this pile and fortunately found one on which I could put a copper collar and bend round a circle to take up the slack on the shaft and on the housing. I prepared two strips of copper of about an inch wide, several inches long and about 5 mm thick and, by bending them into circles, then filing away to bring them down to the correct thickness, I managed to hammer the bearing on to the half shaft. When the bearing was sitting tightly, running freely

TO ALL DRIVERS IN M.E. COMMAND

M.E.T.P. No. 15 Instruction No. 13

COMBINED OPERATIONS— INSTRUCTIONS TO DRIVERS

The following, and **only** the following, jobs will be carried out immediately on landing:—

1. Remove sheet from radiator.

2. Clear breathers of hydraulic and air brakes.

3. Clear crank-case breather.

4. Clear clutch-housing breather.

5. Clear gearbox breather.

6. Clear axle breathers (front and rear).

7. Clear distributor breather.

8. Clear dynamo breather.

Serious trouble will be experienced if any of the above jobs are not carried out at the earliest moment.

The rest of the de-waterproofing may be carried out at any later period when operations permit.

(Signed) **J. S. STEELE**, *Maj.-Gen.,*
for Lt.-Gen.,
Chief of General Staff.

with my copper strip now acting as a distance piece, I put the second circle of copper into the housing of the assembly. The whole bearing on the half shaft all assembled to the wheel, then entered very tightly into the collar that I had made and inserted.

By this time we appeared to have an even larger audience watching us than that looking after the shop and taking care of the army. It was now all over bar the shouting. We assured the red-tabbed officers that the panic was over and well before they were ready to move off, the scout car's wheel was fully assembled. We were not able to test drive it, but it ran very freely. We had jacked up the wheel and it articulated in all directions as required. The footbrake worked beautifully and we knew that our repair was perfectly acceptable. We warned the driver to take it as easy as possible and to remember that the bearing was a little bit smaller on this wheel than the other wheels – and of a different make. He was instructed to take the scout car into a REME workshop at the first opportunity. Everybody was pleased – particularly our commanding officer – and we were offered our customary cup of char by the warrant officer in charge. He was an old regular soldier who normally did not have much time for temporary wartime warrant officers like myself. Secretly he thought the war was interfering with the proper work of the army and he was itching to get back to peacetime and the battles that only happened on Horseguards Parade.

For the next few weeks there was no stopping Craftsman Flynn. He told everybody who would listen, all about his exploits in saving the army headquarters and that he was expecting the arrival at any time of his Victoria Cross, along with his promotion to at least sergeant!

18
Wounded

Field Marshal Kesselring was now receiving reinforcements and was desperately strengthening his army in every possible way. He was banking on stopping the Allies at the Gothic Line between Florence and Rimini. Our division attacked on 25th August. By this time the regiment had become somewhat battle-weary with both the equipment and the men having taken severe poundings. We had been in action for quite a long time with only very short respites.

As I travelled along a small mountain road near to the coastal resort of Rimini, I came across a tank that had obviously broken down. I had to tell the tank commander that this sort of mechanical fault was completely beyond my capability and that it was necessary to arrange recovery facilities. As this was one of my periodic roams around the battlefield in search of spares, I was quite a distance from my own LAD so I told the tank commander that I would alert a tank recovery unit that I had previously called at and inform them that this tank required immediate action.

As I turned away around a corner, a jeep approached me and a red-tabbed staff officer flagged me down. He was a full colonel who wanted to know the whereabouts of this broken down tank and had recognised that I was a REME ASM from my badges of rank. I walked over to him, saluted him very smartly and said, 'Hello, Colonel Robson, sir, how are you?'

He looked at me in amazement and replied, 'Well I never, if it isn't Sanitsky!'

He was delighted to see me and very proud that one of his Leyton lads was now an ASM in the front line area. We chatted for at least an hour and I learnt that he was now a senior REME officer attached to the 8th Army. As he had only been in Italy for a few weeks I, as an old timer, was able to give him an enormous amount of information from the worm's eye view, which was very different from that which he had gleaned from his elevated position at army headquarters.

We spoke about the old days at Leyton and he enquired about Nat Stein's welfare. I was really elated when he said, 'I knew that I could rely on you two lads to do well.' He told me that we were going to have to manage with the equipment that we already had in Italy because the main theatre of war was now centred upon France. Our war, however important it was to us, was now a sideshow. I escorted him to the tank that needed attention, we shook hands and he wished me the best of luck in the future.

In the middle of September 1944 the 53rd Field, along with most of the other units in the brigade, was pulled out of the line for a rest and refit. We were taken back to a mountainous area north of a small town called Foligno. We were informed that we could expect a respite of about four weeks during which time we were to reorganise ourselves and bring the regiment back to its usual proficiency.

I tried to allocate the work to give all the men the opportunity of having as much spare time as possible whilst ensuring that we carried out all the routine inspections necessary. Everybody in the LAD was now very experienced at the cycles of events that we encountered when we were in action, pulled out or actually had some free time.

We were now in a very beautiful part of the mountainous countryside with absolutely perfect weather. As it was not possible to arrange any proper leave we did our best to keep everybody entertained within the facilities of the regiment and division. We had a mobile cinema, ENSA concert parties visits and we arranged a variety of our own impromptu concerts and sing-songs.

We were equipped with mobile shower units that included delousing units, the most unpopular one being a bath/shower facility which included a disinfecting unit. a Maze of screens was erected through which we walked in at one end, handed over every stitch of our clothing to somebody and then walked through the variety of showers that had been rigged up. Some of them contained warmish water, some cold water and some were laced with some mysterious disinfectant. By the time we emerged from the other side we were allegedly free from any foreign bodies. Our clothes were returned in a not quite dry state and for the next few days there was a terrible aroma around everybody. It reminded me of my childhood when large lumps of green carbolic soap had been a very common product.

I was fortunate in having the use of my jeep so, whenever it was possible, I roamed around the high mountains accompanied by either Tommy Sinclair or Terry Lewis or any of my other friends who happened to be off duty at the time. We found one small village that was so isolated that it could only be approached by a primitive cart track for the last two miles. It lay in a small plateau high on the mountain top. Many of the young people there had never been down to the bottom of the mountain and had spent all their lives never having seen a small town and all the modern facilities that one would have found in a small urban area. Due to its isolation the village had hardly seen any German soldiers during the occupation and had only met one other British soldier; a lieutenant who had probably accidentally found his way there and had stayed for about half an hour or so. We were really as great a novelty to the villagers as they were to us. Tommy and I were made extremely welcome and we visited them as often as possible, becoming especially friendly with a young miller and his wife. They taught us a great deal about the life-style of people living in remote mountain areas and we realised that even the violent political changes of Mussolini's Fascist government had had little effect on the lives of these people.

Their remoteness and the war situation meant that this village was completely without any kind of medication and, as a few of the children were suffering from simple illnesses, my friend Lance Montgomery gave us some basic remedies. The villagers were extremely grateful for these drugs and we were delighted that we actually managed to see a marked improvement in the health of these children during our stay in the area.

Lance himself was recovering from a broken arm which he had got just prior to the regiment leaving the battle area. A shell had landed directly on to the house that he was using as a casualty station and it had taken about four hours to rescue him along with three or four soldiers who had also been wounded. Fortunately this shell had caused no fatalities and Lance had escaped with nothing worse than a fractured arm.

As Colonel Robson had previously indicated, we were unable to acquire any new vehicles and only essential replacements of battle casualties were issued. There were no replacements available for vehicles which we considered to be only suitable for rear echelon duties so we had to work very hard to get these damaged vehicles fully repaired, doing the best we could with them.

The entire regiment, from the Colonel down, considered the 25-pounder gun to be the finest weapon that the war had produced. From a reliability point of view it was absolutely superb and from every technical aspect it was superior to the other famous gun of the war, namely the versatile German 88 mm. As an LAD, we managed to carry out all the necessary work on our 25-pounders without too much trouble despite the fact that many hundreds of thousands of rounds of ammunition had already been fired from them. I seem to recall that on one particular day the figure of one million rounds fired by the regiment since leaving home was mentioned.

To subsidise our vehicle numbers we had managed to pick up a few German light trucks which were small beetle-like cars. We had corrected those with minor faults and found them to be a very useful, unofficial addition to our establishment. We painted out the iron cross insignia of the enemy and painted in its place – usually on the top and on the sides – the Royal Air Force roundel which we hoped would identify it as now being British. It had been known, though fortunately not in our regiment, for some captured vehicles to be shot up and strafed by our own planes.

We also converted a few 15-cwt trucks in to two wheeled trailers. This was mostly done to vehicles whose front had been destroyed and we became very adept at removing the wheels and engines, then bending the chassis and welding on a towing eye. We bent the chassis inwards from a point just beyond the box structure where they joined as a 'V' and were able to weld it together, attaching the towing eye.

There was now a continual flow of replacements of both equipment and men. Major changes in personnel took place and many familiar faces began to disappear from the scene. The authorities considered that many of the soldiers had earned a rest and should be used for training purposes with some experienced soldiers being posted to other formations that had not yet seen action. The Adjutant had already been replaced and he was quickly followed by the major second-in-command. Many transfers and promotions now took place amongst the officers, the battery sergeant majors, senior NCOs and all the junior ranks with new officers and men arriving to bring us up to full fighting strength. I had to ensure that I became familiar with all the new personnel with whom I was going to have to deal.

Rodney Howe, the young major commanding Queen Battery, left the regiment at this time. He was the type that I had thought only existed in the imagination of Rudyard Kipling – a regular soldier from a military family of many generations, with many generals and senior officers amongst his forebears. I thought he was one of the finest men I had ever met and he was certainly the bravest, seeming to live an absolutely charmed life. There were several occasions when the rest of his observation party had been badly mauled yet he had escaped with minor cuts that never necessitated medical evacuation. I found talking to him to be very interesting as I tried to understand his whole point of view. He was being removed from the regiment against his own wishes and felt that as far as he was concerned the war was probably over. He was being sent home to go on a three-year course at the Staff College.

Rodney had been fully aware that during his stay with the regiment he would either be fatally injured or receive the battle experience and the Military Cross which he needed to advance his army career. He was happy to accept whichever way his fate decided although, in some respects, he seemed envious of the many fellow cadets of his year at Sandhurst who had remained and died with their regiments in what he considered to be a fitting manner for a soldier. It was expected, he told me, that a percentage of his class would be killed in battle, some would fail to cope with battle conditions in the manner that was expected of the top brass and the few that honourably survived would be removed from the war. This last section were destined to be the nucleus of the senior military people in the post-war period. In many ways I had to admire the long term view that had been taken by the War Office to ensure that they salvaged sufficient of their best people. Rodney was very sad at having to leave the regiment but there was nothing he could to to alter the decision. He made a point of going to each sub-unit to say goodbye to everybody and to wish us all the very best of luck.

I might add that almost everyone else in the regiment would have probably given his eye teeth for the opportunity to be out of the war and to return home. My attitude was similar to most of the others in that whatever we had to do we would approach in the most efficient way possible. We were not heroes and most of the time we were dead scared but there was a job to be done and we just had to get on with it. We would all have been delighted to have been posted to another part of the world where there was no fighting.

A few days prior to our departure I was called upon to give my opinions on the old subject of stripping down the guns in order to fly them over the mountains. Unfortunately I still had to report that even when stripped, the gun carriage was no lighter than the last time the subject had been discussed. During the meeting one very enthusiastic young officer asked whether it was feasible to saw the carriage in half and weld it together at the other side of the mountain range! I expect that this particular officer, with his imaginative ideas, probably got very far in his chosen profession, presuming he survived the war. It does, however, show how desperate they were to find ways to get across the mountains.

By mid-October we were back in the line in the mountains north of Florence. The autumn was fast approaching and the weather was deteriorating. I very quickly realised why the subject of flying the guns had been brought up again as it was pretty obvious that it was going to be one hell of a job getting them there by road. The staff officer that had coined the phrase, 'the soft underbelly of Europe' had patently never been anywhere near the positions we were in. He had probably done all his reconnoitering in the nightclubs of Rome and Capri in the golden pre-war days.

I was reminded on Rosh Hashanah and Yom Kippur when I received a personal message from the army commander. It wasn't just sent to me but was given to all the Jewish forces serving in the 8th Army. Lieutenant-General Oliver Leese sent us seasonal greetings and wished us the best of luck.

A variety of Jewish Palestinian units were now dotted around the 8th Army and their numbers were growing. In actual fact I did occasionally bump into some of these units in my travels and had always stopped for a chat with them. I had become very friendly with two sergeants from a Palestinian Royal Engineer Company

213

when I was in Rome and was told by one of the refugees that these sergeants had given them a great deal of assistance in their search for lost relatives.

The next period was one of heavy fighting in very difficult conditions as we crawled forwards across the mountains, yard by yard, capturing places like Borgo San Lorenza, Marradi, Brisighella, Faenza, Forli, Imola and on to Ravenna – which fell at the end of October. The German line was now firmly established just south of Bologna across Italy to Lake Comacchio on the Adriatic Coast. The regiment was widely dispersed over several mountain ridges so I had to spend much of my time travelling from the remote LAD position on one ridge to the sub-units scattered about on other nearby ridges.

The farmhouse that we had requisitioned was typical of the whole area with the exception that the locals apparently never ate potatoes. Instead they substituted chestnuts. Outside was an enormous barrel filled to the top with chestnuts. During the season the farmer and his family roamed the area picking up these nuts, like squirrels, and during the whole winter they cooked and ate them in the same way that other people consumed potatoes. This farmer and his family were a slightly different type of people, being very sturdy and strong, but we became very friendly with them and this added to our knowledge of the different kinds of Italian peasants.

When we had first arrived in Italy I noticed that many of the Italians were somewhat wary of our Indian troops so we were very pleased to discover that in the rural areas the Italian peasants all got on very well with Indians and I can recall no incidents where there were any problems between the two races. In fact several Indian troops applied for permission to marry Italian girls, but this was not allowed because the War Office had ruled that no British soldier was permitted to marry an ex-enemy national.

Although we did not realise it at the time, the next couple of weeks were to mark another full stop for the 8th Army as we had reached the second winter line. By now General Alexander had only 17 divisions and the Germans had 23 with the assistance of the four Italian divisions. The next assault was being organised but did not take place until the beginning of the following April.

On the morning of 1st November Harry Beaumont handed me the normal bunch of papers consisting of regimental orders, new modification sheets for our equipment and the daily vehicle and gun situation reports from each of the sub-units. Various other documents were included, the usual sundry bumph that came through each day and oiled the machine that the military required for it to operate properly. Amongst this last section of papers was a copy of the latest 8th Army General Routine Orders which provided information that the authorities thought should be widely circulated. When I had a moment to spare I would glance through them to see if there was anything of special concern to me. On this day I was very interested to read that a Jewish Brigade Group was being formed and would be joining the 8th Army. The personnel of the brigade would consist of units that were already in existence but further Jewish soldiers would be allowed to volunteer for this newly formed brigade. The only stipulations were that a suitable vacancy had to exist in the new brigade's establishment and that the commanding officer of the applicant's own unit had to sanction the transfer.

I had been regularly receiving a news-letter for Jewish soldiers, which was edited by Sergeant Sidney Palace whom I had met at one of the synagogue services I had attended. Sidney was with the office of the Jewish Chaplain at 8th Army Headquarters and I found his newsletters very intriguing as they were the only way I could learn about both local and worldwide Jewish matters. These newsletters had already provided me with some very disturbing reports of the deliberate murders of innocent Jewish civilians from the occupied territories.

It seemed to me that since so many of my old friends had been posted, this was the ideal opportunity for me to take part in something that was obviously going to be a landmark in Jewish history. I had always got on very well with all the Palestinian personnel with whom I had come into contact at their depots where I had tried to obtain spares or services, both in the Middle East and in the CMF. It therefore did not take me long to make up my mind to apply. Following the old Sanitsky family motto, 'No sooner said than done'.

I made a point of talking to Terry Lewis who, being the regimental chief clerk, was the first person I had to notify in order to make my transfer request official. He promised that he would pass on my request to the Adjutant and through to the CO, the moment these two officers were free. He kept his word and on the next day I received a message saying that the Colonel would see me that very afternoon, after I had completed my other business at regimental headquarters.

I explained my reasons for wishing to join the Jewish Brigade and he was very understanding, although I do not suppose he had met more than a few Jews in his life. He paid me several compliments about my three years with the 53rd Field Regiment and ended by assuring me that he would instruct the Adjutant to signal the proper channels without any delay, recommending my transfer. He would personally see that a very good reference went with my papers. I thanked him profusely and told him that I would be very sorry to leave the regiment.

I had no idea when or even if this transfer might happen. There may well have been no opening in the new brigade for a WO1

„Habe ich Sie hier nicht schon
vor zwei Jahren gesehen?"

UMSONST

Vom Dnjepr bis zur Wolga — das war ein langer,
blutiger Weg. Heute stehen die deutschen Heere
wieder an ihrem Ausgangspunkt.

Alle Opfer waren umsonst

Die Hunderttausende von Toten, die zwischen Dnjepr
und Wolga liegen, haben weder den Ostraum erobert
noch die russische Offensive aufhalten können. Die
Russen sind im Vormarsch. Der Weg von Stalingrad
an der Wolga bis nach Kiew am Dnjepr, den die Russen

British Propaganda pamphlet to the enemy.

sergeant major in the establishment and, for all I knew, they could already have ten REME ASMs too many. Also, knowing only too well how army bureaucracy sometimes functioned, I would not have been surprised if the war ended before my transfer came through. I therefore put all thoughts of transfer out of my mind, as I returned to my small part of the war and the various jobs that needed my more immediate attention.

Although the CO had told me that it was very common for early winter snow to fall without warning in the high mountains, the weather remained pleasantly sunny and fresh and we did not find it necessary to wear anything heavier than pullovers. We did not realise just how deceptive the climate was for when the snow did suddenly fall, all the narrow tracks became merged into the landscape. Thus divisional headquarters issued orders that all vehicles had to be moved down to within a very short distance of the only road through the mountains. This road would then be kept operative whatever the weather and circumstances.

When I was instructed to move the LAD to the small town of Marradi, I realised that Marradi and its vicinity were going to be bulging at the seams. Therefore, the quicker we moved the better chance we would have to claim suitable cover. This was especially important as there was a distinct possibility that our next position could actually become our winter base, where we would remain for a considerable length of time.

On 3rd November we moved from our mountaintop farm to find ourselves some suitable space down in the town. It appeared that everybody had had the same idea as me because already some parts of Marradi were jammed solid with vehicles, guns, military equipment and very many soldiers. We managed to find ourselves a niche by the railway yard just off the road at Marradi Station. There was some flat space here which gave us our necessary hard standing so we parked our vehicles by the railway track and swiftly set up shop so that we could act as a breakdown service for the whole vicinity.

Billeting was difficult but we managed to occupy the semi-basement of an abandoned house further down the road. Since there was quite a distance between our work site, our vehicles and our place of rest, we had to devise a rota in order to guard our stores and equipment. Each site required a permanent twenty-four hour guard because there was always the possibility of enemy infiltration which could create havoc if Marradi was not sufficiently protected.

On 5th November I had to attend Robert Battery to deal with various problems, one of which concerned a temperamental gun. I managed to solve this problem and returned to the LAD later that afternoon. When I asked Harry Beaumont what had occurred during my absence he told me that a Bedford water truck had come in for urgent repair. These water trucks were my number one priority because whilst any other vehicle could be temporarily replaced, there was no suitable substitute for a vital water truck. Should a water truck be out of action, it created an enormous problem for the Quartermaster who would then have to rustle up cans with which to ferry water to the sub units.

I joined the capable Bert France who was already working on the engine, and he explained that the core plug on the rear of the cylinder block was leaking. As I leaned over the engine to asses the seriousness of this leak and whether or not it could be temporarily plugged, the Germans began shelling. They must have known that we were evacuating our mountain sites because there were plenty of local Italians who would have been informants so, from the German point of view, this was an excellent opportunity to destroy many vehicles and soldiers who were now confined in such a small area. At the same time the enemy could block the only supply route.

The Germans used the 88mm multi-purpose gun which was ideally suited for firing over mountain tops and into the valleys below. Bert and I heard the characteristic sound of these shells coming towards Marradi and then we heard them land.

I remember seeing a violent flash and the smell of cordite burning. Strangely, I do not recall hearing a noise; in fact everything went very quiet. Suddenly I realised that I was lying on the road with Bert sprawled across me. A shell had landed some five yards away from us.

I was stunned. I looked down at my legs because I could feel nothing in my right leg. I saw that one of my rubber boots, the right one, had been ripped apart and there was blood trickling over my numb leg. 'That's funny,' I thought to myself, 'I've been wounded.'

There were some small holes on the right sleeve of my shirt – I had not been wearing a jacket – and parts of my face were stinging, presumably from where the blast had thrown up pieces of stone. Bert had a head-wound and was unconscious. For the moment I did not know what to do. I tried to stand up but found that only my left leg was operative. Then I removed my shirt and wrapped it round Bert's blood-smeared head.

The shelling continued. About 15 yards away I saw two soldiers alight from their jeep to take shelter in a ditch. I called across to them, 'Come over here and help me with this corporal!'

I had to yell a couple of times before they responded for they were rather nervous, even though no more shells seemed to be landing near us. With their help I managed to hop into the jeep and they lifted Bert on to the back seat where I held him in my arms.

I instructed them to drive half a mile straight down the road to the medical aid post. The driver was extremely jittery and I had to keep telling him to stay calm or else we would all suffer further injuries. When we reached the RAMC post, which was a large house standing in its own grounds, some orderlies came out, lifted Bert on to a stretcher and took him away. I felt no pain but was obviously in some sort of state of shock. I was not afraid, I just had a leg devoid of feeling so I attempted to dismount from the jeep. Suddenly I found myself being lifted by two more orderlies who also placed me on a stretcher.

'Take it easy, Sergeant-Major,' I remember them saying. 'We'll take you in to the doctor.'

I was taken into an annexe where a male nurse gave me an injection of morphine. Within a minute or so one of the doctors arrived to examine me and said, 'You'll be fine. We'll take you into surgery as soon as we are free. We'll remove the shrapnel from your leg, clean you up and do whatever is necessary.'

By this time some feeling was returning to my leg and some sort of reaction began to set in. Once the initial trauma was over, I began to realise exactly what had happened but the effects of the morphine were very strong and I was in a very drowsy state. I kept badgering the male nurse, 'How is Bert?' and I remember asking the doctor, 'How is my corporal?' but all they would say was, 'Don't worry. Everything is being done.'

A few minutes later some more casualties arrived including the Company Sergeant-Major of the Royal Engineer Detachment who was a friend of mine. We lay side by side on stretchers awaiting operations on our wounds. His was a chest injury and he was in considerable pain. The surgeon heard us talking and asked me, 'Are you all right? Would you mind if your friend went into the theatre first?'

I said, 'Be my guest,' for by this time I was in a suspended state of mind and practically asleep.

After a while I was taken into the theatre which appeared to be situated in the hallway of a large house. I remember that there were two operating teams working and, as they carried me in, I could see one medical team operating upon my friend. This did not upset me as the drugs had completely calmed me down and I remember looking with mild curiosity at them carrying out this operation. Within seconds of being placed on the table I was unconscious.

I awoke some time later to discover that I was lying on a stretcher in a room with several others also on stretchers. I had various dressings about my body and my leg was completely swathed in bandages; yet I felt fine. Oddly enough I was starving and, when one of the male nurses came over to me to ask how I felt, I replied that I felt all right but would like something to eat. He told me that as it was the middle of the night it might be rather difficult but he would see what he could find in the kitchen. A few minutes later he returned with, of all things, a bully beef sandwich and a cup

THE VICTORIAN FORCES NEWS.

(Formerly The Victorian Soldiers' News formerly The Victorian being the News Sheet of the Victoria Boys' Club, Fordham St., New Rd., E.1)

War Issue No. 16.   MARCH 1944.

EDITORIAL.

To the casual observer it would appear that Victoria has been having a quiet but steady winter. Considering the increase in the frequency & severity of air raids on London, activities both indoor & outdoor have been quite well supported, but the casual observer would not have noted any outstanding success or spectacular event which would make the winter of 1943/44 live in the Club's history.

Yet inside the Club one important change has taken place; one, which may well prove to be of great significance in the years to come. The Victoria Intermediate Club has been revived.

For some time the senior members of the Boys' Club had wanted more independence & more say in the running of their Club. During 1943 a few old boys were invalided out of the services. It was not surprising that on their return from the services, they wished for a self-governing Club.

Before the war the experiment of having an Intermediate Club—a self-governing Club for fellows of 17-22 years of age—had been a great success. The writer, who had been the last Chairman of the Inter-Vics before the war, had always looked forward to the day when the Club could be revived.

The new Inter-Vics, who welcome members up to 25 years old, have not yet "Set the Thames on Fire." It is too much to expect that they would. As long as the war lasts most members of the age group for which the Club provides should remain fit & serve in the forces & the Club's membership must be comparatively small.

Under the energetic leadership of their Chairman, Algy Samuels, & their Hon. Sec. "Ginger" Harris, the Club is, however, making progress & the 2 functions they

News from the boys' club in Fordham Street, received in Italy.

of milk. I quickly devoured the sandwich, drank the milk and promptly fell back into a deep sleep.

I awoke to find that I was being lifted into an ambulance and told that I was to be taken to Florence, twenty miles across the mountain. There I would be seen by the military hospital people who would decide whether to detain me there or transfer me elsewhere. At this point I began to shout at the orderlies demanding to see the doctor and refusing to leave until I knew about the condition of my corporal. The orderlies were somewhat startled because, having been a sergeant-major for a number of years, I knew how to make men do exactly what I desired. Even though I was on a stretcher my voice was perfectly capable of being heard at a great distance. One of the orderlies fetched the doctor who wanted to know what all the fuss was about. When I told him that I would not leave until I knew about Bert he said, 'I am very sorry to tell you that Bert France was dead on arrival at the hospital.'

I was devastated.

I let them lift me into the ambulance and we began our journey to Florence. The ride was very bumpy for the road had been shelled and repaired time and time again and it took us ages to reach our destination of Florence airport. Here a team of doctors examined and assessed the casualties as they came through from the front. Most of the casualties were put on aircraft and flown to the South of Italy where there were many military hospitals away from the war zone.

A South African doctor examined me and he noticed that the journey had caused my leg to bleed considerably. The bandages around it were completely bloodstained. 'We'd better keep you here for a few days,' he said, 'Don't worry, you'll be fine, we'll look after you.'

I was then driven a short distance to the South African hospital which was housed in a huge building that had only just been taken over. To my surprise, I found that I was the only patient in the 600-bed hospital. One of the coloured South African nurses told me that the hospital had just arrived from South Africa and I was its first customer!

The doctor then told me that although the shrapnel had already been removed from my leg, the wound had not been stitched. The idea was to keep the wound open for some days to ensure that there was no infection. Once everything was in order, it would be stitched but, for the moment, I was to go into the theatre to have the wound cleaned and the bandages replaced by fresh ones.

Some while later, I found myself lying in a very comfortable bed with a view of what seemed to be an enormous hallway containing what appeared to be a couple of hundred empty beds awaiting casualties.

I was visited by a woman from the South African WVS who offered me chocolate, cigarettes and something to read. I was delighted to get some reading material and very happy with the chocolate. I told her that although I did not smoke cigarettes, both my pipe and pouch had remained in my pocket, so I asked her if she could possibly find me some tobacco. She soon returned with a large box containing about 100 half pound packets of Afrikaander tobacco! 'This is ridiculous,' I said. 'I don't want all this!'

'That's all right,' she replied. 'You keep it, we've tons more!' I then requested some notepaper to write to my mother. The WVS lady promised to post my letter immediately – and she most certainly did. I was later delighted to discover that my letter informing my mother that I was wounded but well, arrived home an hour before the official telegram.

After a few days I was returned to Florence Airport along with all my possessions: my pipe, my pouch and this huge box of Afrikaander tobacco! (The rest of my kit had been left behind. My trousers had been cut away by the first hospital and my shirt had been destroyed.) About eight of us on stretchers together with three or four walking casualties boarded a Dakota and were flown to Naples where we were transferred to one of the base hospitals.

I was in the 70th British General Hospital which was spread among many buildings over a wide area. The General Orthopaedic section occupied a pre-war nunnery overlooking the main entrance to the excavated ruins of Pompeii. The standard joke amongst us patients was that there were more ruins within the hospital walls than outside in the ancient city.

Most patients slept in two-tier bunks to get the maximum number of men in the space available. Whilst confined to bed and in need of medical treatment, we lay on lower bunks but as soon as we were able to walk we were allocated to one of the upper berths. I was informed that there were about 100 soldiers in this ward but, as I was confined to a lower bunk situated in the corner of a side passage, my vision was limited. All I could see was the few beds surrounding me. I soon became acquainted with the people in my immediate vicinity even though I did not see their faces until I was able to walk. I had to rely on those soldiers who were mobile for all the ward gossip.

Here the ward sisters were females and held the rank of lieutenant. There were very few nurses and a great number of soldiers so there did not seem to be any romances going on. I was told that the nurses were more interested in working on the officers' wards where romance might be more profitable! As the sisters did not consider that they should do any menial tasks, most of the donkey work was done by RAMC orderlies or patients who were pressed into service as soon as they were considered fit enough.

Price **2d.**

Information
FOR JEWISH SERVICE PERSONNEL

AUTUMN 1944/5705

LIBERATION AT LAST ?

The war news is truly exhilarating. Paris, Bukarest, Brussels—are some of the landmarks on the road traversed. One is glad to think that in all the glorious advance of the armies of the United Nations the Jews are playing their full part. One reads with pride of Jews fighting in the underground movements of France and Poland as well as with the Yugoslav Forces under Marshal Tito. It is good to know, too, that the first Soviet detachments in sight of the German border—and likely to cross it—are commanded by a Jew, General Cherniakhovsky. To our great sorrow, however, the towns and villages liberated by the Red Army have been cleared of Jews. The Jewish centres of Minsk, Vilna, Bialystok and Lublin are one vast graveyard of the Jewish people. Only few, who were hiding, survived.

The Great Powers acted too late to save the remnants of the Jews of Poland. The fate of ¾ of a million Jews in Hungary is still in the balance. Here again few have managed to get out into relative safety or still better into the haven of the Jewish National Home.

We had better understand, before it is too late, that even the defeat of Hitlerism will not solve the Jewish problem. Not only is anti-Semitism unlikely to perish from the earth overnight, but the Jewish people as a whole will still be homeless, even though Democracy has won; and the remnants of the Jewish people in Europe will be homeless in more than one sense. They will be uprooted in every sense of the word. Are new efforts to be made in order to recreate what may well be an untenable position—or should not all the available energy go into establishing a secure home for all those who need Palestine or wish in the only land they can call collectively their own?

The eyes of Jewish youth, and of young Jewish men and women in the Forces in particular, turn to the Land of Israel. British Jews, as well as nationals of other Allied countries, wish to join actively in the building of the Jewish State. They wish to have a share in the constructive achievements in agriculture, industry and science of the reborn Jewish people.

The problem of Palestine has recently come very much to the fore. The two great political parties of the U.S.A. demand the opening of Palestine to unrestricted Jewish immigration and the establishment of Palestine as a Jewish Commonwealth. The Labour Party of Great Britain has put forward

News from home, published and circulated by the Association of Jewish Ex-Servicemen.

There were separate wards for commissioned officers but warrant officers and NCOs were mixed in with all the other ranks. We were all treated equally although great care was taken by RAMC personnel to address all patients by their correct rank so we were never allowed to forget that we were in a military hospital. For my confined-to-bed period I was able to ignore all this nonsense and became friendly with the chaps in my vicinity.

The occupant of the bed above me was a South African. He had apparently been shot in the foot but was well on the way to recovery. He told me that as a result of this injury he would always walk with a limp but what he did not say was that there was a sign on the front of his bed, in red paint on a white background, which said SIW. After he had been discharged from the hospital he was to be sent to a military prison to await a court martial. SIW, in military parlance, is the abbreviation for self-inflicted wound.

One of the other patients told me, that in a moment of desperation the South African had shot himself. As I was quite friendly with him I asked him to explain what had happened. He was quite willing to discuss it with me, freely and frankly admitting that he had lost his nerve in a difficult moment, panicked and aimed his rifle at his foot.

He was a fascinating character and I had several interesting discussions with him; after all there was very little else to do. He was a man of quite normal intelligence who had been subjected to violent Afrikaaner nationalistic propaganda for the whole of his life. He came from a small South African village where he had hardly ever spoken to anybody who differed from him in either political or religious views. I doubted whether in his whole life, he had ever spoken to a black or coloured South African, other than to give them an order. He was so indoctrinated that he became quite hysterical when a wounded, coloured soldier was brought into the ward and placed in a nearby bed. As the orderly could not quieten him a medical officer was summoned and he was moved to an isolated corner of the ward where his outbursts could disturb no one. It seemed incredible to the rest of us that any soldier who had shot himself as an act of cowardice could have the nerve to object to the presence of a black fellow countryman who had been seriously injured by a mine. Within a day or two of this incident, he was removed from the ward and things returned to normal.

I was kept fairly comfortable and treated with a variety of medicines. After a few days the marks on my face began to heal and I was told that it was considered unnecessary to operate on my right arm as any tiny splinters would eventually either work their way out or never bother me. As my arm felt perfectly all right and my face was healing I was quite happy with this diagnosis. My leg was examined on several occasions and on the fifth day the orthopaedic surgeon told me that he considered it to be safe from infection. I once again went to the theatre where my leg was cleaned and this time the wound was sewn up.

The orthopaedic MO was a Londoner, about twenty-eight years old. In one of our discussions he told me that he had gained more experience during his one year in Italy than he reckoned he could have acquired in a lifetime at Bart's Hospital where he had been trained and usually practised.

My only complaint was that my leg was stretched out with my foot laid flat on the mattress. As the muscles had been sewn in this position I had trouble straightening my foot. When I began to walk it looked as though I was moving sideways because my foot was at right angles to my leg, and only slowly moved into the normal position.

About three days after the operation I began to feel some burning sensations in my leg and was given a course of M & B tablets as a precaution against infection. Fortunately they seemed to be effective and the burning sensation disappeared. Penicillin had just arrived at the hospital but the only time I saw it used was on a soldier who had crushed his finger after an accident with the breech of a field gun. His finger had become infected and, as a last attempt to save it, a rubber sheath was placed around the wound and injected with penicillin. When the gunner waved his finger we could see the penicillin liquid sloshing about in it. Unfortunately this remedy was not effective and the poor man had to have the finger amputated.

I was pleased when I began to receive some mail which was being redirected by Bill Langley, our friendly postal bombardier at the 53rd Field. He included a very welcome letter which contained everyone's good wishes plus all the latest gossip from Tommy. The really ironic news was that on 5th November, the very day I was injured, my transfer to the Jewish Brigade had come through and I had been supposed to leave the regiment on the 6th. That's fate.

Once the stitches had been removed my leg began to heal satisfactorily. I then received regular daily massage and exercises. I hobbled around on crutches for several days but soon found I could manage with just a stick.

Once, when I crossed the corridor to the storeroom to get my hospital blues, I bumped into none other than the old RSM, Jim Burrows, who was now a lieutenant. We had a long conversation about old times and he told me that he was at the hospital awaiting a Medical Board. He was very worried that they might downgrade him as he was having trouble with an old leg injury he had received years ago in India. As a regular soldier, this was the last thing he wanted, for it could halt his career prospects and wreck his chance to serve out his time, perhaps with luck, as a captain.

My next promotion was my elevation to an upper bunk, although I had to be quite a Tarzan to manoeuvre my way on and off it with only one fit leg and a stick. Now that I could walk around the ward I began to become acquainted with more of the patients. Some were very badly wounded, some were amputees and some had large parts of their limbs missing. Most of the wounds looked dreadful, being left open to the air to heal yet it was truly amazing how friendly and cheerful everybody was. The spirit was fantastic; I suppose we all felt a terrific sense of relief at being out of immediate danger and not having to face another cold, wartime winter.

One afternoon, as I walked through the ward, I was astonished to see no other than Len Mellows, one of the Victoria Club stalwarts. He held the record of being the first Old Victorian to be sent overseas to the British expeditionary forces in France. He was sitting by a bed and nearly fell out of his chair in surprise. He was visiting one of his brother's friends, Morris Leventhal, and although I had said hello to him in passing, I had no idea either that he was a Jewish soldier or that we had any mutual friends. Once again I realised what a small world we live in.

There was a hospital ship going to Britain in a convoy and many soldiers were to be sent home for treatment and rehabilitation; it was pot luck as to who might receive a berth. The very serious cases had first claim and the list worked down to the lesser wounded. For a few hours I was a standby for a place on this ship, but my luck was out and the ship was filled before reaching down to my name. However, I certainly did not envy any of the men that were going home. I had no wish to change my healing wounds for those of the more seriously wounded. This, to me, was a great consolation for not being selected.

After many of the wounded had set sail in the hospital ship, the ward seemed to be half empty but it gradually began to fill up again as newly injured patients arrived and the normal routine continued. I felt well enough to take a short walk, using my stick, and to go outside the hospital. So, with a friend, I crossed the road to visit the ancient remains of Pompeii. I did not see many ruins for the visit was somewhat marred for me when I passed a line of eight blind soldiers. They walked in single file, led by an orderly and each man had stretched out his arm holding the shoulder of the man in front. They were laughing and chatting to each other as though this excursion was the most normal thing in the world. They displayed such incredible spirit and fortitude that it made me feel extremely thankful to be alive and in one piece. Naturally I overdid my walking on the first occasion that I was let out and had to return to bed for the next two days in order to recover. However, this was only a small setback and I soon started to walk without my stick.

One evening I was invited to a party at the RAMC sergeant's mess. After talking to several of the corps, I began to realise some of the difficulties that they faced. Many of the wounded soldiers seemed to consider that the RAMC consisted of shirkers, men too scared to enter the fighting areas. This attitude was greatly resented by the RAMC who were all highly trained and very hard-working men, doing a vital job. Nevertheless, some friction between the hospital staff and the patients was inevitable.

The powers that be wished to have as few patients as possible in hospital over the Christmas period. The ward sister thus informed me that I was to be transferred to a convalescent depot where they would continue to give me the same daily treatment. It would be much more comfortable, she said, with a far better atmosphere than it was possible to provide in a busy hospital. I then had to spend several hours at the Stores collecting an entirely new kit and was totally re-equipped from top to toe. The one exception was a sidearm which, I was told, would be issued to me prior to leaving the convalescent depot.

On the day before my departure I was interviewed by the RAMC commanding officer along with my orthopaedic surgeon and the ward sister. My medical papers were discussed and the CO explained to me that all my wounds had healed satisfactorily. He had no doubt that by the time I was discharged from the depot I would once again be perfectly fit. However, as I had lost part of my leg muscle I would probably suffer from something called 'intermittent claudication' which could mean that any undue exercise would cause me to limp and I could also be subjected to leg cramps. A decision regarding my medical downgrading from the A1 rating that I had previously held, would be taken by the medical officers before I was discharged from the convalescence depot.

The CO then asked me whether I had been satisfied with my entire medical treatment and in particular with the attention I had received at this hospital. As I felt well and had received nothing but help and kindness from everybody, I said so and thanked them all very much. I was then surprised to be asked to sign a paper to this effect, especially as it contained a space on which I was invited to list any complaints. I later discovered that a question had actually been asked in Parliament following some complaints from several wounded men concerning their army medical treatment in Italy. Consequently, the top brass of the medical corps were very nervous and were now trying to cover themselves should any investigations take place.

On the morning of 23rd December I toured the ward, said cheerio to the patients and staff and exchanged best wishes with everybody for a speedy recovery. There was one last minute hitch caused by the fact that I did not have any badges of rank. The stores had contained plenty of stripes and crowns but no WO1 badges. The corporal storeman was so determined to send me off properly attired, that he had driven to a nearby RASC depot where he managed to obtain for me a spare badge from the resident RSM. Correctly attired I, together with three other soldiers, was taken

Dinner

Grapefruit or Orange Juice

Cream of Tomato Soup

Roast Turkey : Bread Sauce

Chestnut Stuffing

Roast Pork : Apple Sauce

Sage Stuffing

Roast Potatoes

Savoury Potatoes

Cauliflower : White Sauce

Green Peas

Xmas Pudding

Cognac Sauce

Devil on Horseback

Cheese : Water Biscuit

Coffee

Christmas menu 1944, signed (see verso) by my fellow patients.

S. Banks (Gunjie)

W.J. John. ("Somerset" alias "Swede")

J. Baxter Sgt.

W.A.Cole. Will... P&P. Rew...

V. L. Neal (R. N.) PO

W.J. Mummo (1st London Scottish) Sgt

F. J. Murphy Sgt (Never to old to learn)

No. 7 CONVALESCENT DEPOT

WOs. and Sgts. MESS

CHRISTMAS
1944

on a short truck ride to a tented camp on the south side of Naples. The sign at the entrance gate proclaimed, 'No 7 Convalescent Depot CMF.' I very soon discovered that this was a far from happy place and that the spirit of comradeship at the hospital had completely disappeared. There seemed to be several reasons for this, as far as I could tell. One was that it was commanded mainly by reservists, who were completely unsuitable to be in charge of this sort of camp. It was one of the rare instances when the army personnel system seemed to have failed; square pegs had been inserted into round holes.

Although a Southern Italian camp site was probably wonderful in the summer, it was far too cold and wet to be suitable for a convalescent base in the autumn and winter, being entirely under canvas. By the time I arrived there was open warfare between the convalescents and the permanent staff. As a large percentage of the patients were liable to go straight back to the forward areas they had no compunction at telling the staff exactly what they thought of them, openly inviting charges of insubordination. They would then refuse the OC's punishment and opt for a trial at a higher court where they could publicly air their grievances. The CO and the CSM had the intelligence to deny them this opportunity by refusing to put people on charges. Everybody in the camp was fully aware that the MP who had asked the question in Parliament about the hospital services, had also asked several questions concerning Italian convalescent depots and that No 7 had been especially picked out as his main target. No wonder the atmosphere was somewhat unpleasant.

I shared a tent with the Regimental Sergeant-Major of the Naples District Military Police who was recovering from a bad case of malaria. Physically he reminded me of a rather unpleasant MP RSM I had previously met at forward army HQ but he was, in fact, a kind, intelligent and thoughtful man whose major concern was for the men that he dealt with. It once more taught me never to judge a person by appearances or by preconceived ideas.

We managed to scrounge an oil heater and were fairly comfortable in our tent. As always the cooks pulled out all the stops for Christmas. We had the complete works on Christmas Day and the cook went to a great deal of trouble, even to the extent of getting somebody at the nearby Service Corps depot to print the menus. There were only seven members in the WOs' and sergeants' mess – which was a 180 lb tent specially allocated for the purpose – and one of these was a Royal Navy Petty Officer. He was amongst us soldiers because the Navy did not possess a convalescent depot. Everybody seemed to enjoy the festivities and even the camp OC and the CSM thawed out somewhat.

At my final medical examination I was told that my medical downgrading would not make me eligible for return to the United

Kingdom. I told them not to bother to alter my medical status from A1 as my job in the REME did not include any long marches. By the third week in January I was feeling very fit and was the only mess member remaining. Consequently I was not at all sorry to move on to the REME holding camp at Naples.

This holding camp was a no nonsense unit, mainly used for new REME arrivals. They were normally given a week to get their land-legs and recover from the voyage before being posted to whichever unit they had been allocated. The REME camp was actually one section of a much larger camp where all the different units had their own record offices through which any posting of personnel was directed. The entire camp was sited only a short distance from the Naples docks and a huge billboard had been erected outside it to make sure that every new arrival read its message. The sign was the size of a large house and its message was painted in large red letters upon a white background; it read, 'Beware, Virulent Venereal Disease In This Area'.

When I arrived at the holding camp the major in charge told me that he was expecting about fifty new REME officers to arrive within a day or two. As they would be completely green, he asked me to give them some lectures on my experiences concerning life in Italian battle areas. Apparently this was his usual method of occupying officers whilst they were in his camp. As his request was merely a diplomatic order, I had no choice but to accept.

I was allocated three one-hour lecture spots which I found a very novel experience. I turned the lectures into a question and answer period by saying that if there were any questions they would like to ask or any information they wished clarified, I would do my best to provide answers. To my astonishment the queries came thick and fast and I was quizzed about events that went right back to the desert campaign. My audience all seemed very interested and I was proud that the three lecture sessions had presented no problems to me whatsoever.

When I spoke to the chief clerk he told me that my posting to the Jewish Brigade was still open and that another ASM was holding the fort until my arrival. I was to travel north to join them within the next few days. Just before my departure, I was called to see the OC who said that my lectures seemed to fill an important need. He had seen a note on my medical chart saying that I could be a candidate for a medical downgrading and so, if I agreed, he would put me on the permanent staff of the REME holding unit. I could then spend the rest of the war helping to condition the new arrivals before they were sent to units in the forward area. It was a very tempting offer but my mind was made up and, for better or for worse, I was determined to join the Jewish Brigade.

19
The Jewish Brigade

The Jewish Brigade was stationed at the small mountain town of Fiugi. A transit truck dropped me on the outskirts of Rome and from there I managed to hitch a lift, arriving in Fiugi's town centre at the end of January 1945. I dumped my kit at a nearby house, occupied by some Royal Army Service Corps and asked the corporal to look after it. He directed me to the brigade headquarters which was a couple of hundred yards down the road, in a house attached to a factory.

This factory seemed to contain about a million lemonade bottles. Its ground floor housed the main brigade office which displayed the usual air of activity that is always found in army offices. I reported to a staff sergeant who was sitting behind a desk which bore a sign indicating that he was the chief clerk. When I told him my name he smiled, held out his hand and said, 'Blimey, Sergeant-Major, where've you been? We've been expecting you for three months!'

On hearing this, the rest of the people present gathered round to welcome me and thus began my introduction to the Jewish Brigade.

Mark Hyatt, the clerk, left his paper work and drove me in a jeep, first to collect my kit and then to install me in the sergeants' mess. I was allocated the room that had been occupied by the temporary, ASM who was leaving for Blighty the very next day after having already spent five years in the Middle East forces.

Mark then took me to the civilian garage that had been requisitioned for my new command; The REME LAD attached to Jewish Brigade Headquarters. Here I met the departing ASM and spent the next few hours being fully briefed by my predecessor. I was very fortunate to have arrived before he left as he was able to give me various pieces of information which were to save me an enormous amount of trouble.

I spent a few days getting to know my new LAD and finding out about the history of the various units of the brigade, together with details concerning Brigade Headquarters' personnel. To any outsider the sub-units of the brigade looked and acted like any other part of the British Army. As I had spent some considerable time in the 8th Indian Division, I was quite familiar with the mixture of English and Urdu which permeated all the units. The Jewish Brigade was very similar – except that the languages used here were English and Ivrit, with some occasional Yiddish thrown in for good measure. As a large part of the HQ staff were British Jews, English was spoken by all HQ personnel but all the routine orders were posted in both English and Ivrit. Out at the battalions and other units, Ivrit alone was normally spoken.

The whole brigade was billeted in Fiugi itself, in places like the local Town Hall and schools. I soon discovered that bottling water was the main industry in this area with Fiugi water being famous throughout Europe for both its purity and supposed medical properties. The area contained several huge, modern factories that had once housed thousands of Southern Italian migrant workers. The bottling operation had ceased some months earlier due to fighting in the region and most of the workers had left to return to their homes.

Throughout the war, vast numbers of Jews had served in the various Allied armies. In 1939, upon the outbreak of war, the Jewish Agency in Palestine had registered over 100,000 Jews and Jewesses as volunteers for any service required by the mandatory power – Great Britain. By the end of 1942 over 20,000 Palestinian Jews were in a variety of purely Jewish units, scattered over the Middle East, and had served with distinction in every campaign. The core of the Palestinians were the three Jewish infantry battalions of the Palestine Regiment that had been formed. For three long years the British Foreign Office's Arab appeasement policy had kept these three battalions on monotonous guard duties in North Africa. It had only been by the support of Winston Churchill, together with several other very senior statesmen, that all the opposition to an active Jewish force had been overcome. Thus, in September 1944, the Jewish Brigade Group had finally been formed and destined to join the 8th British Army fighting in Italy with Brigadier E.F. Benjamin being appointed brigade commander. He was a Canadian Jew who had served twenty-five years as a regular soldier in the British Army.

The brigade had begun to assemble in Fiugi during December and the plan was to spend several weeks getting a series of individual units ready to act as a single fighting formation. We were to be in the line by the early spring, ready to take a major part in, what was hoped would be, the final offensive, leading to the complete defeat of all Axis forces in Italy.

My new LAD had been formed by posting a troop of REME men from a Palestinian workshop company in Haifa. As no Palestinian ASM Warrant Officer Class 1 existed, my application had filled a void but as I had been foolish enough to get wounded, a Scottish ASM had been temporarily put in charge.

My interview with the Brigadier was short and sweet. He said that my records indicated that I was well experienced in running an LAD so I was to get the Brigade LAD in shipshape condition as quickly as possible. Should any major problems occur, he could be seen at any time. As long as I did my job, he would ensure that I was left alone to run my unit as I thought fit. General Benjamin was a man after my own heart and was as good as his word. Once again I was in the happy and unusual position of being a soldier and my own boss.

The only slight fly in the ointment initially was Captain Prensky, the Brigade Headquarter's REME Officer. He was an engineering graduate from Haifa Technical College who had been stationed in Palestine doing some sort of clerical work ever since he had enlisted. He tended to want to do everything by the book. At our first meeting I frightened the life out of him by refusing to carry out some of his more far-fetched ideas and suggesting that we asked the Brigadier to arbitrate. In all fairness to Prensky, he left me alone after this assertion of my experience. Once I realised that he was genuinely enthusiastic and only trying to be helpful. I came to like him a great deal.

In many ways, my job at the brigade was simplified by the fact that I was one of the few battle-experienced people around. Almost anything I said was taken as gospel. I soon discovered that everybody was impatient to get into action and anxious to do as good a job as possible.

The men in my detachment were very similar to craftsmen everywhere and I rapidly became aware of their individual abilities. Dov Hoffman, from Ra-Amana, was the LAD sergeant. He was a perky individual and an excellent motor fitter. He loved to ride motorbikes and to dress up in cavalry breeches, so when he volunteered to act as our despatch rider I promptly agreed as this was not one of the most pleasant of tasks, especially in the mud and the snow of mountain terrain. However, when the going got rough, he never had any complaints, although he told me he now understood why his offer had been so eagerly accepted.

David Geller, our corporal, was a very quiet, dependable man from Haifa. Eliazer Sheinbaum, the sergeant armourer, was a happy, enthusiastic man who came from Kibbutz Beit Oron. Lance Corporal Shmuel Wiseman was from Tel Aviv and was a very efficient storeman. Oddly enough, Shmuel was the double of Harry Beaumont – there must be something about storemen! My driver, Nachum Tarachovsky. was a member of the Haifa Bus Cooperative and was a very sturdy, dependable fellow. He taught me a great deal about the *yishuv* and we became very good friends.

Moishe Avny had originated from General Anders' Polish Forces.

After many adventures he had joined the Palestinians where he had adopted the name Avny, preferring it to Sternberg. He had been a cadet officer in Poland and been captured by the Russians. He told us that together with several other young cadets, he had been removed from the ranks of Polish officers at a place called Katyn where, they were later told, only their youth had saved them. Many years afterwards the world heard the story of the dreadful Katyn massacre.

A. Klinghoffer and Shimon Sutka were both typical *sabras*; bright and cheerful young men from Tel Aviv. Dov Albert was a good all-rounder from Haifa and Zvi Feuder was a quiet dependable man from Kiryat Chaim. Moishe Reichman was a quiet, self-contained soldier and, finally, by the usual type of chance postings that are typical in the services, two non-Jewish men completed my unit; Bob Hamilton, from Glasgow and Jack Muscroft, from Yorkshire. They had apparently delivered two stores lorries to the LAD and somehow remained! However, they were both very good men who integrated very well with everybody else in the detachment.

Outside of the LAD, most of my time was spent getting to know the staff of the brigade headquarters. As the large majority were British Jews, transferred from other units, there were no language difficulties; it was like being back at a Victoria Boys' Club Camp! Major Jackson was the second-in-command and the ten or so other officers included the senior chaplain, Captain Bernard Casper, also from London. Prior to my arrival, the senior person in the sergeants' mess was a WO2 company sergeant-major who was a regular soldier – unusual for Jews. He had spent a lifetime in the service, mostly in pre-war India. He told us many interesting stories about the Jewish communities in India, the very existence of which was unknown to most of us.

Mark Hyatt was the staff sergeant and, as chief clerk, was the key man in administration. He was a pre-war London policeman and we developed a very firm friendship which we continued into civvy street. The sergeant in charge of the defence squad was Gerry Cooper who was a solid and reliable person who would always carry out any assignment in a calm, dependable manner. The three or four other mess members had been attached from the three battalions and they performed the clerical jobs that ensured the smooth functioning of the brigade. Together they formed a very friendly, helpful group which assisted me enormously in preparing the detachment for action in the very short time that was available.

As I was to live in a Dodge 15-cwt truck Nachum asked me to choose a name for it which, in accordance with army custom, could then be painted on the front bumper. Most soldiers opted for the names of their wives or sweethearts but, as my romantic attachment was still in the future, I chose the name of a popular item of Jewish food instead; 'Gefilter Fish'! From then onwards the Dodge was always referred to as 'Gefilter Fish' and later, when I received another vehicle, this was named 'Gefilter Fish 11'. Whenever I was chasing around Italy, well away from the brigade, soldiers would spot the name on the vehicle and frantically wave to me, shouting greetings. Once, when I was able to stop, I was hailed by a private in the Royal Fusiliers who happened to come from London's Commerical Road. Naturally I had to explain to him why my vehicle was so named and then all about the Jewish Brigade. Also, the Magen David symbol, blue with a white background, was painted on all the brigade's vehicles and signs.

When the brigade was not in action, the non-working day was Saturday and, whenever possible, work would stop on a Friday afternoon before the beginning of Shabbat. I managed to get the carpenter to make a folding table for Rabbi Casper. He was delighted to have a mobile prayer desk and carried it around to be used in all sorts of places. Rabbi Casper conducted services at brigade headquarters where there was always a party atmosphere, usually culminating with some home made entertainment followed by a sing-song. The only difference between celebrations in the British Indian Unit and the Jewish Brigade was that the songs sung at the latter were in Ivrit rather than English or Urdu.

I was very pleased that the men of the brigade had a very good rapport with the locals. During my time in Italy, I had found most of the Italians to be a very kind and sympathetic people who had been caught up in a political situation that most of them had never wanted. Many of the Jewish Brigade soldiers had an aptitude for languages and, after only a few weeks, seemed to speak far better Italian than I could after being in the country for eighteen months.

The following weeks were among the busiest and most exciting of my life. Several years had passed, during which my Jewish upbringing and experiences had simmered on the back burner of my life. Sometimes weeks and months had passed with hardly a thought to any event of specific Jewish interest. Now, suddenly, I was in a completely Jewish world where every action was determined by the effect we were making on Jewish history by being a Jewish fighting force. There was a fantastic spirit and feeling that finally we were being allowed to fight back as a people. In our hands and by our actions, we were once again raising the banner of a nation that had, by its traditions, a history of fighting for man's freedom against many tyrannies. For far too long a period we had opted to turn the other cheek but now the fortunes of war had changed. Every single soldier was aware that we were the beginning of a new era that would depend entirely on the courage and skill of Jewish fighting men for our very survival as a people.

I became immediately immersed in Jewish political history and the whole Zionist story from Herzl to the present time. I knew very little about Zionism or its history for these events had never been discussed in any of the boys' clubs. Most of the people who were responsible for financing these institutions were from old settled families that discouraged Zionism and many did not change their attitude until Israel was reborn as a state.

At Fiugi I began to hear eye witness reports of the terrible and almost unbelievable events that were happening to the Jewish people in the various concentration and extermination camps. Once we began to appreciate the horrors that our people had suffered, our priority was to rescue those who had survived by any method we could devise to save Jewish lives.

As more areas became occupied by the Allies, a variety of clandestine operations was set up to save as many Jews as possible. Rabbi Casper organised a voluntary cut in rations by all ranks to enable a store of food to be accumulated in anticipation of finding refugees. As far as I know, nobody knew the whole story. In all the dealings in which I was later involved, at no time was I ever told any more than I needed to know in order to carry out the task that I was allocated.

About a week after I had arrived in Fiugi I had a conversation with a soldier who had brought a 3-tonner that needed a minor repair into the LAD. He casually broached the subject of help to sustain Jews who had been contacted during the advance north in Italy. Apparently there were a few groups at different places so the intention was to send them to Palestine as soon as possible, by any means. As I firmly believed that any Jew who had survived Hitler's occupation should be helped to the safety of Palestine – if that was his wish – I made it clear to this driver where my sentiments lay. I had almost forgotten this incident when a few days later, I was approached by another soldier who told me that there was a need to obtain lorries. These would be used for a few days at a stretch to transport refugees and supplies. He suggested that, maybe, in my position I could help provide such vehicles.

After a great deal of thought I devised a scheme whereby I would call in a 3-ton lorry for a routine check from one of the units under my responsibility. As the driver automatically remained with his vehicle whilst at the LAD he therefore came under my control. I would then swear him to secrecy before sending the lorry to a prearranged destination where it would carry out whatever tasks were required. After a few days the driver would return to the LAD and we would then carry out a blitzkrieg job on his vehicle before returning him to his unit. I successfully used this basic system, with several variations according to the need, over the next several months.

Later, after I had been transferred to the brigade workshops, I had a much larger base from which to operate and could supply a considerable number of vehicles as and when asked. I never questioned the drivers about their missions but from the mileometers, I could tell that they often had travelled long distances. I had to sign documents authorising their journeys, should they be stopped by the military police. These journeys were totally fictitious and generally implied that they were collecting stores. I never spoke about these excursions to anyone. Nobody in the LAD or the workshop company knew anything, other than that many vehicles had taken part in routine checks and repairs.

As always in my army service, my time and energy were concentrated on the tiny area that I happened to occupy at any particular time and I paid very little attention to the news from the other war fronts. When I look back, it seems obvious that the war was coming to a close but at the beginning of 1945 I was busy preparing to re-enter the battle front in the Italian mountains. Experience had taught me that the enemy was very far indeed from being defeated.

When we were told that the brigade was to be attached to none other than the 8th Indian Division, I found myself going back to a very familiar environment. The division was still in the same area that it had occupied when I had been wounded, about twenty-five miles north of Florence. Somebody had noticed in my records that I had served a long time with the 8th Indians so several people came to the detachment to quiz me about the background of the various units which could only be known to somebody who had been with the division from the beginning. I was also able to describe the general layout of the area since I was far more familiar with that part of the battle front than I was with the West End of London, for example.

My main theme was the danger from anti-personnel mines. I tried to hammer home to the LAD the message not to enter places unless it was absolutely necessary and never to handle objects or souvenirs out of curiosity. Naturally very little notice was taken of my warnings but, as I expected, this changed dramatically after the first casualties occurred.

The brigade left Fiugi at the beginning of February with everybody determined to do a good job and behaving as though it was a text book military exercise. It made me realise how different the real war was to the one played by inexperienced units. I also realised how far my ideas had moved since that other world, so long ago, when I had first entered the Western Desert.

Our infantry took over part of the front line and the rest of the brigade settled into the positions that had been allocated to them. At first I found it strange to have no responsibility for the 25-pounders and I soon discovered that running an LAD attached to infantry was far simpler than one with an artillery regiment. My workload was much lighter once the brigade was in action and it took me sometime to get used to the idea that I no longer had the

238

constant worry about guns.

Once the LAD had settled in the area of Borgo San Lorenzo, I was able to meet up with my old friends from the 8th Indian. My reunion with the 53rd Field was like old home week. I was overjoyed to see the lads of the LAD and especially Jack Wragg who was pleased to hand me my kit which he had been looking after. My radio set and wristwatch were intact but Jack was most apologetic that the shotgun and Luger had disappeared. Apparently they had had to leave all the transport in the forward area during their rest period and, on their return, he had discovered that all sorts of objects had been purloined by whoever had been detailed to care for the vehicles.

I spent a very pleasant time reminiscing with Tommy Sinclair and the Quartermaster chaps. Although many changes in personnel had occurred, Lance Montgomery was still medical officer and the indestructible Captain Matthews remained the Regimental Quartermaster. My dealings with the various divisional workshops and supply units were made much easier by dealing with people who were mostly old friends.

One day, when I was at a battalion headquarters, news arrived that a company was needed to make an attack that same night in order to straighten out a dent in the line. This was the sort of thing the staff officers loved. As all the companies volunteered, a draw was held to decide and I was astonished to see the men of the winning company spontaneously dance a *hora* at the news that they would have the privilege of making this attack. Although it was duly successful, there were several casualties among those who had 'won' the lottery.

Towards the end of March the brigade took over from the Indians in new positions near Brisighella, which was intended to be the start line in the forthcoming battle. For the first time since Biblical days, a Jewish fighting force was in action at Passover; this was making history with a vengeance. *Seder** services were held in whatever shelters could be found and I was able to take most of my LAD to join in the *Seder* laid on by the 179 Army Service Corps Company. It was a most memorable service with special *Haggadahs* (Passover prayer books) that had been printed on their Roneo duplicator. Every man present was most conscious of the moment in history in which we were taking part. This certainly dispelled any regrets that I might have had about refusing the cushy post that had been offered to me in Naples. I felt proud to be taking an active part in these events.

I was very pleased with the speed at which the LAD adapted to battle conditions and I had no problems in getting volunteers for the more dangerous jobs that cropped up, like repairing or

*A commemorative meal recording the biblical exodus from Egypt.

recovering faulty Bren gun carriers from the difficult forward position of the front line.

Even during this period in action, news continued to arrive from the refugee front and I felt thankful to be able to help by my small contribution of supplying transport whenever it was required.

20
The Fighting Ends

On 3rd April, a few days after Pesach (Passover), a special ceremony was held formally to consecrate the brigade's colours. The flag was handed to Brigadier Benjamin by Mr. Moishe Shertok, who later Hebraized his name to Sharett, one of the leaders of the Palestine Jewish community who had come from Jerusalem especially for this occasion. As the speeches and ceremony were conducted in Ivrit, I could only understand a little of what was said. However, knowledge of Ivrit was not necessary in order to appreciate the deep feelings of the men present – as many representatives from all the brigade's units that could be spared from their duties. It is interesting to note that our brigade's flag was later adopted as the flag of the State of Israel.

Much to my surprise, Moishe Shertok visited our LAD on the following day, escorted by Captain Prensky. Mr. Shertok spent some time questioning me about our work and how the REME facilities of the Jewish Brigade compared with those of the 8th Indian Division. I thought this to be a most unusual interview until Prensky later informed me that a brigade workshop company was being formed. It was to be constructed from various Palestine REME units who would leave the Middle East to join us in Italy.

Moishe Shertok struck me as a polite, quietly spoken man who appeared to have an instant comprehension of all the points that were made to him. After our discussion he cordially thanked me for my time but on leaving, when no other person was within earshot, he mentioned the secret, vital work that was needed to save as many refugees as possible. It was obvious that he was fully aware of all our operations involving the rescue of Jews and, in retrospect, I realise that he was probably the only man to have total knowledge of the whole picture.

A very important part of the preparations for the forthcoming battle was the clearing and destroying of all enemy strongpoints and positions on our side of the Senio river and establishing complete control of the area by our infantry to prevent any possibility of enemy infiltration. It was a sign of the high esteem the Army Commander had of our men's eagerness to engage the hated enemy that the task was given to the Jewish Brigade to carry out. As a result patrols were continuously covering the battlefield seeking out and attacking the enemy so ferociously that we had complete control of the territory and it was only the strict discipline of the officers that prevented the more hotheaded of our men from pre-empting the battle plans and advancing deep into enemy-held areas.

Reports from captured prisoners said that Jerry morale, which was low as a result of their reverses on every front, became near panic when they learned that they were now facing a Jewish fighting force with a host of scores to settle. The Allied top brass were so impressed with the brigade's results that our men were complimented by none other than General Mark Clark himself for the efficiency and manner in which all its objectives were achieved.

April 9th saw the start of the battle that was to mark the end of the fighting in Italy. The whole brigade was fully engaged spearheading the attack very successfully and in a fighting advance broke through the last of the enemy defences and swiftly carried out its objective at Imola a small town just south of Bologna. One of the Indian brigades then leap-frogged our units to continue the advance, giving our battalions the opportunity to rest and refit after nearly two months in action.

Surrender stories now came in thick and fast from all over Europe. It was widely believed that we would be summoned to attack a so-called last redoubt that Hitler and his hard core SS divisions were supposedly planning in the Alps.

My final REME task during the war ended on a humorous note. A message reached the LAD that a Bren carrier had broken down and needed assistance. When I checked the map reference I saw that it was only about 100 yards from our current position so I walked across to the carrier, spoke to the infantry sergeant in charge and ascertained that the fault was a broken track pin. I returned to the LAD and despatched a couple of fitters to carry out the necessary repair. The war was virtually over and what was left of the organised part of the enemy was a long way away. The Luftwaffe was finished and our only remaining danger was the perennial one of mines not yet made safe. In these relaxed circumstances we were all dressed exceedingly casually and there was no trace of the parade ground bull element to be seen within the detachment. Suddenly Captain Prensky arrived, wearing full battle kit complete with steel helmet and webbing; I think he even had a full water bottle. He announced that as there was a Bren carrier in a very forward position that needed help, he had come personally to lead our gallant fitters to the dangerous site! I roared with laughter and told him that it was not his job to do recovery work. When I checked his map reference, which had somehow turned itself round, I found that it indicated a position about fourteen miles north of Venice – an area that the army had not yet captured!

At the end of April we finally saw the official surrender of all enemy troops in Italy. As the news was released, every gun in Allied hands was fired into the air.

Although the end of our war had been expected it was still very difficult to absorb and to appreciate its significance. My first thoughts were that at last I could go to sleep at night without some sort of interruption. The idea of permanent, peaceful sleep every night seemed too good to be true, after years of hardly two or three hours passing without somebody or something needing my attention. Yet there was still the Far Eastern war to win so we could not allow ourselves to become too excited about returning to civvy street. Strangely enough most soldiers never considered the Japanese war at all, presuming it to be an American responsibility with nothing to do with us. Nevertheless, now that Hitler and the Nazis had been defeated, I could now allow myself to be grateful that I had survived in one piece and to contemplate some sort of future life as a civilian. After nearly six years I had become accustomed to being a soldier and had put thoughts of returning home right out of my mind. Now, quite suddenly, there was the near certainty that I would soon be leaving the army and I found the prospect of all the things that would naturally follow my demob, to be somewhat overwhelming.

However, for the moment I still had a job to do concerning the freeing of the occupied territories. There was also the enormous project of trying to help several million displaced persons to return to their homes and rebuild their lives. There was also the uncertain political activities of the Russians to consider.

As far as I was concerned, my main resolve was to provide as much support in whatever ways possible for as many of the Jewish survivors as I could. I soon realised that my first loyalty was to these unfortunate refugees and, when this sometimes clashed with red tape, officialdom, I had no hesitation whatsoever in using any subterfuge possible. After all, I had no way of knowing if any of my own relatives were among the many death camp survivors that we managed to assist.

One day I had a pleasant surprise when a Royal Artillery officer called into the LAD to request assistance with his vehicle. He turned out to be none other than Eric, the youngest of the three Nabarro brothers who had been stalwart supporters of the Victoria Boys' Club. Eric and I chatted about old times and the whereabouts of various friends whilst my fitters mended his truck. He happened to know that Tommy Kleinman was a cook with an infantry battalion that was currently in a convoy travelling north. As I had some spare time, we set off in a jeep and an hour later had tracked down his unit which had stopped on the road for the night. Lo and behold, there we discovered Tommy busily preparing a meal in the cook's wagon! It reminded us of our annual Seaview summer camps where Tommy had always been the club's Quartermaster. As there was a vacancy for an RA counter mortar officer on the brigade's establishment, Eric was able to arrange a transfer and duly joined the brigade headquarter section.

The army was rapidly moving north. After a few days we moved via Bologna, Ferrara, Padua, skirted Venice, on to Udine and finally stopped at the small town of Tarvisio on the borders of Italy, Yugoslavia and Austria. Now that we were nearing the end of May, we were able to enjoy some beautiful spring weather which we all appreciated. Throughout this journey north, we encountered thousands of Italian partisans who were easily recognised by the red kerchief that they wore over their makeshift uniforms. It was obvious that much of Italy's industrial north had been taken over by these partisan units. As the red kerchief signified that they were supposedly communist it seemed to me that Italy was liable to become a communist state. I realised that from a political point of view, the post-war world was going to be quite different from that which I had known in September 1939.

By placing the Jewish Brigade at Tarvisio at this particular time, fate had played its trump card. The Tarvisio area was ideally situated for our gathering together of refugees. There were many refugees scattered over a huge area which was now under either British, French, American or, most important, Russian occupation. We were now based at the very crossroads of three countries and in the very place where Allied liberated areas met the Soviet-occupied territories. There was also the added bonus that we were but a stone's throw from the Austrian bridge that spanned the river separating the British from the Russian forces.

A series of camps, stretching southwards through Italy, had been established. These were essential refugee stopover places which enabled us to gradually transport the Jews to ports. Here desperate attempts would be made for them to board any type of shipping that could be obtained and let them escape from the European hell to a new, safer life in Palestine.

The British policy in Palestine was a shambles. The government, the War Office and the Foreign Office were all at sixes and sevens for, after all, it was a very small problem for a Britain that had miraculously survived victoriously from six years of war. There were many enormous problems at home for the new government to attempt to solve. We were therefore heartened when the Brigadier told us that there was tremendous goodwill and good wishes towards our actions that assisted any refugees. This encouragement came to us from throughout the hierarchy of the British occupying forces, including Field Marshal Lord Alexander, the General Commanding Officer. He actually made a special visit to the brigade at Tarvisio to inspect several units. It was intimated

---

SPECIAL ORDER OF THE DAY

Soldiers, Sailors and Airmen of the Allied Forces in the Mediterranean Theatre

After nearly two years of hard and continuous fighting which started in Sicily in the summer of 1943, you stand today as the victors of the Italian Campaign.

You have won a victory which has ended in the complete and utter rout of the German armed forces in the Mediterranean. By clearing Italy of the last Nazi aggressor, you have liberated a country of over 40,000,000 people.

Today the remnants of a once proud Army have laid down their arms to you—close on a million men with all their arms, equipment and impedimenta.

You may well be proud of this great and victorious campaign which will long live in history as one of the greatest and most successful ever waged.

No praise is high enough for you sailors, soldiers, airmen and workers of the United Forces in Italy for your magnificent triumph.

My gratitude to you and my admiration is unbounded and only equalled by the pride which is mine in being your Commander-in-Chief.

H. R. Alexander

Field-Marshal,
Supreme Allied Commander,
Mediterranean Theatre.

that we must always strictly adhere to the official line but that every possible help would be given unofficially. We were free to act in any manner which we considered to be necessary, with the one proviso that if problems arose then we would not be able to claim that we were carrying out orders. I was pleased to find the same helpful attitude from most of the junior British ranks on the several occasions that I required their assistance.

Most of the brigade headquarters at Tarvisio occupied a deserted SS army barracks with the LAD being allocated a corner that had obviously been previously used for workshop activities. Within a couple of hours of our arrival I became aware that our garage contained a huge trailer which was completely covered by a canvas tarpaulin. One of our soldiers, whose curiosity had overcome warnings concerning mines, could not resist investigating the contents of this trailer and by the time I discovered what had happened, many boxes of the cargo had been swiftly removed. The word of his discovery spread like wildfire for the trailer was loaded with hundreds of crates of white wine. This was too good an opportunity to miss. Immediately the cooks and orderlies of the various messes came running to help themselves and before long, most of this booty had disappeared. For many weeks our sergeants' mess was enlivened by this white wine and we held many parties whilst we had the means to do so.

Later that first night, a soldier from a Scots regiment turned up. He had apparently been left behind to look after this trailer and he was most upset to learn that most of his unit's spoils were now in the hands of another unit – but such are the fortunes of war. So that he would not get into too much hot water I made sure that he retained the hundred or so cases that still remained on the trailer. That evening, a towing vehicle arrived to collect what bottles were left, but the driver was not too upset because, he told us, his unit already had a whole warehouse full of the stuff and most of their regiment had been holding non-stop celebrations for the last two days.

There was a strict order in operation to the effect that no soldier or civilian was permitted to cross either of the borders without proper authorisation. This was very rigidly enforced by the military police as it was vital to try to establish some law and order in an area where hundreds of thousands of displaced persons were roaming.

On the morning after our arrival I was told that mechanical assistance was needed by a truck just over the Austrian border. As we were the nearest available REME unit, I jumped for joy at this stroke of good fortune and said, 'Get the jeep ready, Nathan. We are going into Austria!'

He looked at me in amazement but I continued, 'I've waited too long to see what it's all about, so get cracking and let's go!'

246

We set off in our jeep which had Magen David signs painted on to the front and back, the emblem of the Jewish Brigade. We also wore flashes on our shoulders which were of a similar design; the shield of David on a blue and white background. When we alighted we felt most peculiar to be standing on German soil. All the shops bore German names and they were all closed. There were very few people about but all of a sudden we saw two young men wearing Wehrmacht uniforms walking down the street. They came up to us and, to our surprise, said, 'Shalom!' When I looked at them closely, I noticed that they wore no insignia of any kind on their uniforms. They began to speak Yiddish and were obviously very excited to see us.

I asked them who they were and they told me that until a couple of days ago they had been held in a concentration camp. Then, suddenly, the Germans had departed and to all the prisoners' utter astonishment, they had been able to walk out of the gates into freedom. They had felt completely bewildered but a group of them had made their way to Allied areas where they thought they would be safe. The young men told us that their particular group consisted of 98 men and 2 women who were presently in a building about two hundred yards from where we were standing. They had found an abandoned German army store where they had exchanged the tattered, filthy, striped nightdress type of uniform that they had been obliged to wear in the camp for fresh Wehrmacht uniforms, discarding any flashes or insignia. They were very short of food and had only spoken to one Allied official, a captain whose job it was to take over the occupied territories. He was responsible for many thousands of homeless people but had only a staff of ten with which to try to set up a military-civil organisation. This captain had to provide all the necessary facilities for some sort of normal life including the supply of water, emergency medical aid and emergency feeding. All this very kind officer had been able to supply had been a daily ration consisting of one very poor bowl of soup together with one slice of bread each.

We immediately put the two men in our jeep and drove to the house where the rest of the Jews were waiting. As we entered the courtyard, pandemonium broke loose and we were immediately surrounded by all of those ninety-eight souls who were able to walk. They just could not believe their eyes. They could not take it in that after so many years under Nazi rule, they were finally free. They were astounded to be actually seeing and touching Jewish soldiers from the Allied side. It was a heart-rending scene that I shall never forget.

Inside the house we tried to pacify these people as we told them that about an hour's journey away there was a whole brigade of several thousand Jewish soldiers who would be only too willing to give them every help that they required. As, unfortunately, we had no food with us, we would have to return to the unit, but we promised to return within a few hours with food, clothing and other help. They were most reluctant indeed to let us go. They all wanted to accompany us and were afraid that if we left they would never see us again. However, after a conference with the two or three men who were their leaders, they accepted our proposals.

They were Hungarian Jews who had been captured at different times in the previous two years. Most of their relatives and friends had been exterminated and the stories that they told us were almost too horrific to believe. We tried to make them feel better by saying, 'Thank God, all these experiences are now behind you, let us look to the future!'

To keep them occupied while we were away, we asked them to make a list of all their names and addresses. They were very anxious to know whether we had any Hungarians with us in the brigade and they wanted to know whether any of these might be acquaintances or even relatives of theirs. We promised that within a few hours we would provide them with as much help as possible and finally drove back to Tarvisio at breakneck speed.

As soon as we arrived at the camp, I went to see Rabbi Bernard Casper. Once he had heard my news he told me that he would attend to all the arrangements and told me to meet him half an hour later outside the regimental office. I was to have a quick meal before returning to Klagenfurt.

The word had spread like wildfire around the whole Brigade and all the Hungarian Jews were very excited that perhaps someone they knew might be among the Jews that we had discovered. It so happened that the sergeants' mess cook was a Hungarian and he came dashing in to beg me to take him with us to Klagenfurt. At first I said that this was impossible as we just did not have the room. Then I remembered that as we had left the house, one very anxious old gentleman had written down his name and address on a piece of paper and, to calm him I had put the note into my pocket. Whilst I was talking to our cook I remembered this scrap of paper and gave it to him. When he saw this name tears came into his eyes. It was a neighbour of his that he had known in Budapest many years ago. After that I had no alternative but to take the cook with me.

Our rescue unit consisted of two 3-ton lorries, our cook, two other cooks with portable ovens and food, two doctors, the Rabbi, two sergeant clerks, Nathan and myself. As we approached Klagenfurt we were met by some of the refugees who had begun to walk towards Tarvisio, having not had the patience to merely sit still and wait for us. We collected these stragglers and finally arrived with all our people intact.

Although our reception was very emotional, our men were very disciplined as we were used to acting correctly and efficiently in emergencies; as far as one can get used to these things. Without wasting any time, the cooks rigged up a temporary cookhouse and soon there were dixies of stew boiling merrily away with tea, coffee and other foods in abundance. The doctors set about giving medical treatment, first attending to the few seriously ill and then working their way through until everybody had been examined. We saw to it that they all ate their fill and were clothed in British army battledress, and gave them flashes bearing the insignia of our own Jewish Brigade which they were proud to pin on to their new uniforms. The clerks meanwhile took over the lists of names of all these people.

My cook was overwhelmed to be reunited with his old friend and was busily engaged in deep conversation with him in Hungarian. He received some tragic news about his family but also heard some hopeful news that his sister had been seen alive only three weeks previously. Before we left, Rabbi Casper held a short service to thank God that we had been able to survive and that our hundred Jews had been able to live through this terrible time. He added that we should all look to the future with hope and that whilst we must never forget the events that had happened, we should, for the moment, put them out of our minds. We should realise that if you live, you live through everything.

We left our two clerks behind with the refugees and finally returned to our camp for the night. The next day many of our soldiers, particularly the Hungarians, went independently to Klagenfurt to search for news about their relatives, friends and neighbours. The lists had been circulated throughout the brigade and there were several instances where people became reunited. Within two or three days about half of our Jews were already being transported through Italy in an attempt to enter Palestine. The remainder, most of whom were not fit to travel, were kept in small groups in various parts of Italy where we hoped they could build up sufficient strength to enable them to make the longer journey. There were a few, however, who returned to Budapest. They were those who could not accept that if any of their family had survived, the information would be passed on to them wherever they were. They first wanted to go back to their homes just in case any of their relatives had returned so that they could be there to greet them. We could not argue with this very natural desire so we helped them with food and money, transporting them as far as we could into the Russian zone.

Within a fortnight of our arrival in Klagenfurt, every one of the hundred Jews had been assisted. About thirty-three were in Italian camps and about six had returned to Hungary. A month later we were able to close this chapter when we heard that all of the Jews that had wanted to, were now in Palestine.

21
On to the Low Countries

The last of the SS had abandoned the barracks just prior to the arrival of our forces in Tarvisio. They tried to hide in a number of places such as among the flood of displaced persons, among the staff of the many German military hospitals and in the various convalescent depots scattered around the area. Our orders were to arrest all enemy soldiers and either forward them to one of the prisoner of war camps or hand them over to the nearest military police unit. There was a special emphasis on SS troops, for they were all considered to be fanatics and thus still dangerous. As many of our brigade had German origins, we did not find it too difficult to distinguish members of the SS who were trying to conceal themselves among other POWs. As their barbaric behaviour gradually became known, it was only by the strong military discipline of our troops, together with a firm belief that nobody should be punished without a trial, that we were able to prevent mayhem upon those SS discovered.

Sometimes, when we had a senior SS waiting to be collected by the MPs from our brigade guardroom, members of our mess decided to frighten these sadists by setting up a fictitious court martial and quickly sentencing them to be shot. After a short period these SS officers would be placed up against the wall but, just before the firing squad were to carry out the order, a dispatch rider would arrive and announce that the execution was to be delayed. The prisoners were then returned to the guardroom where the farce would be repeated after a short interval. By the time the military police arrived our captives had begun to understand how it felt to be on the receiving end of such trickery. In retrospect I realise that these actions of ours were pretty childish and meaningless, but at least it released some of the frustrations that we were all feeling at the time.

The Tarvisio area had long been a bone of contention between the Italians and the Germans with all the locals being fluent in both languages. The last change of ownership had been after the Great

War when Italy had taken over from Austria but there had always been conflict between the two communities and, now that the Italians had the advantage, many acts of revenge took place in respect of age-old feuds.

One day I received a letter from my old friend, Mark Rosenfeld. He was serving with an artillery regiment in the 78th Division and was now stationed in Austria. As the flow of work at the LAD was well under control, I was able to institute a rota of 24 or 48-hour leave passes. On one of my free days I decided to visit Mark. I was very impressed with the beauty of the countryside and saw little sign of any bomb damage in the small villages through which I passed. In fact, if it had not been for the refugees who were everywhere, one would hardly have known that any of the past few years' events had taken place. The largest refugee congregation comprised of thousands of Ukrainians, camped in tents lining the road around Villach. Most of the men wore badgeless German army uniforms and they appeared to be accompanied by their wives and children. I was told that they were USSR citizens who had deserted to the Germans to fight against the Soviet forces. Britain allowed all these men to be handed over to the Russians in accordance with the Yalta agreement.

It took me far longer than I had expected to find Mark and it was not until mid-afternoon that I discovered him on guard duty in a farmhouse. He could not believe his eyes when I stepped out of my jeep. He had been trying to carry on a conversation with the farmer's eight-year old daughter and was struggling to find similarities with his Yiddish and her German. I stayed with him for about an hour and we spoke about how this chain of events had so greatly altered our lives. Together we looked forward to our release into civvy street where we could restart our lives with our families and friends.

On another occasion a couple of friends and I took a day trip to Venice. I found it to be certainly one of the world's most remarkable cities, quite different from any of the other places that I had seen in my travels. As we were sitting in St Mark's Square drinking coffee, like all tourists, I suddenly heard my name being called out. I turned round and, to my amazement, saw Gaby Marsh sitting at a nearby table. Gaby was a close friend of Manny, my brother, who was now serving in a Royal Engineer unit and, like all of us, was anxiously awaiting his discharge. This was yet another of the several extraordinary happy meetings that I was fortunate to have throughout my travels.

The military police who were responsible for the three borders, were situated in another part of Tarvisio. One day I was approached by their Regimental Sergeant-Major, a jovial Geordie, as they needed some urgent repairs on a few of their trucks. He was very grateful for my help and we invited his mess to one of our parties.

This was reciprocated by the MPs and we spent some very enjoyable evenings in their company. As a result, I became friendly with many of the MP mess members which enabled me to move freely across the borders without any problems arising.

In the middle of June a group of Palestinian REME arrived and set up camp a few miles away at Valbruna. I paid them a visit and spoke to Major Levin, the OC, who explained that the idea was to collect the establishment required for a brigade workshop company built around his recently arrived group, previously known as the 319 Palestine REME Workshop Company. A little while later I received a visit from Captain Prensky who told me that, in keeping with the British Army practice of not promoting colonial troops to be warrant officers class 1, there was no Palestinian suitable to take over the ASM job of principal workshop foreman in the new company. He had discussed this with Major Levin and the outcome was that I was being offered this position. Should I accept, it would entail leaving the LAD and transferring to the workshops.

It was obvious that running the brigade workshop, consisting of a few hundred men, was a much bigger task than running the LAD. Naturally, I would lose my independence for I would no longer be in charge of the whole unit, but I would have the compensation of being in charge of the workshops, which would be an extremely good experience. It was certainly a challenge and, after some thought, I accepted the offer. In accordance with the old family motto, 'No sooner said than done.' the very next day saw me exchanging places with the AQMS – the WO2 from the workshop – and I joined my new unit.

In the very early part of the war, many Palestinian Jewish volunteers had joined the British army and, among the various units raised, there had been three REME workshop companies. The 319 had originally been stationed at Haifa where it had provided REME facilities stretching across the entire Middle East, Persia and Iraq forces.

Second-in-command to Major Levin was Captain Weiss, and the senior WO2 was CSM Kramer who had once served as a night raider under the legendary Chindit leader Captain Orde Wingate. The unit had been suddenly sent to Italy in February 1945 where it had been divided into two parts soon after landing in Taranto. It was this larger part that was destined to become the Jewish Brigade workshop, although by the time they had organised, ready to join the brigade, the war had ended.

A few other small REME troops from various Middle Eastern camps had also arrived to swell the numbers and, out of this somewhat mixed up collection, we now had to try to incorporate everyone into the establishment framework of an independent infantry brigade workshop company.

This move heralded a complete change in my personal situation as I was now living in a totally Jewish Palestinian environment where Ivrit was the first language. Most of the men had gleaned some English during their military lives but for some their only knowledge of my tongue was confined to simple drill commands. I thought that communication was going to be my largest problem but, surprisingly, I never had the slightest difficulty on that score. One way or another I was able to get on perfectly well with everybody, all my instructions and discussion being perfectly comprehended. All the senior ranks spoke English as did most of the office staff. Among the handful of British Jews were the NCOs Staff Sergeant Harry Carton and Lance-Corporal Bert Rosenberg.

I had no responsibility as far as the organisation of the unit was concerned for all administrative and disciplinarian chores were the province of CSM Vitis and CSM Kramer. My duties were very clearly defined as being in charge of the workshop office and controlling the workshop with all that affected its proper functioning. Unlike the LAD we were not expected to operate whilst on the move and we could set up static sites wherever suitable. I was the PWF with a senior staff of two WO2s who were AQMSs, plus about twenty sergeants and staff sergeants who were in charge of the various sections. The senior, junior NCOs and other ranks were all classified as tradesmen apart from the few clerical staff. On most working days there were between two and three hundred people toiling in our workshops.

We managed to find good accommodation for the regimental office, quartermaster section, officers' and sergeants' messes together with adequate sleeping and mess quarters for all the men. However there were no suitable buildings for workshop use in the village itself but, as the weather was fine, we chose a field about half a mile from the men's living quarters. I was pleased since using an open field gave us almost unrestricted space in which to operate. Our workshop office was housed in a suitably furnished lorry, with a tent attached to give us more covered space and we had other tents which were used for stores, tools etc. We had a couple of machinery lorries to carry items such as lathes and drills with further lorries allocated to the electricians, welders, body repairers and other sections.

At first circumstances forced me to organise the workshop according to what skilled men were available but gradually, as more men and equipment arrived, we were able to function more efficiently. We were a most comprehensive unit, competent to tackle almost anything that could possibly be required. The motor transport repair sections were, as always, the core of the whole operation but there was also an enormous amount of other equipment – including weapons, instruments and radioes – that often needed our attention. We had every type of craftsman imaginable and I never encountered any problems in finding an expert to deal with any specific electrical or mechanical engineering task.

My first duty was to sort out the tradesmen and assign them to appropriate sections. This was very easy as far as motor fitters were concerned for there was always a terrific shortage of their talents, but some trades were overstaffed whilst others, such as vehicle electricians, presented a problem that we never solved. It was essential that we attained a proper, balanced staff if we were to avoid the occurrence of terrible bottlenecks so we had to use some men in trades other than those for which they were classified. Fortunately many had considerable experience in skills allied to their prime ones so, by combining one semi-skilled man with a skilled man we devised teams that managed to solve most of the staffing problems. Above all my job was made much easier by the men's willingness to cooperate together with their very high standard of craftsmanship.

Sorting out the tools and workshop equipment was virtually impossible as nobody knew exactly what equipment was present. Therefore equipment could neither be allocated to its correct section nor could we indent for missing items that were essential according to the establishment tables. I proposed that there should be a three-day cessation of all workshop activities in order that all tools and equipment could be placed where I could take a team of men to assess it all. The OC concurred with my plan and I took six men to spend three days submerged in huge piles of hardware and we duly straightened out the whole mess.

Within a few days of this reorganisation things began to click into position and I was delighted at how smoothly the whole system was operating. As an example, a 15-cwt truck would arrive at the Receipt and Issue office and then on to the light MT (Motor Transport) unit where it would be mechanically attended to by the fitters, welders, blacksmiths, carpenters, panel beaters, painters and electricians. Finally the vehicle would pass through a rigorous road test by one of the staff sergeant motor transport armament artificers. Any spares that were needed would be supplied by the stores section, led by Captain Glucksman, a South African settler in Palestine, who had exactly the right temperament for this job. As I had spent many long periods at my previous LADs chasing around for spare parts, it was a great relief to have somebody else responsible for this work. Nobody appreciated as well as I the amount of time and effort that Captain Glucksman and his merry men had to spend in successfully obtaining the necessary spares. Without their efforts we would have simply become bogged down with dozens of useless vehicles.

During all this activity I got to know more of the people in the unit. Major Levin was an older man who always appeared to have the world's troubles on his shoulders. He was always politely friendly to me and whenever I suggested important changes he would agree to them without any discussion. Captain Weiss was his complete opposite, being a tall, breezy type of person with whom it was very easy to communicate. Once, when we happened to be in a room containing a piano, he astonished me by sitting down and giving an hour's impromptu virtuoso performance. The other two officers were Lieutenant Glicksman – a very likeable young man – and Lieutenant Morduc, a decent but rather fussy individual. I got on very well with all of them for they had the good sense to allow everybody in the workshop division to perform their duties without the imposition of too much regimentation.

We had a wonderful collection of characters in our sergeants' mess, each of whom had enough reminiscences to fill volumes. CSM Kramer told us stories about night fighting, guarding and protecting kibbutzim and other small communities from marauding Arabs and the Grand Mufti's assassins. Sergeant Tabor told stories of his childhood in Bulgaria where, from the age of ten, he had carried a pistol to protect himself from bandits. He was busy writing a thesis for his PH.D.; the subject was, 'How to set up a chain of garage repair depots to service the Jewish settlers in Palestine'. Tabor, who was renowned for his extremely strict ideas of morality, had a daily cold shower followed by a road run to assist him to remain faithful to his beloved wife back home.

CSM Vitis was a perfect chief clerk being quietly spoken, never flustered and fully aware of everything concerning the unit. Staff Sergeant Harry Carton was a dependable Londoner and Sergeant Yasher Disenshiks had a huge figure with a voice to match – he looked like a Russian General and certainly acted like one. Sergeant Finkelstein, who claimed to be a plumber but seemed expert in a wide variety of trades, was as short as Yasher was tall.

The same pioneering spirit that dominated the whole Yishuv in Palestine was very marked and was apparent in all the mess discussions. Most of the talk was centred around the political drama that was occurring in both Europe and Palestine. Every hour seemed to bring fresh momentous news and we were all very aware that we were living through historic times.

I managed to collect a small efficient staff for my workshop office and two of these clerks later became lifelong friends. Yehuda Sharlin, a seventh generation *sabra* from Jerusalem, was a cheerful, bright young man who was training to be a schoolteacher. David Ben Dov was just as bright but a bit more serious in outlook. He was hoping to continue his studies after the war at Hebrew University to prepare himself to serve in the foreign Service of an independent Jewish State. Bert Rosenberg became a very close friend and contributed a great deal to the smooth running of the workshop.

My move to the workshop coincided with a great deal of activity on the refugee front and, now that I could call on the whole brigade transport system, it became far easier to step up the number of vehicles I could supply. When a stopover refugee camp was needed on our side of the border, a site was chosen in a mountain clearing near Valbruna. It was an old abandoned prison camp containing utterly derelict huts. When we asked for volunteers, the entire unit responded by working in their spare time for several days to make the camp habitable for the imminent arrival of the first refugees. These poor Jews were in a pitiful state and the heartfelt stories that they told us stiffened our resolve to make their stay as comfortable as possible. We wanted to help them regain as much of their health as possible before continuing on the next stage of their journey to the Promised Land.

I kept in touch with my military police friends for I often had to cross the Austrian border in order to check on the recovery detachment we had been asked to maintain there. As the War Office had been getting complaints concerning our mercy missions from the military in Palestine, the MPs had begun to make more stringent checks to prevent illegal border crossings. As particular attention was given to vehicles driven by soldiers who spoke English with a foreign accent, it was hoped that my cockney tones coupled with excellent reasons for my journeys, would enable me to continue to smuggle refugees into Italy. One day I drove a three-ton lorry into the Villach area of Austria where I collected some twenty people. As we neared the border, we closed the back tarpaulin and told everybody inside to make no noise whatsoever. I duly stopped at the Italian border and casually chatted to the MP who I happened to know quite well. He then waved me through and I completed my mission without any problems. As this ruse was so effective, I had no compunction at repeating it on the few subsequent occasions that I was asked.

The most remarkable aspect of these journeys was that although the political and refugee problems were continually discussed. I never said nor heard one word spoken about the organisation that was coordinating the saving of refugees. I always did whatever I was asked to do, never querying the requests. I was always discreetly approached by soldiers who were personally unknown to me and I never discussed my operations with any other person. As a result, I had no way of knowing how large the operation was, nor the identities of those behind our work. It was obvious to me that most of the gossip I heard from different soldiers was pure guesswork, by people who were not themselves involved.

Sometimes something unusual would occur but, as long as the soldiers concerned were known to me to be conscientious people, I used Nelson's blind eye and did not investigate matters any further. For example, there was a WO2 on the company roll who I had never actually seen. Purely by chance, some weeks after I had joined the unit, I discovered that he, accompanied by a couple of fitters and an electrician, was at the Southern Italian port of Bari. Apparently some kind of ship had been obtained and, as the AQMS had been a Marine Engineer in civvy street, he was attempting to make it sufficiently seaworthy to sail refugees across the Mediterranean. In my view, this work was fully justifiable and I was pleased to be able to contribute in any way possible to the successful salvage of any of these unfortunate people.

A group of men, who had originally served in the Polish Army, joined the unit. They had endured some most incredible adventures and survived every type of villainy in the book. I was faced with the task of making good use of them for, without any doubt, they were the toughest characters that I had ever met. I had to make it crystal clear that they had to operate within my rigidly enforced rules. Yiddish was discouraged in the brigade as the Zionist concept was to make Ivrit the national language but, like myself, these Poles hardly spoke any Ivrit. However they were completely at home with Yiddish. Thus I managed to communicate with them and was accepted by this group who never once performed any action that stepped outside the code of conduct that I had established. Much to the surprise of most of the senior people in the unit, who had been most unhappy when this group had arrived, within a few weeks the Poles had completely settled into the workshop and were indistinguishable from the other men. The man with the worst reputation, who had been court-martialled and found guilty of several serious crimes, turned out to be the hardest worker of them all. I was delighted when, many years later, David Ben Dov told me that this man had become a model citizen, a successful businessman and an eminent charity worker.

Due to all this activity the weeks seemed to fly by. Then, quite out of the blue, the brigade received orders to move. On 29th July 1945, after a few days of furious preparation, the convoy left Valbruna to begin its long trek to join the British Liberation Army in North-west Europe. As we wound our way through the Brenner Pass, I recalled the stories of Hannibal taking his elephants on the same journey and could not help but wonder if any future historian would remember the time that the Jewish Brigade followed in Hannibal's footsteps. Although we had no elephants we did have vehicles that decided to develop faults on the most awkward of bends or upon the steepest of slopes. I had spent so much time in different mountain ranges that I thought I had seen all the horrors they could offer, but the Brenner was the king of the mountain passes. Whilst I fully appreciated that it was quite an experience to shepherd a whole brigade through the Alps, I was more than delighted to leave them behind although the scenery was magnificent. Suddenly a whole panorama opened up before us and there, nestling in the distant valley, was the city of Innsbruck, looking like a fairy tale picture.

The rest of the journey was on major trunk roads or autobahns which soon became rather monotonous. As I usually travelled some distance behind the main convoy, most minor troubles had been attended to before my arrival. Consequently my workload was light and I was able to read a very interesting book that I had obtained from a friend before leaving Italy. This upset my driver who complained that I had hardly spoken a word to him for days as my nose was continually stuck in this book. I had some sympathy for him and made a point of periodically talking to him but I am sure that he was very relieved when at last we arrived at our destination.

We drove through Austria entering Germany via Stuttgart. We felt that there was something unreal about this countryside probably because we found it difficult to accept that we were actually travelling through the heart of enemy territory. It was hard to realise that the dwellings we passed housed the very people who were responsible for Hitler's rise to power, the war and its terrible consequences. We saw plenty of evidence of fighting on our route and much damage that looked like it had been caused by falling bombs. There were many German refugees trudging along the roads. They either carried bundles or dragged handcarts, giving us a very wide berth as soon as they realised that we were a Jewish convoy of soldiers. There was a marked contrast when we neared a Bavarian camp. Here, as we passed by, a group of Jews greeted us with hysterical cheering and joyful flag waving. We had to enforce our strict 'no stopping rule', otherwise the whole convoy would have come to a standstill, but Rabbi Casper ensured that these people received as much help as possible.

After Stuttgart, one of my staff sergeants left the convoy unofficially in order to visit Heidelberg, where he had lived from birth until leaving Germany as a refugee. On his return to us, he told us that he had seen his old home, which had escaped any bomb damage, and visited the local bank where he had collected a small sum of money that he had left behind. His account had remained open and the Germans had even added interest, year by year. He bought a second-hand flute with this money and it must have given him some satisfaction to have salvaged something to recompense him for all that he had been forced to abandon.

The night before we left Germany we laagered on the side of the autobahn which was littered with several damaged aircraft. Apparently, after the Allied bombers had destroyed their aerodromes, the Luftwaffe had used this road as a runway for fighter planes. Our laager site was several miles away from any cities or villages with only the odd farmhouse in the vicinity. The night passed uneventfully and the convoy departed at about 7 a.m. I had to wait for a minor repair to be carried out on a 3-ton lorry but this was completed very quickly. Just as I was about to get into my vehicle, so as to catch up with the main convoy, a jeep with French insignia drew up alongside me. An officer dismounted and quizzed me about the convoy that had been laagering that night on the autobahn. Apparently we were in the French zone of Germany and this officer was responsible for an area about the size of Middlesex.

He told me that during the previous night, somebody had set fire to a farmhouse causing its four inhabitants to be burned to death. From his attitude I could see that he was pretty certain that men from our convoy were responsible but there was no concrete evidence and, in fact, it could have been an attack by any of the various individuals or gangs that roamed the countryside.

I told the officer that it was impossible to know for sure whether the arson had been performed by anyone from our convoy. I would not make excuses for any of them, I said, but if we did find the culprit then he would definitely be charged and punished. However, under the circumstances, I felt that this would be an extremely difficult case to solve, so perhaps it would be better for him to presume that I had actually left five minutes earlier. He could then explain that when he had reached our site, there was no one left on the scene.

He thought about this for a moment and said, 'Yes, my friend, you are probably right. This is one of the terrible happenings we shall have to add to the enormous number of atrocitites that we are discovering about the Second World War.'

We all felt a great sense of relief when we left Germany and its foul associations behind. We crossed the Rhine and travelled on into France, where we received friendly greetings in contrast to the attitudes which we had experienced in Austria and Germany. There was always a special cheer for us whenever we were recognised as a Jewish Military formation.

We passed many First World War cemeteries and very shortly entered Belgium. We went on to Turnhout and soon arrived at our destination; Rotterdam in Holland. Here I had been allocated a large disused factory and, as I had no other responsibilities, I was able to concentrate all my energies upon constructing an efficient workshop.

We were comfortably billeted in a large school and, with all the civilians being so amiable and helpful we felt that this was a wonderfully happy environment. Many of our soldiers had grown up in this type of area so they were completely at home both with the local dialects and customs which helped us enormously in our dealings with the civilians. A close cooperation developed between us all and the atmosphere here was most pleasant.

On 6th August, a few days after our arrival at Rotterdam, we were astounded to hear of the atom bomb attack on Hiroshima. This was

259

PERSONAL MESSAGE
from the
ARMY COMMANDER

On the occasion of the Jewish New Year, I send to all Jewish soldiers serving in the British, Dominion and Allied formations of the Eighth Army, my good wishes.

Jewish soldiers, several thousands of whom are serving in the Eighth Army, have borne their full share in our battles. I hope that the Day of Victory, for which they, with their comrades of this Army, have fought so long and so hard, is now close at hand.

Oliver Leese.

Lieutenant-General.

260

followed by the attack on Nagasaki on 9th August. Whilst we were trying to absorb the implications of these events, we heard the most amazing news of all when, on 14th August, Japan surrendered and, all of a sudden, the Second World War was over.

It took several days for us to absorb all of this news. In my case it was somewhat overshadowed by the leave roster that the brigade had started for British personnel. I could hardly believe that I would be going home very shortly.

All the same, we still had to quickly settle into our workshop routine. The brigade was now spread all over Belgium and Holland so it was only necessary to keep an emergency squad on duty outside normal working hours. I had plenty of spare time to explore the whole area at will. Holland had obviously suffered very badly and, now that the guilder was rapidly inflating itself out of existence, the black market had come to the fore, with bartering also being the order of the day. The soldiers stopped taking money from the regular payday parades, for the value of a week's military printed currency was about equal to the sale of five cigarettes from his official issue. Thus cigarettes replaced currency for, apart from those issued by the army, they could be freely bought in Belgium and taken across the border to Holland where they could be sold for twice their original cost. However, as the profit on this transaction was in near-worthless guilders, this project became a pointless waste of time.

The brigade naturally became a rallying point for every Jew in the area. We later discovered that our move to North-West Europe had been designed to satisfy the British military in Palestine who thought it would impede our ability to smuggle refugees into the Protectorate. In this objective, they were effective for our salvage work was greatly curtailed due to our further distance from Palestine. There were still plenty of rumours floating around the brigade about refugee operations, but I, personally, was not approached for any more transportation assistance, so this activity of mine therefore ceased.

I knew of several individuals who had gone to various countries under Russian occupation to search for their families and to gather as many Jews that they could find. Application had been made to army headquarters in BAOR for us to send official teams of men for this purpose. After a great deal of pressure, two teams were allowed to go. HQ 21st Army Group were more obliging and gave permission for several other teams who managed to operate all over the Russian occupied zone for some weeks, before being recalled by an order from the War Office. When I heard that a team was going into Poland, I requested permission to join them as their route could pass through Gombin. I hoped to find some of my relatives who might have survived or, at least, garner some news of them. However, before this journey could be organised my leave date was decided. As wild horses could not have prevented me from going home, another soldier took my place on the Polish team. Several weeks later this man told me that they had indeed stopped in Gombin, but they had been unable to discover a single living Jew in the entire district.

British soldiers in Italy were entitled to four weeks' home leave. As I was now in BAOR, which was considered home service, only twelve days was the norm. This was a classic administrative muck up but, in an attempt to redress the balance for those men who had spent several years overseas, The Brigadier said that we would have another twelve days after a very short interval.

On 4th September 1945 I embarked at the Hook of Holland for Folkestone. My mind was in a complete whirl as I recalled the route I travelled since that day in July 1942, when I had sailed from Scotland. I could not help but compare this short channel crossing to the long sea voyage around Africa. Both the world and I had drastically changed. I was now twenty-five years old and, in these lost years, I had crammed so many different experiences and learned the sort of authority that a lifetime in civvy street could never have taught me. Above all, I was completely confident in my own ability and had developed a personal philosophy that I felt would stand me in good stead to cope with whatever the future decided to hold for me.

From the windows of the train to Victoria I observed the terrible damage caused by such Nazi weapons as flying bombs and rockets. Soon I transferred to the Metropolitan Railway which passed through such familiar stations as Farringdon Road and Liverpool Street. Finally I arrived at Whitechapel station. I dumped my kitbag and my faithful portable wireless in the barber's shop a few yards away, saying that I would collect my gear later. I crossed the road to the London Hospital, dashed down Turner Street and ... suddenly, I was there.

Festooned across the entrance to the shop was a series of paper decorations that joyously proclaimed, 'WELCOME HOME LEN'! Then everything seemed to happen at once. My mother was serving a customer when she looked up and saw me. When I flung my arms around her neither of us knew whether to laugh or to cry, but at least we both knew that I was now safely home and that she could stop worrying about me.

My first impression was how tiny everything appeared, it was all so much smaller than I had remembered. The shop and the house seemed shrunken and the streets were much narrower than I had expected. The next few hours were like a dream as I met Uncle Sam, my stepfather and was briefly introduced to his youngest daughter Sonia, who said, 'Cheerio!' and then left. I was so busy talking to my mother, Uncle Sam and other callers, that I did not realise until much later that I was taking over what was now Sonia's bed. I was told that she had gone to stay with one of her sisters in Ilford.

Although during the next few days I was reunited with my family and as many friends as possible, my main memory of this leave is of something completely different; for Sonia returned the next day. From almost the first moment that I saw her clearly and spoke to her, I had no doubts whatsoever that I was head over heels in love. Fate had certainly played its trump card. My plan upon being demobbed had been to concentrate all my energies into establishing my career and to make up for the lost years. The very last thought in my mind had concerned marriage. However, within a few days I asked Sonia to be my wife and my future plans had changed completely. Sonia claims that my proposal was more of an order than a request and I can only excuse this impression by saying that all my recent experiences had been in dealing with the male side of the population. Yet, even though many other men may be capable of more romantic proposals – with flowers and violins playing – no man could ever have proposed to any girl with more sincerity than I did.

After travelling the world I had been lucky enough to return home where I had found this most beautiful, intelligent and *molta sympatica* girl who was to become my lifelong wife and partner. We both knew without any shadow of a doubt that we would always face the future with love, and we were confident that together we could surmount whatever problems were thrust into our lives.

Sonia, of course, was my stepsister and I was duly presented to her elder sisters, Freda, Mary and Frances, brothers-in-law to be Abe, Stanley, Ruby, and her brother, Leslie. They were probably astonished to learn that we were to be married but, if they were surprised at this turn of events, they, like all the members of my own family, appeared to be delighted and wished us a hearty *mazeltov*.

One evening we went to the Troxy Cinema, accompanied by my mother and Uncle Sam, where we saw the latest Betty Grable film Sonia and I managed to sneak off to sit on our own, some distance from our parents. The theme song of this film was 'I Wish I Knew' and, as in all great love affairs, we adopted it as 'our' song.

I managed to visit the Victoria Club in Fordham Street where I heard the latest news about many of my friends. The boys present were mostly too young for the services but there were one or two managers of my age who had been invalided out of the army. One of these was my very special friend Ginger, who was now living in a flat in Stoke Newington. Sonia and I spent a very happy evening with Ginger and his wife Dodie, who was now expecting a baby. I was overjoyed that Sonia and Dodie seemed to have an immediate rapport and became good friends.

My short leave finished on the eve of Rosh Hashanah and I

returned to Holland on 16th September. This time, however, I felt very different for I now had a fiancée to consider and I began to count off the days before I could return home again.

Time now passed much more slowly and throughout autumn, with the prospect of winter weather looming, life was a matter of working and of being involved in the political discussions that dominated our lives. At least I could look forward to Sonia's letters and remain as cheerful as possible. I tried to learn Ivrit but once again realised that I had no aptitude at all for languages.

We were next told that we were being moved to take over the main line of communication REME in the Belgium town of Lier. Here we would be responsible for all the military requirements in the area, as well as retaining our duties with the Jewish Brigade. This move and takeover kept me very busy and was still incomplete by the time I left for the second leave that I had been promised.

I arrived home on 5th November and spent twelve wonderful days with Sonia. We were both aware that this was to be my last leave and that the next time I came home I would be a civilian. We spoke a great deal about our future and made a million plans. We visited all the members of both our families and met as my friends as possible. I learned about rationing and began to get some indication of the hardships and shortages of London life. I also learned a great deal more about the hardships so heroically suffered by the ordinary men and women in the street during the years I had been abroad.

Sonia's story was itself an illustration of how difficult life had been for a young person growing up during the war years. Her mother had died just prior to the outbreak and she and her brother were part of the massive evacuation programme for London's children. She was sent to a family who were the bakers in a Suffolk village, separated from her brother Leslie and although the baker and his family were very kind to her, the pain of separation was distressing and bewildering to an 11-year-old child.

For several years after many unhappy experiences being shunted from one member of her family to another usually as an afterthought during which time she started a commercial course of shorthand and typewriting at school, with additional lessons at evening classes. As she was expected to help financially towards her keep, she left school at the age of fourteen and began working in an office in Ilford.

The enemy attack on London then entered a new phase by unmanned rockets and on one occasion she was in the house in Empress Avenue with her sisters Freda and Frances when it was very badly damaged. She was badly cut by glass and taken to the ARP First Aid Post for treatment, being fortunate in not being killed. Towards the end of the war she went to live in Turner Street with her father and my mother and was there when the war finished.

She did not consider her experiences unusual but considered herself lucky compared with the many unfortunate people who had suffered death and permanent injury as a result of the war. In many ways the difficult years had strengthened her character and she was looking forward to a new and happy future.

Some people in the brigade believed that the authorities planned to deliberately delay the demobilisation of Palestinian troops on the grounds that it was undesirable to have thousands of trained Jewish ex-soldiers available to join the Haganah and other underground forces operating in Palestine. I was asked to discuss this with my local Member of Parliament, the communist Phil Piratin. Accordingly, I went to his office and explained the situation as we saw it. He tabled a question about it in the House but whether he had any effect I do not know. However, from then on, there was no more talk of delays. Palestinians were demobbed by the same criteria of age and length of service as all the other soldiers.

Prior to my second leave, I had been asked by Private Hammerman to oblige him by making a telephone call to his cousin John while I was on leave. He had apparently been with the Polish army in Britain and was now demobbed and they had not met since the German invasion of Poland in 1940. I promised to telephone and to send his cousin greetings and best wishes. A few days into my leave I made the telephone call and the cousin, who was delighted to hear Hammerman's news from me, invited both Sonia and me to lunch at a club he was now running. The next day we duly went to Hamilton Place, off Piccadilly and near Hyde Park Corner. We took a bus to the West End and eventually found the address which turned out to be a large building off Park Lane. We rang the bell above the plate which said 'Les Ambassadeurs' and a uniformed porter ushered us into a world which we had never imagined still existed. There was a massive hallway which contained a huge spiral staircase and led to a large room which was scattered with leather bound chairs and beautiful objets d'art. The walls were covered with magnificent paintings, mostly of horses and portraits of aristocratic-looking individuals from a bygone era. Here we were greeted by John Mills, a giant of a man, who escorted us to one of the small tables where he insisted that a waiter took our drink orders. John explained that we were now his guests in this private club which he had founded with three of his friends.

There was a variety of people sitting around the room and at the large bar in the corner. They were all dressed in officer's uniform, not only of our own army services but those of our Allies too. I, as the only non-officer present, seemed to be surrounded by all sorts of generals and staff officers.

John was very interested to hear all my news about his cousin and I promised to help Private Hammerman to obtain leave to visit

England. Sonia and I kept exchanging winks during the whole period and she behaved as though lounging in such an opulent environment was quite a normal occurrence to her. Our host told us that among the club's members were several Royal personages, some very senior people in the services and members of governments from both our own and Allied countries. He showed me a cigarette case that had about thirty signatures engraved on the inside, explaining that each time a celebrated guest signed his name, the case was then sent to a jeweller to be engraved over the written signature. The most prominent name that we noticed was that of Princess Margaret, so I was not at all surprised that Sonia and I were not invited to provide our autographs.

After a while John escorted us to the main restaurant where we were served by dinner-jacketed waiters using impeccably starched linen and polished cutlery. Our host pointed out that immense care was taken not to breach any of the food rationing regulations, so I pointed out to Sonia that I was confident that, once we were married, she would arrange for our meals to be presented in a similar silver-service manner. All in all it was a most unexpected and enjoyable afternoon. It was with some regret that we left this fairy story existence, which we had accidentally glimpsed, to return to the real life of Turner Street and my imminent return to the army.

22
The Last Lap

During my absence the rest of the workshop company had settled in at Lier. Belgium appeared to have escaped the sort of war damage that much of Europe had suffered, and I was surprised to see many flourishing shops where one could purchase many items that were in short supply elsewhere.

The workshop here was considerably larger than I had previously experienced. Not only did it cover more space but it employed more craftsmen and, for the first time, I had authority over a large number of civilians. They were part of the original staff who had been taken over with the workshop at the time of the liberation. Contrary to my expectations, I found it easy to organise such a huge work force for I now had a complete and fully manned group of sub-units, each of which had a responsible military or civilian foreman in charge.

Major Levin had returned home shortly before my first leave, and had been replaced by Major S. Naicrog, who was a very different character. I found him most approachable and encountered no difficulties with this changeover.

From my point of view, all was progressing smoothly but time certainly seemed to pass more slowly than it had before I knew Sonia. Meanwhile I looked forward to the future and had her letters to read.

Yehuda Sharlin, one of my clerks, introduced me to a girl he had met. She had been among the Jewish group of refugees we had encountered soon after our arrival in Holland. Her name was Ruth and she had been brought up in Germany. After the most terrible experiences she had miraculously survived the death camps and now she and Yehuda had fallen in love and wanted to get married. She had managed to find a Jewish family near Lier who had willingly offered her a temporary home until such time as she could be sent, as a soldier's wife, to Yehuda's home in Palestine.

This was where their problems began, for the victorious Allies had a strict policy that there was to be no fraternising with the enemy – although this was never intended to include Jewish refugees. Yet, as Ruth was officially a German national, special

267

permission had to be granted by the London War Office before they could wed. Rabbi Casper had forwarded the necessary application and there was nothing further anybody could do to hasten permission. All they could do was to wait patiently.

I did my best to cheer Yehuda up, pointing out that he, at least, could still see his sweetheart, whereas I could only exchange letters with mine. Since they were willing meanwhile to have a religious ceremony, he decided to approach the *chazzen* (cantor) in the Brussels synagogue. This *chazzen* was the only synagogue official to have survived the war and should have been sympathetic towards this couple. However, as he had received some official communications on the subject, he refused point blank to marry them, saying that it was against the law.

In the meantime the situation in Palestine was deteriorating daily. All the high hopes we had held that the newly-elected British Labour government would be more sympathetic to the terrible plight of our refugees, were dashed to the ground. The Foreign Office, under Ernest Bevin, attempted to carry out the most inhuman of policies and things became desperate. Only the high discipline and intelligence of our soldiers prevented open mutiny against the government and a mass desertion from the ranks. On several occasions I needed to utilise all my powers of tact and good humour to bring in a sense of reality and calm among such inflamed tempers.

One day the word went round that, as a protest, there was to be a spontaneous twenty-four hour fast. At each mealtime in the men's mess, for the entire day, all personnel walked past the serving tables of prepared food without taking a morsel. They filed past in silence and great care was taken that no military rules were breached. When I asked several soldiers for their reasons, I was told that it was their personal way of legally protesting against the British government's attitude towards Palestine. I reported all this to the major who passed the information to brigade headquarters. Apparently this hunger strike was being repeated throughout the entire brigade and a report was sent to army headquarters by Brigadier Benjamin. The only touch of humour in this incident was that most people managed to eat something on the quiet, for as Yasher said, when he popped into my room with some sandwiches, 'This is a political, not a religious protest, I would not want to confuse the heavenly clerks that Yom Kippur had come early this year!'

Cultural life was gradually returning in Belgium and, apart from the cinema and a couple of concerts, the cafés had re-opened, many offering a pianist or a singer to entertain the customers. It certainly made a change to sit with friends drinking coffee and eating pastries in the continental style. The conversation was always political and the future of the *yishuv* dominated every gathering.

One day my old driver Nachum approached me to ask if I would be interested in becoming a member of the Haifa bus corporative. Apparently, in the plans that were being made, a suitable person was required to take charge of the transport maintenance workshop and my name had been suggested to fill the vacancy. The Haifa transport system was rapidly growing and, to encourage me to accept, I would only be required to pay a nominal sum to become a full member, instead of something like the usual cost of about £10,000. I was very flattered and surprised by this offer and, after some discussion with Nachum, we decided that it would be left open for three months after my demobilisation, which would give me some time to spend with Sonia and my family before making such a major decision.

On a Thursday morning in the middle of January a movement order arrived at the company HQ. It had been decided that all schoolteachers were to be given immediate demobilisation as they were desperately required at home. Yehuda, the only official school teacher in our unit, was required to be at Brigade HQ at 2 p.m. that Saturday for onward transmission with several other soldiers from different units. At first he refused point blank to go, aware that, in the present climate, it could take Ruth years to get permission to join him. I told him that he had no choice as it was an order from above but I promised to do everything possible to help him in what was now an emergency situation.

I spoke to Rabbi Casper who explained that the fraternisation order was so strict that if he broke it his standing with his seniors would be jeopardized. This in turn would affect too many other negotiations in which he was involved concerning a great number of desperate people.

As an official marriage was not possible we decided that the best hope was to get them married by the civil religious authority which would be accepted by Jewish people everywhere. The marriage contract alone would be sufficient proof. Knowing that the *chazzen* in Brussels had already refused, our only alternative was in Rotterdam. Yehuda and I travelled into Holland and finally arrived at the synagogue. This was a huge, beautiful, candlelit, old temple built over a canal. Fortunately the Germans had used it as a storage dump and had not harmed it in any way. The only official present was a *shummus*, (beadle) a kind, pathetic remnant of a man who had tragically lost his entire family. He was totally dazed by all the events and it was obvious that this was a dead end, from our point of view. As a memento of our visit the *shummus* gave me an old prayer book that was lying on one of the boxes in the main office. Some years later, I learned that his wife had managed to survive and had returned to Rotterdam a few weeks after our visit.

It was now late afternoon and we realised that our only chance was to return to the *chazzen* in Brussels. It was late evening by the time we entered his synagogue office. We explained our dilemma to him and promised that if he carried out the ceremony the civilian authorities need never know. He did not need to enter the marriage in the official records for all that we required was a ceremony and a *ksibah* (marriage contract). He said that he wanted to help, but was afraid. We offered him a few hundred cigarettes and some tinned food that I had in the jeep but to no avail. Finally I got so frustrated that I told him that his behaviour was no better than that of the Germans, particularly as we were pleading with him and not in any way threatening him. Eventually he very reluctantly agreed and arranged the ceremony for 2 p.m. the next day, Friday.

We arrived promptly at 2 p.m. The bride looked lovely in the prettiest clothes that she and her adopted family had been able to arrange in the circumstances. She carried a suitable floral decoration and Yehuda was dressed in his best uniform with a flower in his buttonhole. David Ben Dov and Oded Yarkoni, Yehuda's other closest friends, accompanied us. The ceremony was short but very moving for we were all well aware of the background events. When I wished this young couple *mazeltov* and a happy future, I sincerely meant it with all my heart.

We dropped the bride and groom at a small hotel where Yehuda had arranged to spend his short honeymoon and I returned to collect them the next morning. We drove to Yehuda's billet to collect his kit and then back to the house in which Ruth was staying. After a short interval, during which the tearful goodbyes were said, I delivered a very dejected soldier to Brigade headquarters at the specified time. Before he left, Yehuda thanked me for my help and said that he was leaving his wife in my hands. He knew that I would do everything possible to help her to join him in Palestine.

I made arrangements for Ruth's food rations to be taken care of, but a couple of weeks passed without the permission arriving from the War Office. Ruth daily called in at the workshop office and became more desperate as the days went by.

By now the date of my own discharge had come through and I began to count the days I had left. Around 14th February I was told that a Greek-owned ship had been hired to smuggle refugees to Palestine. They were being assembled near Marseilles in a camp run by a Jewish American army major. I discussed this venture with Ruth and kitted her out in army battledress. I wrote out the necessary papers and sent her off in a truck, driven by a trustworthy man from the workshop. I gave them a week's food and petrol and my last instruction to the driver was that by hook or by crook he should deliver her to the American major in time to board this ship. Once I had waved Ruth goodbye, I could now turn all my attention to winding down my own affairs and handing over my work.

The truck duly returned after six days and, to my astonishment, both the driver and Ruth dismounted. They had had many adventures on the way to Marseilles but, when they had arrived, they had been told that the ship's captain had reneged on the arrangement. A large number of people were now trapped in this camp whilst the major attempted to arrange another ship to transport them to Palestine. Ruth had refused to stay and was now our responsibility once more.

I spent a couple of days chasing around trying to organise something but the outlook appeared very bleak. Then, suddenly, the *mazel* turned when Vitis came running over to my office, excitedly waving a paper which declared that the permission to marry had now arrived. This was such a relief that we forgot that for a wedding to take place, we needed a groom – ours was miles away somewhere on the route to Palestine! I decided that now was the time to stick my neck out so I instructed Vitis to insert the marriage in our unit part 1 orders which would thus make it official. I reasoned that nobody was likely to notice the fact that Yehuda had not actually been with the unit on the date he was supposed to have got married. The entry in orders was duly made and forwarded to army records. Then we immediately asked area HQ transport section to arrange the transport of Mrs Sharlin, an army wife, to her home in Jerusalem. It was now only a question of time for this arrangement to come through so I asked Vitis to keep chasing the transport people and to claim that it was most urgent as she was expecting a child.

Most of my last few days were spent in saying cheerio and shalom to all my acquaintances and friends within the brigade. We held a

271

56066

PAY
FORM
R.16

To *Mr L Panitsky*

RELEASE.

POST OFFICE SAVINGS BANK ACCOUNT No. **LE** 6512

1 The amount of War Gratuity and Post War Credit as shown below is being deposited in your name in the Post Office Savings Bank :—

		£	s.	d.
	78 months at £1 per month W.O.I	78	–	–
WAR GRATUITY	Less deductions (brief particulars)			
	Balance of War Gratuity due	78	–	–
POST WAR CREDITS DUE From 1/1/42 to 16/6/46		40	14	
OTHER CREDITS				
TOTAL AMOUNT DEPOSITED IN POST OFFICE SAVINGS BANK		£118	14	–

P.T.O.

War Gratuity – 78 months' service at £1 per month = £78.

272

mess party with many visitors and I could not help but compare my leaving the army with my very hesitant entry many years before in Leyton. The one golden rule that I had adhered to since becoming a lance corporal, was never to raise my voice to anybody that was junior to me in rank but I was always willing to tell a senior officer exactly what I thought about a situation, before the addition of the word 'Sir' at the end of my statement. I was given my soldier's release book and was quite overwhelmed by the testimonial written within. Quoted verbatim this is what it said:

A most loyal and reliable Warrant Officer. Outstanding power of organisation, combined with an excellent theoretical and practical knowledge of his trade. Excellent power of command and ability in dealing tactfully with his superiors and subordinates.

Mark Hyatt was being discharged on the same day as me so during the morning of 9th March 1946, he called for me in an HQ truck. Once again I reminded Vitis that he had now inherited the responsibility of keeping an eye on Ruth and making sure that she was not forgotten by the authorities. (This story did have a happy ending for, about two months after my return home, I heard that Ruth and Yehuda had indeed been happily reunited in Palestine.)

After saying our final farewells, Mark and I left the amazing world of the Jewish Brigade behind us and began our journey home.

Our demob leave began at Shorncliffe Release Centre where I was told that my pay would cease as from 16th June. On that date I would officially no longer be a soldier although I would be put on to the army 'Z' reserve for an indefinite period and be liable for recall should an emergency be declared by Parliament. Our last call was to Olympia Stadium, which had been converted into a huge clothing depot. Here, the normal procedure was reversed, for this time one entered at one end in uniform, shedded army issue as we progressed and eventually emerged with civilian clothing that still had a very uniform look about it, despite there being a choice of design for each item. We were allowed to retain our battle dress.

I bade Mark farewell, and travelled for the final time as a soldier along the route to Whitechapel Station. I had written to Sonia saying that I expected to arrive home on the 11th so, when I entered the shop a day earlier, they were all somewhat pleasantly surprised. I dumped my kit bag and my new cardboard box of clothes on the floor. My welcome was overwhelming.

All I could say was, 'Well I'm home!'

This is my story. I apologise to the very many friends and comrades that I have not mentioned. Let me assure you all, that you are there somewhere in my mind. In some cases I have

probably mixed up names, places and incidents and for this I hope
to be forgiven as every word is the true story of my life when I was

ON PARADE

Index

Index